Grammar Plus Writing

3

저자 약력

전지원 미국 오리건 주립대 Linguistics 석사
(현) 한국 외국어대학교 외국어연수 평가원 영어 전임 강사
〈내공 중학 영작문〉 (다락원), 〈Grammar Mate〉 (다락원),
〈Grammar's Cool〉 (YBM), 〈빠르게 잡는 영문법〉 (천재교육) 등 다수의 교재 공저

박혜영 미국 하와이 주립대 Second Language Studies 석사
(현) 한국 외국어대학교 외국어연수 평가원 영어 전임 강사
〈내공 중학 영작문〉 (다락원), 〈Grammar Mate〉 (다락원),
〈Grammar's Cool〉 (YBM), 〈빠르게 잡는 영문법〉 (천재교육) 등 다수의 교재 공저

Grammar Plus Writing 3

지은이 전지원, 박혜영

펴낸이 정규도
펴낸곳 (주)다락원

개정판 1쇄 발행 2023년 12월 11일
개정판 2쇄 발행 2024년 2월 26일

편집 서정아, 신채영
디자인 구수정, 포레스트
삽화 강정연
영문 감수 Michael A. Putlack

다락원 경기도 파주시 문발로 211
내용문의 (02)736-2031 내선 503
구입문의 (02)736-2031 내선 250~252

Fax (02)732-2037
출판등록 1977년 9월 16일 제 406-2008-000007호

ISBN 978-89-277-8066-3 54740
978-89-277-8063-2 54740(set)

http://www.darakwon.co.kr
다락원 홈페이지를 방문하시면 상세한 출판정보와 함께
동영상강좌, MP3 자료 등 다양한 어학 정보를 얻으실 수 있습니다.

Grammar Plus Writing

3

STRUCTURES | 구성과 특징

Grammar Plus Writing 시리즈는

- 중등 필수 영문법을 쉽고 빠르게 습득할 수 있습니다.
- 학습한 문법 요소를 영작과 연계하여 문법 지식과 영작 능력을 동시에 향상시킬 수 있습니다.
- 최신 기출 유형과 고난도 문제로 내신 및 서술형 시험에 효과적으로 대비할 수 있습니다.

GRAMMAR FOCUS

내신뿐 아니라 영작을 할 때 꼭 필요한 중등 필수 영문법을 선별하여 쉽고 간결하게 제시했습니다. 문법 학습 후에는 단계별 Exercise를 통해 학습한 내용을 체계적으로 점검할 수 있습니다.

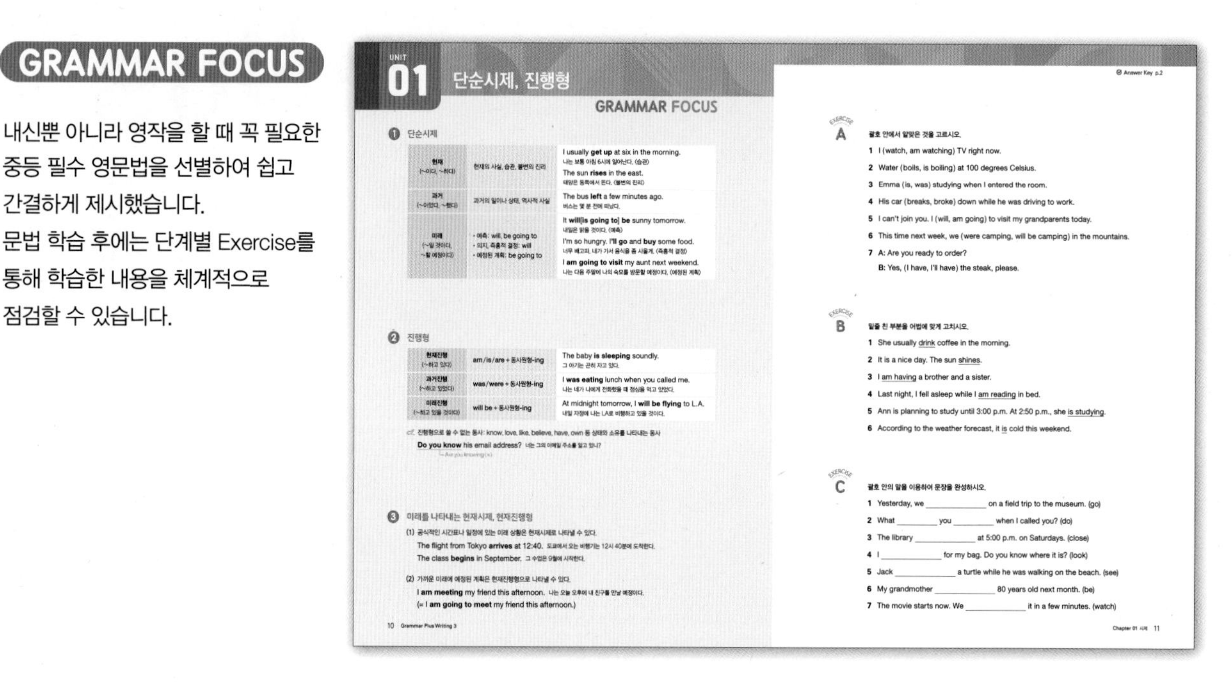

UNIT 01 단순시제, 진행형

GRAMMAR FOCUS

❶ 단순시제

현재 (~이다, ~하다)	현재의 사실, 습관, 불변의 진리	I usually **get up** at six in the morning. 나는 보통 아침 6시에 일어난다. 〈습관〉 The sun **rises** in the east. 태양은 동쪽에서 뜬다. 〈불변의 진리〉
과거 (~이었다, ~했다)	과거의 일이나 상태, 역사적 사실	The bus **left** a few minutes ago. 버스는 몇 분 전에 떠났다.
미래 (~일 것이다, ~할 예정이다)	· 예측: will, be going to · 의지, 즉흥적 결정: will · 예정된 계획: be going to	It **will[is going to] be** sunny tomorrow. 내일은 맑을 것이다. 〈예측〉 I'm so hungry. **I'll go** and **buy** some food. 너무 배고파. 내가 가서 음식을 좀 사올게. 〈즉흥적 결정〉 **I am going to visit** my aunt next weekend. 나는 다음 주말에 나의 숙모를 방문할 예정이다. 〈예정된 계획〉

❷ 진행형

현재진행 (~하고 있다)	am/is/are + 동사원형-ing	The baby **is sleeping** soundly. 그 아기는 곤히 자고 있다.
과거진행 (~하고 있었다)	was/were + 동사원형-ing	I **was eating** lunch when you called me. 나는 네가 나에게 전화했을 때 점심을 먹고 있었다.
미래진행 (~하고 있을 것이다)	will be + 동사원형-ing	At midnight tomorrow, I **will be flying** to L.A. 내일 자정에 나는 LA로 비행하고 있을 것이다.

cf. 진행형으로 쓸 수 없는 동사: know, love, like, believe, have, own 등 상태와 소유를 나타내는 동사

Do you know his email address? 너는 그의 이메일 주소를 알고 있니?
— Are you knowing(×)

❸ 미래를 나타내는 현재시제, 현재진행형

(1) 공식적인 시간표나 일정에 있는 미래 상황은 현재시제로 나타낼 수 있다.

The flight from Tokyo **arrives** at 12:40. 도쿄에서 오는 비행기는 12시 40분에 도착한다.

The class **begins** in September. 그 수업은 9월에 시작한다.

(2) 가까운 미래에 예정된 계획은 현재진행형으로 나타낼 수 있다.

I **am meeting** my friend this afternoon. 나는 오늘 오후에 내 친구를 만날 예정이다.

(= I **am going to meet** my friend this afternoon.)

10 Grammar Plus Writing 3

Answer Key p.2

EXERCISE A 괄호 안에서 알맞은 것을 고르시오.

1 I (watch, am watching) TV right now.
2 Water (boils, is boiling) at 100 degrees Celsius.
3 Emma (is, was) studying when I entered the room.
4 His car (breaks, broke) down while he was driving to work.
5 I can't join you. I (will, am going) to visit my grandparents today.
6 This time next week, we (were camping, will be camping) in the mountains.
7 A: Are you ready to order?
B: Yes, (I have, I'll have) the steak, please.

EXERCISE B 밑줄 친 부분을 어법에 맞게 고치시오.

1 She usually drink coffee in the morning.
2 It is a nice day. The sun shines.
3 I am having a brother and a sister.
4 Last night, I fell asleep while I am reading in bed.
5 Ann is planning to study until 3:00 p.m. At 2:50 p.m., she is studying.
6 According to the weather forecast, it is cold this weekend.

EXERCISE C 괄호 안의 말을 이용하여 문장을 완성하시오.

1 Yesterday, we ______ on a field trip to the museum. (go)
2 What ______ you ______ when I called you? (do)
3 The library ______ at 5:00 p.m. on Saturdays. (close)
4 I ______ for my bag. Do you know where it is? (look)
5 Jack ______ a turtle while he was walking on the beach. (see)
6 My grandmother ______ 80 years old next month. (be)
7 The movie starts now. We ______ it in a few minutes. (watch)

Chapter 01 시제 11

WRITING FOCUS

학습한 문법 요소를 활용하여 영작 훈련을 하는 코너입니다. 영작에 대한 자신감을 키우고 학교 시험에 자주 나오는 문제 유형(배열 영작, 문장 완성, 문장 전환, 오류 수정 등)을 통해 서술형 시험에 효과적으로 대비할 수 있습니다.

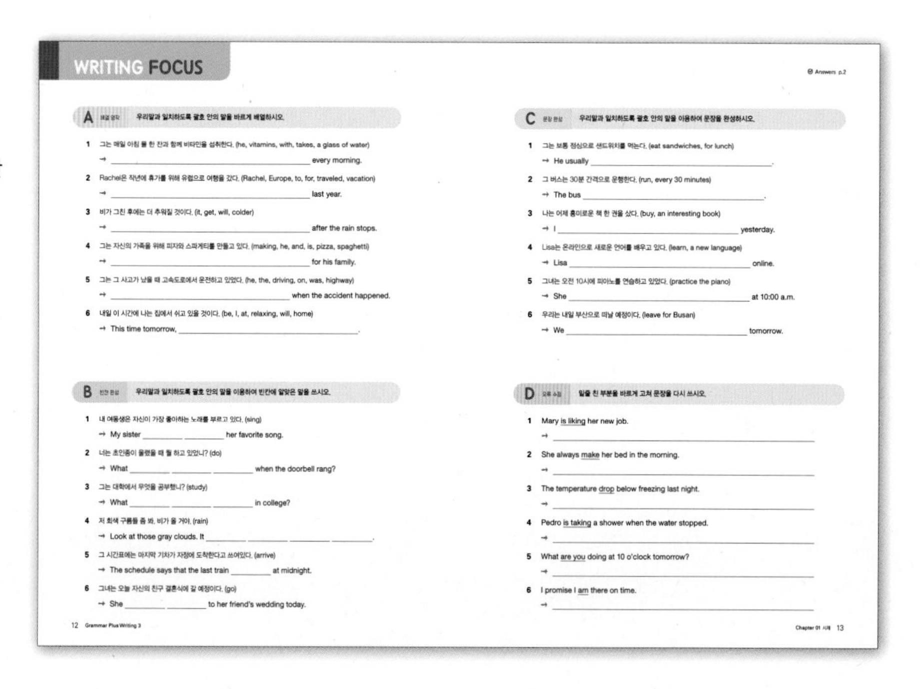

WRITING FOCUS

A 배열 영작 우리말과 일치하도록 괄호 안의 말을 바르게 배열하시오.

1 그는 매일 아침 물 한 잔과 함께 비타민을 섭취한다. (he, vitamins, with, takes, a glass of water)
→ ______ every morning.
2 Rachel은 작년에 휴가를 위해 유럽으로 여행을 갔다. (Rachel, Europe, to, for, traveled, vacation)
→ ______ last year.
3 비가 그친 후에는 더 추워질 것이다. (it, get, will, colder)
→ ______ after the rain stops.
4 그는 자신의 가족을 위해 피자와 스파게티를 만들고 있다. (making, he, and, is, pizza, spaghetti)
→ ______ for his family.
5 그는 그 사고가 났을 때 고속도로에서 운전하고 있었다. (he, the, driving, on, was, highway)
→ ______ when the accident happened.
6 내일 이 시간에 나는 집에서 쉬고 있을 것이다. (be, I, at, relaxing, will, home)
→ This time tomorrow, ______.

B 빈칸 완성 우리말과 일치하도록 괄호 안의 말을 이용하여 빈칸에 알맞은 말을 쓰시오.

1 내 여동생은 자신이 가장 좋아하는 노래를 부르고 있다. (sing)
→ My sister ______ ______ her favorite song.
2 너는 초인종이 울렸을 때 뭘 하고 있었니? (do)
→ What ______ ______ ______ when the doorbell rang?
3 그는 대학에서 무엇을 공부했니? (study)
→ What ______ ______ ______ in college?
4 저 회색 구름들 좀 봐. 비가 올 거야. (rain)
→ Look at those gray clouds. It ______ ______ ______ ______.
5 그 시간표에는 마지막 기차가 자정에 도착한다고 쓰여있다. (arrive)
→ The schedule says that the last train ______ at midnight.
6 그녀는 오늘 자신의 친구 결혼식에 갈 예정이다. (go)
→ She ______ ______ to her friend's wedding today.

12 Grammar Plus Writing 3

Answers p.2

C 문장 완성 우리말과 일치하도록 괄호 안의 말을 이용하여 문장을 완성하시오.

1 그는 보통 점심으로 샌드위치를 먹는다. (eat sandwiches, for lunch)
→ He usually ______.
2 그 버스는 30분 간격으로 운행한다. (run, every 30 minutes)
→ The bus ______.
3 나는 어제 흥미로운 책 한 권을 샀다. (buy, an interesting book)
→ I ______ yesterday.
4 Lisa는 온라인으로 새로운 언어를 배우고 있다. (learn, a new language)
→ Lisa ______ online.
5 그녀는 오전 10시에 피아노를 연습하고 있었다. (practice the piano)
→ She ______ at 10:00 a.m.
6 우리는 내일 부산으로 떠날 예정이다. (leave for Busan)
→ We ______ tomorrow.

D 오류 수정 밑줄 친 부분을 바르게 고쳐 문장을 다시 쓰시오.

1 Mary is liking her new job.
→ ______
2 She always make her bed in the morning.
→ ______
3 The temperature drop below freezing last night.
→ ______
4 Pedro is taking a shower when the water stopped.
→ ______
5 What are you doing at 10 o'clock tomorrow?
→ ______
6 I promise I am there on time.
→ ______

Chapter 01 시제 13

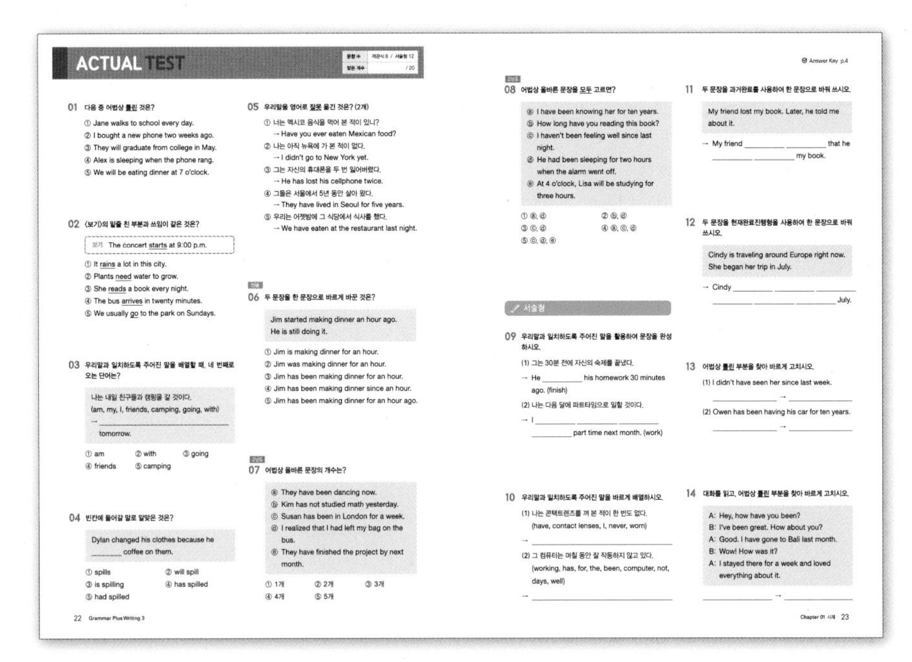

ACTUAL TEST

문항 수	객관식 8 / 서술형 12
맞은 개수	/ 20

01 다음 중 어법상 틀린 것은?
① Jane walks to school every day.
② I bought a new phone two weeks ago.
③ They will graduate from college in May.
④ Alex is sleeping when the phone rang.
⑤ We will be eating dinner at 7 o'clock.

02 〈보기〉의 밑줄 친 부분과 쓰임이 같은 것은?
보기 The concert starts at 9:00 p.m.
① It rains a lot in this city.
② Plants need water to grow.
③ She reads a book every night.
④ The bus arrives in twenty minutes.
⑤ We usually go to the park on Sundays.

03 우리말과 일치하도록 주어진 말을 배열할 때, 네 번째로 오는 단어는?
나는 내일 친구들과 캠핑을 갈 것이다.
(am, my, I, friends, camping, going, with)
→ ______ tomorrow.
① am ② with ③ going
④ friends ⑤ camping

04 빈칸에 들어갈 말로 알맞은 것은?
Dylan changed his clothes because he ______ coffee on them.
① spills ② will spill
③ is spilling ④ has spilled
⑤ had spilled

05 우리말을 영어로 잘못 옮긴 것은? (2개)
① 너는 멕시코 음식을 먹어 본 적이 있니?
→ Have you ever eaten Mexican food?
② 나는 아직 뉴욕에 가 본 적이 없다.
→ I didn't go to New York yet.
③ 그는 자신의 휴대폰을 두 번 잃어버렸다.
→ He has lost his cellphone twice.
④ 그들은 서울에서 5년 동안 살아 왔다.
→ They have lived in Seoul for five years.
⑤ 우리는 어젯밤에 그 식당에서 식사를 했다.
→ We have eaten at the restaurant last night.

06 두 문장을 한 문장으로 바르게 바꾼 것은?
Jim started making dinner an hour ago.
He is still doing it.
① Jim is making dinner for an hour.
② Jim was making dinner for an hour.
③ Jim has been making dinner for an hour.
④ Jim has been making dinner since an hour.
⑤ Jim has been making dinner for an hour ago.

07 어법상 올바른 문장의 개수는?
ⓐ They have been dancing now.
ⓑ Kim has not studied math yesterday.
ⓒ Susan has been in London for a week.
ⓓ I realized that I had left my bag on the bus.
ⓔ They have finished the project by next month.
① 1개 ② 2개 ③ 3개
④ 4개 ⑤ 5개

22 Grammar Plus Writing 3

Answer Key p.4

08 어법상 올바른 문장을 모두 고르면?
ⓐ I have been knowing her for ten years.
ⓑ How long have you reading this book?
ⓒ I haven't been feeling well since last night.
ⓓ He had been sleeping for two hours when the alarm went off.
ⓔ At 4 o'clock, Lisa will be studying for three hours.
① ⓐ, ⓓ ② ⓑ, ⓓ
③ ⓒ, ⓓ ④ ⓐ, ⓒ, ⓓ
⑤ ⓒ, ⓓ, ⓔ

서술형

09 우리말과 일치하도록 주어진 말을 활용하여 문장을 완성하시오.
(1) 그는 30분 전에 자신의 숙제를 끝냈다.
→ He ______ his homework 30 minutes ago. (finish)
(2) 나는 다음 달에 파트타임으로 일할 것이다.
→ I ______ ______ ______ ______ part time next month. (work)

10 우리말과 일치하도록 주어진 말을 바르게 배열하시오.
(1) 나는 콘택트렌즈를 껴 본 적이 한 번도 없다.
(have, contact lenses, I, never, worn)
→ ______
(2) 그 컴퓨터는 며칠 동안 잘 작동하지 않고 있다.
(working, has, for, the, been, computer, not, days, well)
→ ______

11 두 문장을 과거완료를 사용하여 한 문장으로 바꿔 쓰시오.
My friend lost my book. Later, he told me about it.
→ My friend ______ ______ that he ______ ______ my book.

12 두 문장을 현재완료진행형을 사용하여 한 문장으로 바꿔 쓰시오.
Cindy is traveling around Europe right now.
She began her trip in July.
→ Cindy ______ ______ ______ ______ ______ ______ July.

13 어법상 틀린 부분을 찾아 바르게 고치시오.
(1) I didn't have seen her since last week.
______ → ______
(2) Owen has been having his car for ten years.
______ → ______

14 대화를 읽고, 어법상 틀린 부분을 찾아 바르게 고치시오.
A: Hey, how have you been?
B: I've been great. How about you?
A: Good. I have gone to Bali last month.
B: Wow! How was it?
A: I stayed there for a week and loved everything about it.
______ → ______

Chapter 01 시제 23

ACTUAL TEST

챕터 학습이 끝난 후, 내신 유형의 문제를 풀어보며 학습한 내용을 정리합니다. 최신 빈출 유형과 고난도 유형을 수록했으며, 50% 이상이 서술형 문제로 구성되어 어려워진 내신 시험에 철저히 대비할 수 있습니다.

WORKBOOK

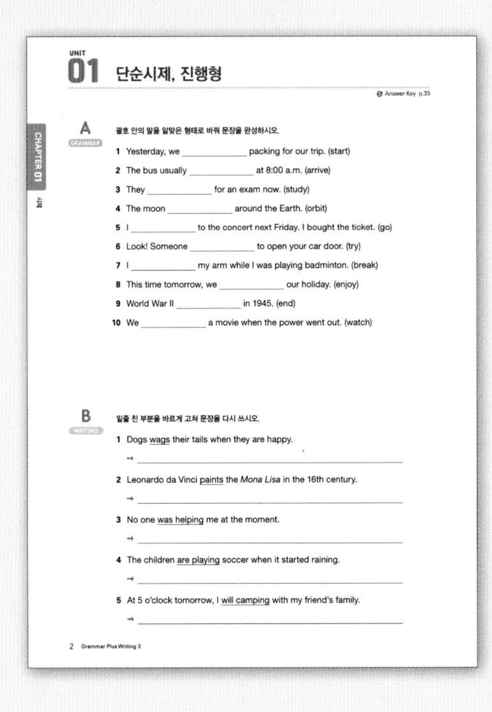

UNIT 01 단순시제, 진행형

Answer Key p.33

CHAPTER 01 시제

A GRAMMAR 괄호 안의 말을 알맞은 형태로 바꿔 문장을 완성하시오.
1 Yesterday, we ______ packing for our trip. (start)
2 The bus usually ______ at 8:00 a.m. (arrive)
3 They ______ for an exam now. (study)
4 The moon ______ around the Earth. (orbit)
5 I ______ to the concert next Friday. I bought the ticket. (go)
6 Look! Someone ______ to open your car door. (try)
7 I ______ my arm while I was playing badminton. (break)
8 This time tomorrow, we ______ our holiday. (enjoy)
9 World War II ______ in 1945. (end)
10 We ______ a movie when the power went out. (watch)

B WRITING 밑줄 친 부분을 바르게 고쳐 문장을 다시 쓰시오.
1 Dogs wags their tails when they are happy.
→ ______
2 Leonardo da Vinci paints the *Mona Lisa* in the 16th century.
→ ______
3 No one was helping me at the moment.
→ ______
4 The children are playing soccer when it started raining.
→ ______
5 At 5 o'clock tomorrow, I will camping with my friend's family.
→ ______

2 Grammar Plus Writing 3

별책으로 제공되는 워크북에서는 각 Unit의 문법사항을 Worksheet 형태로 제공하여 학습한 내용을 빠르게 복습하고 실력을 점검할 수 있습니다.

온라인 부가자료 | www.darakwon.co.kr

다락원 홈페이지에서 무료로 부가자료를 다운로드하거나 웹에서 이용하실 수 있습니다.

CONTENTS | 목차

Chapter 01

시제

UNIT 01 단순시제, 진행형
UNIT 02 완료시제
UNIT 03 완료진행형

UNIT
01 단순시제, 진행형

GRAMMAR FOCUS

❶ 단순시제

현재 (~이다, ~하다)	현재의 사실, 습관, 불변의 진리	I usually **get up** at six in the morning. 나는 보통 아침 6시에 일어난다. 〈습관〉 The sun **rises** in the east. 태양은 동쪽에서 뜬다. 〈불변의 진리〉
과거 (~이었다, ~했다)	과거의 일이나 상태, 역사적 사실	The bus **left** a few minutes ago. 버스는 몇 분 전에 떠났다.
미래 (~일 것이다, ~할 예정이다)	• 예측: will, be going to • 의지, 즉흥적 결정: will • 예정된 계획: be going to	It **will[is going to] be** sunny tomorrow. 내일은 맑을 것이다. 〈예측〉 I'm so hungry. **I'll go** and **buy** some food. 너무 배고파. 내가 가서 음식을 좀 사 올게. 〈즉흥적 결정〉 I **am going to visit** my aunt next weekend. 나는 다음 주말에 나의 숙모를 방문할 예정이다. 〈예정된 계획〉

plus 현재, 과거, 미래시제를 나타내는 시간 표현
- 현재: 빈도부사, every day, on Sundays 등
- 과거: yesterday, last ~, ~ ago, in 1999 등
- 미래: tomorrow, next ~, soon, in two weeks 등

❷ 진행형

현재진행 (~하고 있다)	am/is/are + 동사원형-ing	The baby **is sleeping** soundly. 그 아기는 곤히 자고 있다.
과거진행 (~하고 있었다)	was/were + 동사원형-ing	I **was eating** lunch when you called me. 나는 네가 나에게 전화했을 때 점심을 먹고 있었다.
미래진행 (~하고 있을 것이다)	will be + 동사원형-ing	At midnight tomorrow, I **will be flying** to L.A. 내일 자정에 나는 LA로 비행하고 있을 것이다.

cf. 진행형으로 쓸 수 없는 동사: know, love, like, believe, have, own 등 상태와 소유를 나타내는 동사

Do you know his email address? 너는 그의 이메일 주소를 알고 있니?
└ Are you knowing (×)

❸ 미래를 나타내는 현재시제, 현재진행형

(1) 공식적인 시간표나 일정에 있는 미래의 일은 현재시제로 나타낼 수 있다.

The flight from Tokyo **arrives** at 12:40. 도쿄에서 오는 비행기는 12시 40분에 도착한다.

The class **begins** in September. 그 수업은 9월에 시작한다.

(2) 가까운 미래에 예정된 계획은 현재진행형으로 나타낼 수 있다.

I **am meeting** my friend this afternoon. 나는 오늘 오후에 내 친구를 만날 예정이다.

(= I **am going to meet** my friend this afternoon.)

Answer Key p.2

괄호 안에서 알맞은 것을 고르시오.

1 I (watch, am watching) TV right now.

2 Water (boils, is boiling) at 100 degrees Celsius.

3 Emma (is, was) studying when I entered the room.

4 His car (breaks, broke) down while he was driving to work.

5 I can't join you. I (will, am going) to visit my grandparents today.

6 This time next week, we (were camping, will be camping) in the mountains.

7 **A:** Are you ready to order?

B: Yes, (I have, I'll have) the steak, please.

밑줄 친 부분을 어법에 맞게 고치시오.

1 She usually drink coffee in the morning.

2 It is a nice day. The sun shines.

3 I am having a brother and a sister.

4 Last night, I fell asleep while I am reading in bed.

5 Ann is planning to study until 3:00 p.m. At 2:50 p.m., she is studying.

6 According to the weather forecast, it is cold this weekend.

괄호 안의 말을 이용하여 문장을 완성하시오.

1 Yesterday, we ______________ on a field trip to the museum. (go)

2 What __________ you __________ when I called you? (do)

3 The library ______________ at 5:00 p.m. on Saturdays. (close)

4 I ______________ for my bag. Do you know where it is? (look)

5 Jack ______________ a turtle while he was walking on the beach. (see)

6 My grandmother ______________ 80 years old next month. (be)

7 The movie starts now. We ______________ it in a few minutes. (watch)

WRITING FOCUS

A 배열 영작 우리말과 일치하도록 괄호 안의 말을 바르게 배열하시오.

1 그는 매일 아침 물 한 잔과 함께 비타민을 섭취한다. (he, vitamins, with, takes, a glass of water)

→ ______________________________ every morning.

2 Rachel은 작년에 휴가를 위해 유럽으로 여행을 갔다. (Rachel, Europe, to, for, traveled, vacation)

→ ______________________________ last year.

3 비가 그친 후에는 더 추워질 것이다. (it, get, will, colder)

→ ______________________________ after the rain stops.

4 그는 자신의 가족을 위해 피자와 스파게티를 만들고 있다. (making, he, and, is, pizza, spaghetti)

→ ______________________________ for his family.

5 그는 그 사고가 났을 때 고속도로에서 운전하고 있었다. (he, the, driving, on, was, highway)

→ ______________________________ when the accident happened.

6 내일 이 시간에 나는 집에서 쉬고 있을 것이다. (be, I, at, relaxing, will, home)

→ This time tomorrow, ______________________________.

B 빈칸 완성 우리말과 일치하도록 괄호 안의 말을 이용하여 빈칸에 알맞은 말을 쓰시오.

1 내 여동생은 자신이 가장 좋아하는 노래를 부르고 있다. (sing)

→ My sister ________ ________ her favorite song.

2 너는 초인종이 울렸을 때 뭘 하고 있었니? (do)

→ What ________ ________ ________ when the doorbell rang?

3 그는 대학에서 무엇을 공부했니? (study)

→ What ________ ________ ________ in college?

4 저 회색 구름들 좀 봐. 비가 올 거야. (rain)

→ Look at those gray clouds. It ________ ________ ________ ________.

5 그 시간표에는 마지막 기차가 자정에 도착한다고 쓰여 있다. (arrive)

→ The schedule says that the last train ________ at midnight.

6 그녀는 오늘 자신의 친구 결혼식에 갈 예정이다. (go)

→ She ________ ________ to her friend's wedding today.

Answers p.2

C 문장 완성 우리말과 일치하도록 괄호 안의 말을 이용하여 문장을 완성하시오.

1 그는 보통 점심으로 샌드위치를 먹는다. (eat sandwiches, for lunch)

→ He usually ______________________.

2 그 버스는 30분 간격으로 운행한다. (run, every 30 minutes)

→ The bus ______________________.

3 나는 어제 흥미로운 책 한 권을 샀다. (buy, an interesting book)

→ I ______________________ yesterday.

4 Lisa는 온라인으로 새로운 언어를 배우고 있다. (learn, a new language)

→ Lisa ______________________ online.

5 그녀는 오전 10시에 피아노를 연습하고 있었다. (practice the piano)

→ She ______________________ at 10:00 a.m.

6 우리는 내일 부산으로 떠날 예정이다. (leave for Busan)

→ We ______________________ tomorrow.

D 오류 수정 밑줄 친 부분을 바르게 고쳐 문장을 다시 쓰시오.

1 Mary is liking her new job.

→ ______________________

2 She always make her bed in the morning.

→ ______________________

3 The temperature drop below freezing last night.

→ ______________________

4 Pedro is taking a shower when the water stopped.

→ ______________________

5 What are you doing at 10 o'clock tomorrow?

→ ______________________

6 I promise I am there on time.

→ ______________________

UNIT

02 완료시제

GRAMMAR FOCUS

1 현재완료: have/has + p.p.

과거에 일어난 일이 현재까지 영향을 미치거나 지속된 상태를 나타낸다. 완료, 경험, 결과, 계속의 의미로 쓰인다.

		함께 쓰이는 표현
완료 (방금/이미 ~했다, 아직 ~하지 않았다)	Susan **has** *just* **finished** her homework. Susan은 방금 숙제를 끝냈다. I **haven't packed** my suitcase *yet*. 나는 아직 내 여행 가방을 싸지 않았다.	just, already, yet 등
경험 (~한 적이 있다)	A: **Have** you *ever* **been** to India? 너는 인도에 가 본 적이 있니? B: Yes, I **have**. / No, I **haven't**. 응, 있어. / 아니, 없어.	ever, never, before, once, twice, many times 등
결과 (~했다)	She **has gone** to Paris to study fashion design. 그녀는 패션 디자인을 공부하기 위해 파리로 갔다. (현재 여기 없음)	go, leave, lose 등
계속 (~해 왔다)	He **has lived** in this neighborhood *for ten years*. 그는 이 동네에서 10년 동안 살아 왔다. (현재도 살고 있음)	「for + 기간」, 「since + 시점」, how long ~? 등

plus 현재완료는 어떤 일이 언제 일어났는지는 중요하지 않다. 따라서 yesterday, last ~, ~ ago, when ~ 등 명백한 과거 시점을 나타내는 표현과는 함께 쓸 수 없다.

Susan **finished** her homework *an hour ago*. Susan은 한 시간 전에 숙제를 끝냈다.
└ has finished (×)

2 과거완료: had + p.p.

과거의 특정 시점 이전에 완료된 일이나 그 시점까지 지속되었던 상태를 나타낸다. 과거 기준 시점보다 앞선 과거를 나타내므로 '대과거'라고도 한다.

The train **had left**. — I **arrived** at the station. — now

The train **had** already **left** when I *arrived* at the station. 그 기차는 내가 역에 도착했을 때 이미 떠났다.

I *recognized* him because I **had met** him before. 나는 전에 그를 만난 적이 있기 때문에 그를 알아보았다.

cf. 접속사 before나 after가 쓰여 시간의 전후 관계가 분명할 때는 과거완료 대신 과거시제를 쓸 수 있다.

After I **took** the medicine, I felt much better. 그 약을 복용한 후에 나는 몸이 훨씬 더 나아졌다.
(= *After* I **had taken** the medicine, I felt much better.)

3 미래완료: will have + p.p.

미래의 특정 시점까지 완료될 일이나 지속될 상태를 나타낸다. (미래의 어느 시점에는) '~한 상태일 것이다, ~한 셈이 될 것이다'로 해석한다.

The snowman **will have melted** before the weekend. 그 눈사람은 주말 전에는 녹아 있을 것이다.

The laundry **will have dried** by the time I come back. 그 빨래는 내가 돌아올 때까지는 다 말라 있을 것이다.

By next year, they **will have been married** for 25 years. 내년이면 그들은 25년 동안 결혼한 셈이 될 것이다.

Answer Key p.2

괄호 안에서 알맞은 것을 고르시오.

1 I (ate, have eaten) at the new restaurant twice.

2 She (started, has started) playing the piano when she was seven.

3 Emily doesn't have any money because she (has, had) lost her purse.

4 When we arrived at the theater, the movie (has, had) already started.

5 By next year, we (have lived, will have lived) in this city for five years.

6 They (didn't go, haven't gone) on a family trip since last summer.

밑줄 친 부분을 어법에 맞게 고치시오.

1 We haven't seen each other for last month.

2 Have you ever try sushi before? It's delicious.

3 Luke is still waiting for the bus. It hadn't come yet.

4 My mom was angry because I have forgotten to call her.

5 They have finished cooking by the time the guests arrive.

6 I thought that I have seen her somewhere before.

우리말과 일치하도록 괄호 안의 말을 이용하여 문장을 완성하시오.

1 우리는 방금 호텔에 도착했다. (just, arrive)

→ We __________ __________ __________ at the hotel.

2 나는 10년 동안 영어를 가르쳐 왔으며, 이 일을 정말 좋아한다. (teach)

→ I __________ __________ English for ten years, and I love this job.

3 Isabel은 나에게 자신이 스페인에 가 본 적이 있다고 말했다. (be)

→ Isabel told me that she __________ __________ to Spain.

4 다음 주면 그녀는 1년 동안 프랑스어를 공부한 셈이 될 것이다. (study)

→ By next week, she __________ __________ __________ French for a year.

WRITING FOCUS

A 배열 영작 우리말과 일치하도록 괄호 안의 말을 바르게 배열하시오.

1 Joe는 최근에 체중이 많이 늘었다. (weight, has, Joe, a lot of, gained)

→ ______________________________ recently.

2 너는 두리안을 먹어 본 적이 있니? (have, ever, you, eaten)

→ ______________________________ durian?

3 그녀는 병원에 얼마나 오래 있었니? (how, has, long, she, been)

→ ______________________________ in the hospital?

4 Chris는 이미 그의 모든 용돈을 썼다. (already, Chris, spent, has)

→ ______________________________ all his pocket money.

5 Bill은 자신의 휴대폰을 집에 두고 왔다는 것을 깨달았다. (left, he, at, his, had, cellphone, home)

→ Bill realized that ______________________________.

6 내년이면 Amy는 대학을 졸업해 있을 것이다. (have, will, graduated, university, from, Amy)

→ By next year, ______________________________.

B 빈칸 완성 우리말과 일치하도록 괄호 안의 말을 이용하여 빈칸에 알맞은 말을 쓰시오.

1 Pam과 Rosie는 그들이 10살 때부터 친구였다. (be)

→ Pam and Rosie __________ __________ friends since they __________ ten.

2 그들은 저녁 식사 후 아직 설거지를 하지 않았다. (wash)

→ They __________ __________ the dishes after dinner yet.

3 너는 지금까지 몇 권의 책을 읽었니? (read)

→ How many books __________ __________ __________ so far?

4 내가 식당에 도착했을 때 내 친구들은 이미 주문을 했다. (already, order)

→ When I got to the restaurant, my friends __________ __________ __________.

5 그는 이 도시에 오기 전에 눈을 본 적이 한 번도 없었다. (never, see)

→ He __________ __________ __________ snow before he came to this city.

6 비는 공연이 시작할 때까지는 그쳐 있을 것이다. (stop)

→ The rain __________ __________ __________ by the time the concert starts.

Answer Key p.3

C 문장 완성 우리말과 일치하도록 괄호 안의 말을 이용하여 문장을 완성하시오.

1 나는 바이올린을 연주해 본 적이 한 번도 없다. (never, play the violin)

→ I ______________________.

2 그들은 방금 기차역에 도착했다. (just, arrive, at the train station)

→ They ______________________.

3 Jack은 13년 동안 같은 일을 해 왔다. (have, the same job, thirteen years)

→ Jack ______________________.

4 Martin은 나에게 자신이 전에 런던에서 일을 했었다고 말했다. (work, in London, before)

→ Martin told me that ______________________.

5 Andy는 그의 오래된 차가 고장 났기 때문에 새 차를 샀다. (old one, break down)

→ Andy bought a new car because ______________________.

6 다음 주면 그녀는 자신의 프로젝트를 완료했을 것이다. (complete, project)

→ By next week, ______________________.

D 오류 수정 밑줄 친 부분을 바르게 고쳐 문장을 다시 쓰시오.

1 Have you ever learn to dance?

→ ______________________

2 Mr. Brown has gone to Egypt twice.

→ ______________________

3 The old couple has lived in the country since many years.

→ ______________________

4 He didn't know that someone has stolen his wallet.

→ ______________________

5 My brother already eaten the cake when I got home.

→ ______________________

6 By the time I wake up, my mom will gone to work.

→ ______________________

UNIT 03

완료진행형

GRAMMAR FOCUS

1 현재완료진행: have / has been + 동사원형-ing

현재완료와 진행형을 모두 포함하는 시제로, 과거에 시작되어 지금도 진행 중인 일을 나타낸다.

It **has been raining** for a week. 일주일째 비가 내리고 있다.

I **have been cleaning** my room since 1 o'clock. 나는 1시부터 내 방을 청소하고 있다.

He **has been thinking** about changing his job recently. 그는 최근에 이직을 하는 것에 대해 생각하고 있다.

cf. 상태와 소유를 나타내는 동사는 현재완료진행형으로 쓸 수 없으며 현재완료로 대신한다.

I **have known** him for many years. 나는 그를 수년 동안 알고 지냈다.
└ have been knowing (×)

plus 현재진행형 vs. 현재완료진행형

현재진행형은 지금 진행 중인 일을 나타내지만, 현재완료진행형은 과거부터 지금까지 진행 중인 일을 나타내며, for ~, since ~, how long ~ 등 기간을 나타내는 말과 자주 함께 쓰인다.

He **is studying** *now*. 그는 지금 공부를 하고 있다. 〈지금 진행 중임을 강조〉

He **has been studying** *for three hours*. 그는 세 시간째 공부를 하고 있다. 〈활동의 기간을 강조〉

2 과거완료진행: had been + 동사원형-ing

과거의 특정 시점 이전에 시작되어 그 시점에도 진행 중이었던 일을 나타낸다.

He **had been sleeping** for an hour when the phone rang.
그는 그 전화벨이 울렸을 때 한 시간째 자고 있었다.

By the time I arrived, they **had been waiting** for over an hour.
내가 도착했을 때까지 그들은 한 시간이 넘게 기다리고 있었다.

We **had been living** here for ten years before we moved to Canada.
우리는 캐나다로 이주하기 전에 10년 동안 여기서 살고 있었다.

3 미래완료진행: will have been + 동사원형-ing

미래의 특정 시점까지 계속되어 그 시점에도 진행 중일 일을 나타낸다.

At 9 o'clock tonight, I **will have been studying** for four hours.
오늘 밤 9시가 되면 나는 네 시간 동안 공부하고 있는 셈이 될 것이다.

By the time we arrive in New York, we **will have been flying** for seven hours.
뉴욕에 도착할 때까지 우리는 일곱 시간 동안 비행하고 있는 셈이 될 것이다.

He **will have been working** as a professor for 30 years next year.
그는 내년이면 30년 동안 교수로 일하고 있는 셈이 될 것이다.

Answer Key p.3

EXERCISE A

괄호 안에서 알맞은 것을 고르시오.

1 Look outside. It (is raining, has been raining) right now.

2 Chris (is studying, has been studying) since 2 o'clock.

3 My father (has had, has been having) his car for ten years.

4 Lisa (is listening, has been listening) to Christmas music all day.

5 How long (are you painting, have you been painting) this picture?

6 Judy (is singing, has been singing) the same song for an hour.

EXERCISE B

밑줄 친 부분을 어법에 맞게 고치시오.

1 I am looking for my keys since this morning.

2 Jim was running for an hour when I called him.

3 He will be driving for three hours by the time he gets home.

4 Sue and Eric are playing tennis. They had been playing it for two hours.

5 David was tired because he has been working for a long time.

6 Andy hasn't come yet. At 2 o'clock, I have been waiting for him for an hour.

EXERCISE C

우리말과 일치하도록 괄호 안의 말을 이용하여 문장을 완성하시오.

1 그들은 쉬지 않고 세 시간째 걷고 있다. (walk)

→ They ________ ________ ________ for three hours without a break.

2 Mark는 9시부터 샤워를 하고 있다. (take)

→ Mark ________ ________ ________ a shower since 9 o'clock.

3 그가 방에 들어왔을 때, 나는 한 시간째 공부하고 있었다. (study)

→ When he entered the room, I ________ ________ ________ for an hour.

4 정오가 되면, 나는 두 시간 동안 책을 읽고 있는 셈이 될 것이다. (read)

→ At noon, I ________ ________ ________ ________ for two hours.

WRITING FOCUS

A 배열 영작 우리말과 일치하도록 괄호 안의 말을 바르게 배열하시오.

1 Fred는 세 시간째 컴퓨터 게임을 하고 있다. (been, a, Fred, computer game, has, playing)

→ ________________________________ for three hours.

2 너는 얼마나 오랫동안 그 버스를 기다리고 있니? (how, you, been, long, have, waiting)

→ ________________________________ for the bus?

3 아침부터 비가 내리고 있다. (has, it, raining, been)

→ ________________________________ since morning.

4 그는 내가 그를 깨웠을 때 열 시간째 자고 있었다. (been, he, ten, sleeping, hours, for, had)

→ ________________________________ when I woke him up.

5 나는 하루 종일 해변에서 놀았기 때문에 햇볕에 탔다. (beach, on, playing, I, been, had, the)

→ I got sunburned because ________________________________ all day.

6 6시가 되면 우리는 다섯 시간 동안 쇼핑을 하고 있는 셈이 될 것이다. (we, been, will, shopping, have)

→ At six o'clock, ________________________________ for five hours.

B 빈칸 완성 우리말과 일치하도록 괄호 안의 말을 이용하여 빈칸에 알맞은 말을 쓰시오.

1 Sue와 Jin은 몇 시간째 통화를 하고 있다. (talk)

→ Sue and Jin __________ __________ __________ on the phone for hours.

2 나는 최근에 파트타임으로 일하고 있다. (work)

→ I __________ __________ __________ part time recently.

3 너희는 서로를 안 지 얼마나 되었니? (know, you)

→ How long __________ __________ __________ each other?

4 나는 지금 공부를 하고 있지 않다. 나는 영화를 보고 있다. (study, watch)

→ I __________ __________ __________ now. I __________ __________ a movie.

5 그 전화기가 작동을 멈췄을 때, 그는 일 년째 그것을 사용하고 있었다. (use)

→ When the phone stopped working, he __________ __________ __________ it for a year.

6 내일이면 3일 동안 비가 내리고 있는 셈이 될 것이다. (rain)

→ It __________ __________ __________ __________ for three days tomorrow.

C 문장 완성 우리말과 일치하도록 괄호 안의 말을 이용하여 문장을 완성하시오.

1 Sam은 한 시간째 수영을 하고 있다. (swim, an hour)

→ Sam ______________________.

2 지금 눈이 내리고 있어? (it, snow)

→ ______________________ right now?

3 그는 3시부터 그 컴퓨터를 사용하고 있다. (use the computer, 3 o'clock)

→ He ______________________.

4 비가 내리기 시작했을 때 그들은 두 시간째 하이킹을 하고 있었다. (hike, two hours)

→ When it started raining, ______________________.

5 정오가 되면 그는 열 시간 동안 자고 있는 셈이 될 것이다. (sleep, ten hours)

→ At noon, ______________________.

6 9월이면, 우리는 새 집에서 1년 동안 살고 있는 셈이 될 것이다. (in our new house, a year)

→ In September, we ______________________.

D 오류 수정 밑줄 친 부분을 바르게 고쳐 문장을 다시 쓰시오.

1 Eric is taking a nap for 30 minutes.

→ ______________________

2 Liam has been knowing Amy for fifteen years.

→ ______________________

3 The children had been playing since they woke up.

→ ______________________

4 She has been studying for two hours when her friend called.

→ ______________________

5 By next June, I will be attending this school for three years.

→ ______________________

6 By tomorrow, Jessica will have working here for a year.

→ ______________________

ACTUAL TEST

문항 수	객관식 8 / 서술형 12
맞은 개수	/ 20

01 다음 중 어법상 틀린 것은?

① Jane walks to school every day.
② I bought a new phone two weeks ago.
③ They will graduate from college in May.
④ Alex is sleeping when the phone rang.
⑤ We will be eating dinner at 7 o'clock.

02 <보기>의 밑줄 친 부분과 쓰임이 같은 것은?

보기 The concert starts at 9:00 p.m.

① It rains a lot in this city.
② Plants need water to grow.
③ She reads a book every night.
④ The bus arrives in twenty minutes.
⑤ We usually go to the park on Sundays.

03 우리말과 일치하도록 주어진 말을 배열할 때, 네 번째로 오는 단어는?

나는 내일 친구들과 캠핑을 갈 것이다.
(am, my, I, friends, camping, going, with)
→ ______________________
tomorrow.

① am ② with ③ going
④ friends ⑤ camping

04 빈칸에 들어갈 말로 알맞은 것은?

Dylan changed his clothes because he ________ coffee on them.

① spills ② will spill
③ is spilling ④ has spilled
⑤ had spilled

05 우리말을 영어로 잘못 옮긴 것은? (2개)

① 너는 멕시코 음식을 먹어 본 적이 있니?
→ Have you ever eaten Mexican food?
② 나는 아직 뉴욕에 가 본 적이 없다.
→ I didn't go to New York yet.
③ 그는 자신의 휴대폰을 두 번 잃어버렸다.
→ He has lost his cellphone twice.
④ 그들은 서울에서 5년 동안 살아 왔다.
→ They have lived in Seoul for five years.
⑤ 우리는 어젯밤에 그 식당에서 식사를 했다.
→ We have eaten at the restaurant last night.

빈출
06 두 문장을 한 문장으로 바르게 바꾼 것은?

Jim started making dinner an hour ago.
He is still doing it.

① Jim is making dinner for an hour.
② Jim was making dinner for an hour.
③ Jim has been making dinner for an hour.
④ Jim has been making dinner since an hour.
⑤ Jim has been making dinner for an hour ago.

고난도
07 어법상 올바른 문장의 개수는?

ⓐ They have been dancing now.
ⓑ Kim has not studied math yesterday.
ⓒ Susan has been in London for a week.
ⓓ I realized that I had left my bag on the bus.
ⓔ They have finished the project by next month.

① 1개 ② 2개 ③ 3개
④ 4개 ⑤ 5개

고난도

08 어법상 올바른 문장을 모두 고르면?

ⓐ I have been knowing her for ten years.
ⓑ How long have you reading this book?
ⓒ I haven't been feeling well since last night.
ⓓ He had been sleeping for two hours when the alarm went off.
ⓔ At 4 o'clock, Lisa will be studying for three hours.

① ⓐ, ⓓ
② ⓑ, ⓓ
③ ⓒ, ⓓ
④ ⓐ, ⓒ, ⓓ
⑤ ⓒ, ⓓ, ⓔ

서술형

09 우리말과 일치하도록 주어진 말을 활용하여 문장을 완성하시오.

(1) 그는 30분 전에 자신의 숙제를 끝냈다.

→ He ________ his homework 30 minutes ago. (finish)

(2) 나는 다음 달에 파트타임으로 일할 것이다.

→ I ________ ________ ________ ________ part time next month. (work)

10 우리말과 일치하도록 주어진 말을 바르게 배열하시오.

(1) 나는 콘택트렌즈를 껴 본 적이 한 번도 없다.
(have, contact lenses, I, never, worn)

→ ________________________

(2) 그 컴퓨터는 며칠 동안 잘 작동하지 않고 있다.
(working, has, for, the, been, computer, not, days, well)

→ ________________________

11 두 문장을 과거완료를 사용하여 한 문장으로 바꿔 쓰시오.

My friend lost my book. Later, he told me about it.

→ My friend ________ ________ that he ________ ________ my book.

12 두 문장을 현재완료진행형을 사용하여 한 문장으로 바꿔 쓰시오.

Cindy is traveling around Europe right now. She began her trip in July.

→ Cindy ________ ________ ________ ________ ________ ________ July.

13 어법상 틀린 부분을 찾아 바르게 고치시오.

(1) I didn't have seen her since last week.

________ → ________

(2) Owen has been having his car for ten years.

________ → ________

14 대화를 읽고, 어법상 틀린 부분을 찾아 바르게 고치시오.

A: Hey, how have you been?
B: I've been great. How about you?
A: Good. I have gone to Bali last month.
B: Wow! How was it?
A: I stayed there for a week and loved everything about it.

________ → ________

15 우리말과 일치하도록 〈보기〉에서 필요한 단어들만 골라 배열하여 문장을 완성하시오.

(1) 나는 그가 도착했을 때 설거지를 하고 있었다.

보기	he am was arrives arrived doing did the dishes when

→ I ______________________.

(2) 나는 오후 3시에 도서관에서 공부하고 있을 것이다.

보기	I be am at the library study studying will

→ ______________________ at 3:00 p.m.

16 그림을 보고, 〈조건〉에 맞게 문장을 완성하시오.

two hours ago now

조건	1. do, her homework를 활용할 것 2. 알맞은 시제를 사용할 것

(1) She ______________________ now.

(2) She ______________________ for two hours.

17 어법상 틀린 것을 찾아 기호를 쓰고 바르게 고치시오.

> Chris ⓐis waiting for Lucy. He ⓑbegan to wait for her at 2 o'clock. It ⓒis 3 o'clock now. He ⓓhad been waiting for her for an hour. By 4 o'clock, he ⓔwill have been waiting for her for two hours.

( ) → ______________

18 우리말과 일치하도록 〈조건〉에 맞게 문장을 완성하시오.

(1) 그 콘서트는 우리가 도착했을 때 이미 시작했다.

조건	1. concert, already, start, arrive를 순서대로 활용할 것 2. 총 8단어로 쓸 것

→ ______________________

(2) 내일이면 그는 그 차를 고쳤을 것이다.

조건	1. by, fix, the car를 순서대로 활용할 것 2. 총 8단어로 쓸 것

→ ______________________

[19-20] 대화를 읽고, 물음에 답하시오.

> A: (A) 너는 수의사가 되는 것을 생각해 본 적이 있니?
> B: Yes, I have. I love animals, especially dogs and cats.
> A: That's great! (B) 너는 네 꿈을 이루기 위해 무엇을 하고 있니? (do)
> B: I am doing volunteer work at the local animal shelter and reading books about animals.
> A: Wonderful! I believe you will make a great vet.

19 밑줄 친 (A)와 일치하도록 주어진 말을 바르게 배열하시오.

> you, vet, about, becoming, thought, ever, a, have

→ ______________________

20 밑줄 친 (B)와 일치하도록 주어진 말을 활용하여 문장을 완성하시오.

→ ________ ________ ________ ________ to make your dream come true?

Chapter 02

조동사

UNIT 01 조동사

GRAMMAR FOCUS

❶ 조동사의 의미

can	능력	I **can**(= **am able to**) run fast. *can의 과거형은 could를 쓴다.	나는 빨리 달릴 **수 있다.**
	허가	You **can** use my phone.	너는 내 전화기를 사용**해도 된다.**
	요청	**Can**(= **Will**) you pass me the salt? *정중한 요청은 Could / Would you ~?를 쓴다.	내게 소금 좀 건네 **줄래**?
	강한 추측	That **can't be** true.	그것은 사실**일 리가 없다.**
may	허가	**May** I leave the table? *May you ~?는 쓰지 않는다.	자리에서 먼저 일어나**도 될까요?**
	약한 추측	He **may**(= **might**) be at home.	그는 집에 있을지**도 모른다.**
must	의무	You **must** follow the rules.	너는 그 규칙을 따라**야 한다.**
	강한 추측	He **must** be very upset.	그는 매우 화난 것**이 틀림없다.**
	금지	You **must not** drink the water.	너는 그 물을 마시**면 안 된다.**
have to	의무	She **has to** go to class today.	그녀는 오늘 수업에 가**야 한다.**
	불필요	We **don't have to** hurry.	우리는 서두를 **필요가 없다.**
should	조언	We **should**(= **ought to**) leave now. *ought to의 부정형은 ought not to를 쓴다.	우리는 지금 출발해**야 한다.**

cf. 1. 조동사는 두 개를 나란히 쓸 수 없으며, '~할 수 있을 것이다'는 will be able to로 쓴다.

We **will be able to** meet again soon. 우리는 곧 다시 만날 **수 있을 것이다.**
(└ will can (×))

2. 의무를 나타내는 must와 have to의 과거형은 둘 다 had to를 쓴다.

I **had to** go to the dentist yesterday. 나는 어제 치과에 갔**어야 했다.**

❷ 주의해야 할 조동사

had better	경고	You **had better** go now. You **had better not** go now.	너는 지금 가**는 것이 좋겠다.** 너는 지금 가**지 않는 것이 좋겠다.**
would rather	선호	I **would rather** walk (*than* drive). I **would rather not** walk.	나는 (운전 하느니) **차라리** 걷**겠다.** 나는 **차라리** 걷**지 않겠다.**
used to	과거의 습관	She **used to**(= **would**) travel a lot.	그녀는 여행을 많이 **하곤 했다.**
	과거의 상태	We **used to** be very close. *과거의 상태는 would로 바꿔 쓸 수 없다.	우리는 아주 친**했었다.**

plus used to가 포함된 표현 구분하기

- He **used to fix** cars. 그는 차를 **수리하곤 했다.** 〈used to + 동사원형: ~하곤 했다〉
- He **is used to fixing** cars. 그는 차를 **수리하는 데 익숙하다.** 〈be used to + 동명사: ~하는 데 익숙하다〉
- The tools **are used to fix** cars. 그 도구들은 차를 **수리하기 위해 사용된다.** 〈be used to + 동사원형: ~하기 위해 사용되다〉

Answer Key p.5

〈보기〉에서 밑줄 친 부분에 해당하는 의미를 골라 기호를 쓰시오.

보기	ⓐ 능력	ⓑ 허가	ⓒ 추측	ⓓ 의무	ⓔ 금지	ⓕ 불필요

1 Jessica may be in the classroom. ______

2 Passengers must fasten their seatbelts. ______

3 Teenagers must not drink alcohol. ______

4 Eric doesn't have to wear a suit to work. ______

5 You can use my car while I am on vacation. ______

6 Scott could play the guitar when he was 10 years old. ______

EXERCISE

B

괄호 안에서 알맞은 것을 고르시오.

1 (Can, May) you buy some milk on your way home?

2 The story does not make sense. It (must, can't) be true.

3 He (might, should) stop smoking and eat healthy food.

4 We (must not, don't have to) wait in line. We have VIP passes.

5 You (had not better, had better not) be late for your job interview.

6 I (have to, would rather) go to the gym than watch sports.

7 Sally (used to, would) love eating chocolate, but now she hates it.

EXERCISE

C

두 문장의 의미가 같도록 빈칸에 알맞은 말을 쓰시오.

1 I can write with my left hand.

→ I ______ ______ ______ write with my left hand.

2 Ryan must finish his report by Friday.

→ Ryan ______ ______ finish his report by Friday.

3 You should not buy the grapes. They look bad.

→ You ______ ______ ______ buy the grapes. They look bad.

4 Kim and Greg used to go snowboarding together.

→ Kim and Greg ______ go snowboarding together.

WRITING FOCUS

A 배열 영작 우리말과 일치하도록 괄호 안의 말을 바르게 배열하시오.

1 그는 100미터를 15초에 달릴 수 있다. (can, 100m, he, run)

→ ________________________________ in 15 seconds.

2 내가 주말 동안 네 차를 빌릴 수 있을까? (I, your, borrow, can, car)

→ ________________________________ for the weekend?

3 이번 주말은 맑을 지도 모른다. (may, sunny, it, be)

→ ________________________________ this weekend.

4 나는 어제 내 과학 프로젝트를 끝내야 했다. (had, I, my, to, science project, finish)

→ ________________________________ yesterday.

5 방문객들은 박물관 내에서 사진을 찍으면 안 된다. (not, visitors, take, must, pictures)

→ ________________________________ in the museum.

6 너는 파티에 아무것도 가져올 필요가 없어. (don't, anything, have, you, bring, to)

→ ________________________________ to the party.

B 빈칸 완성 우리말과 일치하도록 괄호 안의 말을 이용하여 빈칸에 알맞은 말을 쓰시오.

1 너는 그것을 하지 않아도 돼. 내가 나중에 할게. (do)

→ You ________ ________ ________ ________ it. I'll do it later.

2 나는 이제 가야 할 것 같아. 벌써 9시야. (go)

→ I think I ________ ________ now. It's already 9 o'clock.

3 Lisa는 내일까지 독후감을 써야 한다. (write)

→ Lisa ________ ________ ________ a book report by tomorrow.

4 너는 코트는 입는 것이 좋겠어. 밖이 매우 춥거든. (wear)

→ You ________ ________ ________ a coat. It's very cold outside.

5 나는 그 영화를 차라리 보지 않겠어. (watch)

→ I ________ ________ ________ ________ the movie.

6 나의 어머니는 비 오는 날에 우리에게 전을 만들어 주시곤 하셨다. (make)

→ My mother ________ ________ ________ us *jeon* on rainy days.

Answer Key p.6

C 문장 완성 우리말과 일치하도록 괄호 안의 말을 이용하여 문장을 완성하시오.

1 Jackson 씨는 지금 사무실에 있는 것이 틀림없다. (at the office)

→ Mr. Jackson ______________________________ now.

2 나는 내년 여름에 유럽으로 배낭여행을 갈지도 모른다. (go backpacking in Europe)

→ ______________________________ next summer.

3 그는 어젯밤에 야근을 해야 했다. (work overtime)

→ ______________________________ last night.

4 당신은 쇼핑하러 갈 때 현금을 들고 다닐 필요가 없다. (carry, cash)

→ ______________________________ when you go shopping.

5 그는 언젠가 자신의 목표를 이룰 수 있을 것이다. (will, achieve, goal)

→ ______________________________ someday.

6 우리는 공항까지 택시를 타는 것이 좋겠다. (take a taxi)

→ ______________________________ to the airport.

D 오류 수정 밑줄 친 부분을 바르게 고쳐 문장을 다시 쓰시오.

1 You <u>must not</u> pay for parking. (너는 주차비를 낼 필요가 없다.)

→ ______________________________

2 She <u>shouldn't</u> be at home now. (그녀는 지금 집에 있을 리가 없다.)

→ ______________________________

3 In the future, robots <u>will can</u> do more jobs. (미래에는 로봇이 더 많은 일을 할 수 있을 것이다.)

→ ______________________________

4 You <u>don't have to</u> forget your passport. (너는 네 여권을 잊어서는 안 된다.)

→ ______________________________

5 You <u>had not better</u> leave your bag here. (너는 네 가방을 여기 두지 않는 것이 좋겠어.)

→ ______________________________

6 I <u>would</u> have long hair when I was in middle school. (나는 중학교 때 머리가 길었다.)

→ ______________________________

UNIT

02 조동사 + have p.p.

GRAMMAR FOCUS

1 may[might] have p.p.

'~했을지도 모른다'의 의미로 과거의 일에 대한 약한 추측을 나타낸다.

They	**may[might] have gone**	home.	그들은 집에 **갔을지도 모른다.**
	may[might] not have gone		그들은 집에 **가지 않았을지도 모른다.**

Nick didn't come to class yesterday. He **may have been** sick.
Nick은 어제 수업에 오지 않았다. 그는 아팠을지도 모른다.

Sue looks tired. She **may not have slept** well last night.
Sue는 피곤해 보인다. 그녀는 어젯밤에 잠을 잘 못 잤을지도 모른다.

2 must have p.p. / can't have p.p.

'~했음에 틀림없다'의 의미로 과거의 일에 대한 강한 추측이나 확신을 나타낸다. 부정형인 '~했을 리가 없다'는 can't have p.p.로 나타낸다.

He	**must have made**	a big mistake.	그가 큰 실수를 **했음에 틀림없다.**
	can't have made		그가 큰 실수를 **했을 리가 없다.**

The ground is wet. It **must have rained** last night.
땅이 젖어 있다. 어젯밤에 비가 왔음에 틀림없다.

It's a holiday today. She **can't have gone** to school.
오늘은 공휴일이다. 그녀는 학교에 갔을 리가 없다.

3 should have p.p.

'~했어야 했다 (그런데 했다)'의 의미로 과거의 일에 대한 후회를 나타낸다.

You	**should have followed**	the advice.	너는 그 충고를 **따랐어야 했다.**
	shouldn't have followed		너는 그 충고를 **따르지 말았어야 했다.**

Owen failed the test. He **should have studied** harder.
Owen은 그 시험에 떨어졌다. 그는 더 열심히 공부했어야 했다.

My stomach hurts. I **shouldn't have eaten** too much.
나는 배가 아프다. 나는 너무 많이 먹지 말았어야 했다.

Answer Key p.6

괄호 안에서 알맞은 것을 고르시오.

1 Let's hurry up. We may (be, have been) late for class.

2 I can't find my umbrella. I may (leave, have left) it on the bus.

3 Joe fell off his bike. He (must, should) have been more careful.

4 We (can't, shouldn't) have watched the movie. It was terrible.

5 Tom (can't, should) have written this letter. This is not his handwriting.

6 She drank three glasses of water. She (must, may not) have been very thirsty.

〈보기〉에서 알맞은 조동사를 고른 후, 괄호 안의 말과 함께 써서 문장을 완성하시오.

보기	may not	must	can't	should

1 **A:** The tickets sold out quickly.
B: We __________ __________ __________ them in advance. (buy)

2 **A:** The oven is warm.
B: Someone __________ __________ __________ it. (use)

3 **A:** Where's the dog?
B: It __________ __________ __________ __________. The door is closed. (go out)

4 **A:** Dave hasn't responded to my email.
B: He __________ __________ __________ __________ it yet. (read)

EXERCISE
C

우리말과 일치하도록 괄호 안의 말을 이용하여 문장을 완성하시오.

1 Tim은 숙제를 했어야 했지만 하지 않았다. (do)
→ Tim __________ __________ __________ his homework, but he didn't.

2 그녀는 단것을 싫어한다. 그녀가 그 케이크를 다 먹었을 리가 없다. (eat)
→ She hates sweets. She __________ __________ __________ all the cake.

3 그들은 기분이 안 좋아 보인다. 그들은 그 경기에서 졌을지도 모른다. (lose)
→ They look unhappy. They __________ __________ __________ the game.

WRITING FOCUS

A 배열 영작 **우리말과 일치하도록 괄호 안의 말을 바르게 배열하시오.**

1 그녀에게 무슨 일이 일어났을지도 모른다. (may, to, something, have, her, happened)

→ ______________________________

2 Liam은 내 메시지를 받지 못했을지도 모른다. (Liam, may, have, not, my, gotten, message)

→ ______________________________

3 그는 그 모임에 대해 잊고 있었음에 틀림없다. (he, have, must, the, forgotten, meeting, about)

→ ______________________________

4 Jones 씨는 진실을 알고 있었을 리가 없다. (Mr. Jones, can't, the, known, truth, have)

→ ______________________________

5 우리는 그 경기를 위해 더 많이 연습했어야 했다. (have, we, for, more, the, practiced, should, game)

→ ______________________________

6 그는 거짓말을 하지 말았어야 했다. (shouldn't, he, a, have, lie, told)

→ ______________________________

B 빈칸 완성 **우리말과 일치하도록 괄호 안의 말을 이용하여 빈칸에 알맞은 말을 쓰시오.**

1 그는 버스를 잘못 탔을지도 모른다. (take)

→ He __________ __________ __________ the wrong bus.

2 그 경기는 아직 시작하지 않았을지도 모른다. (start)

→ The game __________ __________ __________ __________ yet.

3 누군가 내 컴퓨터를 사용했음에 틀림없다. (use)

→ Somebody __________ __________ __________ my computer.

4 그녀는 어제 학교에 있었을 리가 없다. (be)

→ She __________ __________ __________ at school yesterday.

5 나는 어젯밤에 알람을 맞춰 놓았어야 했다. (set)

→ I __________ __________ __________ the alarm last night.

6 그는 예일 대신 하버드를 선택하지 말았어야 했다. (choose)

→ He __________ __________ __________ Harvard over Yale.

C 문장 완성 우리말과 일치하도록 괄호 안의 말을 이용하여 문장을 완성하시오.

1 그는 아파서 조퇴했는지도 모른다. (feel sick)
→ ______________________________ and left early.

2 그녀는 백화점에서 많은 돈을 썼음에 틀림없다. (spend, a lot of)
→ ______________________________ at the department store.

3 그 버스가 우리 없이 떠났을 리가 없다. (the bus, leave)
→ ______________________________ without us.

4 그는 오늘 아침에 체육관에 있었는지도 모른다. (at the gym)
→ ______________________________ this morning.

5 너는 나에게 직접 이야기를 했어야 했다. (talk to)
→ ______________________________ in person.

6 나는 밤을 새지 말았어야 했다. (stay up)
→ ______________________________ all night.

D 오류 수정 어법상 틀린 부분을 바르게 고쳐 문장을 다시 쓰시오.

1 Bob may have went shopping. (Bob은 쇼핑을 갔을지도 모른다.)
→ ______________________________

2 She may have not seen me there. (그녀는 거기서 나를 보지 못했을지도 모른다.)
→ ______________________________

3 I must left my wallet in the car. (나는 내 지갑을 차에 두고 왔음에 틀림없다.)
→ ______________________________

4 She can't forget her own birthday. (그녀가 자신의 생일을 잊어버렸을 리가 없다.)
→ ______________________________

5 He should quit smoking a long time ago. (그는 오래 전에 금연을 했어야 했다.)
→ ______________________________

6 Somebody must steal my bike last night. (누군가 어젯밤에 내 자전거를 훔쳐갔음에 틀림없다.)
→ ______________________________

ACTUAL TEST

문항 수	객관식 8 / 서술형 12
맞은 개수	/ 20

01 빈칸에 공통으로 들어갈 말은?

- Students ________ use the computers in the library.
- The remote control is not working. The batteries ________ be dead.

① can ② can't
③ may ④ should
⑤ have to

02 빈칸에 들어갈 말로 알맞은 것은?

We bought groceries for the week. We ________ go shopping until Sunday.

① should ② cannot
③ must not ④ had better
⑤ don't have to

[03-04] 우리말을 영어로 바르게 옮긴 것을 고르시오.

03 그녀의 이야기는 사실일 리가 없다.

① Her story must be true.
② Her story can't be true.
③ Her story may not be true.
④ Her story shouldn't be true.
⑤ Her story doesn't have to be true.

04 우리는 더 일찍 예약을 했어야 했다.

① We could make a reservation earlier.
② We should make a reservation earlier.
③ We may have made a reservation earlier.
④ We must have made a reservation earlier.
⑤ We should have made a reservation earlier.

05 밑줄 친 부분과 바꿔 쓴 것 중 알맞지 않은 것은?

① May I borrow your pen? (→ Can)
② James can type very fast. (→ is able to)
③ You should eat more vegetables. (→ ought to)
④ They must clean their room every day. (→ have to)
⑤ There used to be a pond in the garden. (→ would)

[06-07] 밑줄 친 부분의 쓰임이 어색한 것을 고르시오.

06 ① A: I have a backache.
B: You should not carry heavy things.
② A: Tomorrow is a holiday.
B: Yes, we don't have to go to school.
③ A: Ian solved the difficult math problems.
B: He must be a very clever boy.
④ A: There will be a storm tonight.
B: We had not better go out.
⑤ A: The buses are full.
B: I would rather take the subway.

빈출

07 ① It's getting cold. I should have brought my coat.
② He ate very little. He may not have been hungry.
③ The TV is on. I must have forgotten to turn it off.
④ She can't have left the house. Her shoes are still here.
⑤ Tom shouldn't have studied for the exam, but he didn't.

고난도

08 어법상 올바른 문장을 모두 고르면?

ⓐ I'll be able to see you tomorrow.
ⓑ Joe has to pay his speeding ticket yesterday.
ⓒ You ought not to speak rudely to your parents.
ⓓ We had better to hurry, or we'll be late.
ⓔ I am used to be shy when I was young.

① 1개 ② 2개 ③ 3개
④ 4개 ⑤ 5개

서술형

09 〈보기〉에서 알맞은 조동사를 골라 문장을 완성하시오.

보기 must may not should shouldn't

(1) He drives a luxurious car and owns a private jet. He __________ be rich.

(2) You __________ sit so near the TV. It's bad for your eyes.

(3) I remember his name, but he __________ remember my name.

10 〈보기〉에서 알맞은 조동사를 고른 후, 주어진 말을 활용하여 문장을 완성하시오.

보기 may must can't should

(1) 그는 첫 기차를 놓쳤을지도 모른다. (miss)
→ He ____________________ the first train.

(2) 너는 어딘가에 네 지갑을 떨어뜨렸음에 틀림없다. (drop)
→ You ____________________ your wallet somewhere.

(3) 그녀는 그 재킷을 샀어야 했다. (buy)
→ She ____________________ the jacket.

11 우리말과 일치하도록 주어진 말을 사용하여 문장을 완성하시오.

(1) 너는 나를 기다릴 필요가 없어. (wait for)
→ ______________________________

(2) 너는 말하기 전에 다시 한번 생각해 보는 게 좋겠어. (better, think twice)
→ ______________________________ before you speak.

12 우리말과 일치하도록 주어진 말을 바르게 배열하시오.

(1) 너는 그 생선을 먹지 말았어야 했다. (should, have, that, not, you, eaten, fish)
→ ______________________________

(2) Dan이 그 테니스 경기에서 이겼을 리가 없다. (have, tennis match, Dan, won, the, can't)
→ ______________________________

13 밑줄 친 부분을 어법에 맞게 고치시오.

(1) You don't have to touch the pot. You might burn yourself.
→ ____________________

(2) Jane came in first in the piano contest. She must practice hard.
→ ____________________

14 주어진 문장을 〈조건〉에 맞게 바꿔 쓰시오.

I was afraid of flying, but I'm not anymore.

조건 used to를 사용하여 총 7단어로 쓸 것

→ ______________________________

15 그림을 보고, 주어진 말을 사용하여 문장을 완성하시오.

→ You ______________________ here. You will get a parking ticket. (better, park)

16 주어진 문장과 의미가 같도록 「조동사+have p.p.」를 사용하여 문장을 바꿔 쓰시오.

(1) I regret that I didn't do my homework.

→ I ________ ________ ________ my homework.

(2) I am certain that it rained during the night.

→ It ________ ________ ________ during the night.

17 〈보기〉에서 필요한 단어들만 골라 대화를 완성하시오.

보기	must	must not	don't have to

A: Oh, no! The science test is tomorrow. We (1) ______________ start studying immediately.
B: Relax. The test was rescheduled for next Friday. We (2) ______________ study right now.
A: What a relief! We can take a break then.

18 주어진 문장을 〈조건〉에 맞게 바꿔 쓰시오.

조건 1. should 또는 shouldn't를 사용할 것
2. 주어진 문장에 나온 단어를 활용할 것

(1) He wasn't careful enough.

→ He ______________________ more careful.

(2) I ate too many sweets, and now I have a toothache.

→ I ______________________ too many sweets.

[19-20] 다음 글을 읽고, 물음에 답하시오.

I grew up near the beach in Florida. When I was a kid, my sister and I used to going to the beach to collect seashells. We loved watching sea creatures like crabs and shrimp. <u>나는 해양 생물학자가 되었을지도 모른다.</u> However, I chose to be a math teacher. I enjoy teaching students, but in my free time, I visit small islands to go diving. It is exciting to dive somewhere no one has ever been before.

고난도

19 어법상 <u>틀린</u> 문장을 찾아 바르게 고쳐 문장을 다시 쓰시오.

→ ______________________________

____

20 밑줄 친 우리말과 일치하도록 〈조건〉에 맞게 문장을 완성하시오.

조건 1. may, become, a marine biologist를 순서대로 활용할 것
2. 총 7단어로 쓸 것

→ ______________________________

Chapter 03

수동태

UNIT 01

수동태의 의미와 형태

GRAMMAR FOCUS

1 수동태

주어가 행위를 받거나 당하는 것을 나타내는 문장 형식이다. 수동태의 동사는 「be동사 + p.p.」 형태로 쓰고, 행위자는 동사 뒤에 「by + 목적격」으로 나타낸다.

능동태	My sister	**wrote**	the letter.	내 여동생이 그 편지를 **썼다.**
수동태	The letter	**was written**	**by** my sister.	그 편지는 내 여동생**에 의해 쓰였다.**

The students **elect** the class president. 그 학생들은 학급 회장을 선출한다.
→ The class president **is elected by** the students. 학급 회장은 그 학생들에 의해 선출된다.

A famous designer **made** the dress. 한 유명한 디자이너가 그 드레스를 만들었다.
→ The dress **was made by** a famous designer. 그 드레스는 한 유명한 디자이너에 의해 만들어졌다.

cf. 수동태로 쓰지 않는 동사: happen(일어나다), disappear(사라지다), belong to(~의 것이다), resemble(~을 닮다) 등

The accident **happened** suddenly. 그 사고는 갑자기 일어났다.
└ was happened (×)

Davis **resembles** his father. Davis는 그의 아버지를 닮았다.
└ is resembled (×)

2 행위자의 생략

행위자가 일반인(you, we, they, people 등)일 때, 알 수 없거나 중요하지 않을 때는 「by + 행위자」를 생략할 수 있다.

German **is spoken** in Germany, Austria, and Switzerland. 독일어는 독일, 오스트리아, 스위스에서 사용된다.
Billy's bicycle **was stolen** outside his house. Billy의 자전거는 그의 집 밖에서 도난당했다.
The road **was closed** due to heavy snowfall. 그 도로는 폭설로 인해 폐쇄되었다.

3 수동태의 여러 형태

(1) 진행형: be동사 + being + p.p.

The dishes **are being washed** by the dishwasher. 그 접시들은 식기세척기로 **세척되고 있다.**
The car **was being repaired** when I arrived. 그 차는 내가 도착했을 때 **수리되고 있었다.**

(2) 완료형: have/has/had + been + p.p.

The book **has been read** by many people. 그 책은 많은 사람들에게 **읽혀져 왔다.**
The food **had been prepared** before the guests arrived. 음식은 손님들이 도착하기 전에 **준비되어 있었다.**

(3) 조동사가 있는 문장의 수동태: 조동사 + be + p.p.

The package **will be delivered** tomorrow. 그 소포는 내일 **배송될 것이다.**
The clothes **must be washed** in cold water. 그 옷은 찬물에 **세탁되어야 한다.**

Answer Key p.8

괄호 안에서 알맞은 것을 고르시오.

1 John (coaches, is coached) the basketball team.

2 My mom was (baking, being baked) a cake an hour ago.

3 The food can (cook, be cooked) in the microwave oven.

4 The music video has (watched, been watched) by millions of people.

5 The car had (stolen, been stolen) before the police arrived.

6 I will (clean, be cleaned) my room before my parents get home.

7 The ship (disappeared, was disappeared) in the Bermuda Triangle.

밑줄 친 부분을 어법에 맞게 고치시오.

1 The window broken during the storm last night.

2 The password should change every six months.

3 The flowers are watering by the gardener right now.

4 The book has translated into several different languages.

5 The accident was happened on the highway this morning.

6 My sister and I are twins, but we aren't resembled each other.

다음 문장을 수동태로 바꿔 쓰시오.

1 My brother ate all the cookies.

→ All the cookies ________ ________ by my brother.

2 The man is asking some questions.

→ Some questions ________ ________ ________ by the man.

3 J.K. Rowling has written many books.

→ Many books ________ ________ ________ by J.K. Rowling.

4 The company will launch a new product.

→ A new product ________ ________ ________ by the company.

WRITING FOCUS

A 배열 영작 우리말과 일치하도록 괄호 안의 말을 바르게 배열하시오.

1 그 식당은 한 유명한 요리사에 의해 운영된다. (run, a, chef, by, famous, is)

→ The restaurant ______________________________.

2 그 건물은 30년 전에 지어졌다. (ago, was, 30 years, built)

→ The building ______________________________.

3 내 컴퓨터는 지금 수리되고 있다. (fixed, my, being, computer, is)

→ ______________________________ now.

4 그 책은 도서관에서 빌릴 수 있다. (be, the, can, borrowed, book)

→ ______________________________ from the library.

5 그 가게는 지난달부터 문이 닫혀 있다. (the, been, shop, closed, has)

→ ______________________________ since last month.

6 그 파티는 우리가 도착했을 때 이미 취소되었다. (canceled, the, had, already, party, been)

→ ______________________________ when we arrived.

B 빈칸 완성 우리말과 일치하도록 괄호 안의 말을 이용하여 빈칸에 알맞은 말을 쓰시오.

1 그 콘서트는 관객 모두가 즐겼다. (enjoy)

→ The concert ________ ________ by everyone in the audience.

2 그 음식은 지금 부엌에서 요리되고 있다. (cook)

→ The food ________ ________ ________ in the kitchen now.

3 아름다운 노래가 그 밴드에 의해 연주되고 있었다. (play)

→ A beautiful song ________ ________ ________ by the band.

4 그 전화기는 한 시간 이내에 충전될 수 있다. (can, charge)

→ The phone ________ ________ ________ in less than an hour.

5 그 차는 어제부터 차고에 주차되어 있다. (park)

→ The car ________ ________ ________ in the garage since yesterday.

6 그 보고서는 마감일 이전에 이미 완성되었다. (complete)

→ The report ________ already ________ ________ before the deadline.

C 문장 완성 우리말과 일치하도록 괄호 안의 말을 이용하여 문장을 완성하시오.

1 지구는 지금 파괴되고 있다. (the Earth, destroy)

→ ______________________________ now.

2 그 시험은 지난주 금요일에 치러졌다. (the test, take)

→ ______________________________ last Friday.

3 새로운 다리가 그 마을에 건설될 것이다. (a new bridge, build, will)

→ ______________________________ in the town.

4 예약은 온라인으로 할 수 있다. (reservations, make, can)

→ ______________________________ online.

5 그 만화는 많은 아이들에게 사랑을 받아 왔다. (the animation, love)

→ ______________________________ by many children.

6 그 방은 그녀가 오기 전에 이미 치워져 있었다. (the room, already, clean)

→ ______________________________ before she came.

D 오류 수정 밑줄 친 부분을 바르게 고쳐 문장을 다시 쓰시오.

1 The door fixed by my father yesterday. (그 문은 어제 나의 아버지에 의해 고쳐졌다.)

→ ______________________________

2 The house is painted by the workers now. (그 집은 지금 작업자들에 의해 칠해지고 있다.)

→ ______________________________

3 Payments can be make through the app. (결제는 앱을 통해 할 수 있다.)

→ ______________________________

4 The book is belonged to the school library. (그 책은 학교 도서관의 것이다.)

→ ______________________________

5 The flight has canceled due to the bad weather. (그 비행편은 악천후로 인해 취소되었다.)

→ ______________________________

6 New computers will buy for students. (새 컴퓨터가 학생들을 위해 구입될 것이다.)

→ ______________________________

UNIT 02

4형식, 5형식 문장의 수동태

GRAMMAR FOCUS

1 4형식 문장의 수동태

4형식 문장은 간접목적어와 직접목적어를 각각 주어로 하는 수동태를 만들 수 있다. 직접목적어가 문장의 주어일 때는 간접목적어 앞에 to나 for 등의 전치사를 쓴다.

She **gave** *me a present*. 그녀는 나에게 선물을 주었다. 〈능동태〉

→ *I* **was given** *a present* by her. 나는 그녀에게 선물을 받았다. 〈수동태: 간접목적어가 주어〉

→ *A present* **was given** to *me* by her. 선물은 그녀에 의해 나에게 주어졌다. 〈수동태: 직접목적어가 주어〉

plus 간접목적어 앞에 쓰는 전치사

- to를 쓰는 동사: give, write, send, tell, teach, show, lend, bring, award 등
- for를 쓰는 동사: make, cook, buy, get 등

cf. make, cook, buy, get, read, sell, write 등의 동사는 간접목적어가 주어인 수동태로는 쓰지 않는다.

My friend **bought** *me a bracelet*. 내 친구는 나에게 팔찌를 사 주었다.

→ *A bracelet* **was bought for** *me* by my friend. (○)

→ *I* **was bought** *a bracelet* by my friend. (×)

2 5형식 문장의 수동태

(1) 목적격보어를 그대로 쓰는 경우

목적격보어가 명사, 형용사, 분사, to부정사일 때는 수동태 문장에서 형태가 바뀌지 않는다.

They named the dog *Lucky*. 그들은 그 개를 Lucky라고 이름 지었다.

→ The dog **was named Lucky** by them. 그 개는 그들에 의해 Lucky라고 이름 지어졌다.

We painted the door *white*. 우리는 그 문을 흰색으로 칠했다.

→ The door **was painted white** by us. 그 문은 우리에 의해 흰색으로 칠해졌다.

Lucia kept me *waiting* for an hour. Lucia는 한 시간 동안 나를 기다리게 했다.

→ I **was kept waiting** for an hour by Lucia. 나는 Lucia에 의해 한 시간 동안 기다리게 되었다.

His doctor advised him *to exercise* regularly. 그의 의사는 그에게 규칙적으로 운동하라고 조언했다.

→ He **was advised to exercise** regularly by his doctor. 그는 자신의 의사로부터 규칙적으로 운동하라는 조언을 들었다.

(2) 목적격보어가 바뀌는 경우

사역동사와 지각동사의 목적격보어로 쓰인 동사원형은 to부정사로 바뀐다.

He made the children *clean* their room. 그는 그 아이들에게 그들의 방을 청소하도록 시켰다.

→ The children **were made** to clean their room by him. 그 아이들은 그에 의해 그들의 방을 청소하도록 시켜졌다.

I saw Jane *enter* the room. 나는 Jane이 방에 들어간 것을 보았다.

→ Jane **was seen** to enter the room by me. Jane이 방에 들어간 것이 나에 의해 목격되었다.

cf. 지각동사의 목적격보어가 분사일 때는 그대로 쓴다.

I saw Jane *entering* the room. 나는 Jane이 방으로 들어가고 있는 것을 보았다.

→ Jane **was seen entering** the room by me. Jane이 방에 들어가고 있는 것이 나에 의해 목격되었다

Answer Key p.9

괄호 안에서 알맞은 것을 고르시오.

1 Ten pianos will be given (to, for) the school.

2 The ticket was bought (to, for) her by her friend.

3 The invitation has been sent (to, for) you by email.

4 The cat is called (Kitty, by Kitty) by my family.

5 The driver was told (stop, to stop) by the police officer.

6 I was made (study, to study) harder by my parents.

7 The baby was seen (smile, smiling) by her mother.

다음 문장을 주어진 말로 시작하는 수동태로 바꿔 쓰시오.

1 My friend wrote me a letter.

→ A letter ______________________________.

2 Mr. Jones teaches us English.

→ We ______________________________.

3 The police saw the thief running away.

→ The thief ______________________________.

4 The staff made us wait in line.

→ We ______________________________.

밑줄 친 부분을 어법에 맞게 고치시오.

1 They are taught to Korean at school.

2 Some surprising news was told us by Jane.

3 The soup was cooked to me by my mother.

4 The children are made go to bed before 9:00 p.m.

5 She was seen cry alone in her room.

6 He was asked singing by the audience.

WRITING FOCUS

A 배열 영작 우리말과 일치하도록 괄호 안의 말을 바르게 배열하시오.

1 그들은 학교에서 스페인어를 배운다. (they, taught, are, Spanish)

→ ______________________________ at school.

2 그 소포는 내 친구에 의해 나에게 보내졌다. (package, me, was, to, the, sent)

→ ______________________________ by my friend.

3 그 미역국은 내 생일에 나를 위해 만들어졌다. (the, for, made, me, was, seaweed soup)

→ ______________________________ on my birthday.

4 나는 그 노래로 기분이 좋아졌다. (made, I, happy, was)

→ ______________________________ by the song.

5 그 아이들은 점심 식사 전에 손을 씻도록 시켜졌다. (kids, their, made, the, wash, to, were, hands)

→ ______________________________ before lunch.

6 그 아기가 밤새 우는 것이 들렸다. (was, cry, to, heard, baby, the)

→ ______________________________ all night.

B 빈칸 완성 우리말과 일치하도록 괄호 안의 말을 이용하여 빈칸에 알맞은 말을 쓰시오.

1 Susan은 그녀의 어머니에게 그 목걸이를 받았다. (give, the necklace)

→ Susan ________ ________ ________ ________ by her mother.

2 그 상은 그 대회의 우승자에게 수여되었다. (award)

→ The prize ________ ________ ________ the winner of the competition.

3 그 생쥐는 그 만화에서 Jerry라고 불린다. (call, Jerry)

→ The mouse ________ ________ ________ in the animation.

4 우리는 그 웨이터로부터 몇 분 동안 기다리라는 말을 들었다. (tell, wait)

→ We ________ ________ ________ ________ for a few minutes by the waiter.

5 그들은 도서관에서 조용히 하도록 시켜졌다. (make, quiet)

→ They ________ ________ ________ ________ ________ in the library.

6 그 남자가 그 집에 침입하고 있는 것이 목격되었다. (see, break into)

→ The man ________ ________ ________ ________ the house.

Answer Key p.9

C 문장 전환 다음 문장을 주어진 말로 시작하는 수동태로 바꿔 쓰시오.

1 The teacher gave us an assignment.
→ An assignment ____________________.

2 My dad cooks us breakfast every Sunday.
→ Breakfast ____________________.

3 His rude comment made her angry.
→ She ____________________.

4 I heard the girl playing the piano.
→ The girl ____________________.

5 He made the dog sit and stay.
→ The dog ____________________.

6 The driver asked the passengers to fasten their seatbelts.
→ The passengers ____________________.

D 오류 수정 어법상 틀린 부분을 바르게 고쳐 문장을 다시 쓰시오.

1 I was given to useful information by Jackie. (나는 Jackie에게 유용한 정보를 받았다.)
→ ____________________

2 The book was bought to me by my friend. (그 책은 내 친구가 나에게 사 준 것이다.)
→ ____________________

3 The story was told me by my grandmother. (그 이야기는 나의 할머니께서 나에게 들려 주신 것이다.)
→ ____________________

4 They were asked following the rules by the coach. (그들은 그 코치로부터 규칙을 따르라는 요청을 받았다.)
→ ____________________

5 He was seen sleep in class by the teacher. (그는 수업 시간에 자고 있는 것이 선생님에 의해 목격되었다.)
→ ____________________

6 I was made take piano lessons by my mom. (나는 엄마에 의해 피아노 레슨을 받도록 시켜졌다.)
→ ____________________

UNIT 03 주의해야 할 수동태

GRAMMAR FOCUS

❶ 구동사의 수동태

구동사는 수동태에서 한 단어처럼 취급하여 붙여 쓴다.

· look at	~을 보다	· laugh at	~을 비웃다	· put off	미루다, 연기하다
· look after	~을 돌보다	· deal with	~을 처리하다	· call off	취소하다
· look up to	~을 존경하다	· take care of	~을 돌보다	· turn down	거절하다
· look down on	~을 무시하다	· hand in	~을 제출하다	· turn on/off	켜다/끄다

The babysitter *takes care of* the baby. 그 베이비시터는 그 아기를 돌본다.

→ The baby **is taken care of** by the babysitter. 그 아기는 그 베이비시터에 의해 돌봐진다.

Mr. Jobs *dealt with* the issue. Jobs 씨가 그 문제를 처리했다.

→ The issue **was dealt with** by Mr. Jobs. 그 문제는 Jobs 씨에 의해 처리되었다.

cf. 구동사의 목적어가 동사와 부사 사이에 있는 경우, 수동태 문장에서 부사를 빠뜨리지 않도록 주의한다.

The DJ *turned* the music *on*. 그 DJ는 음악을 틀었다.

→ The music **was turned on** by the DJ. 음악이 그 DJ에 의해 틀어졌다.

❷ 목적어가 that절인 문장의 수동태

목적어가 that절인 문장은 가주어 it 또는 that절의 주어를 수동태 문장의 주어로 쓴다. that절의 주어가 수동태 문장의 주어일 때 that절의 동사는 to부정사로 바뀐다.

People say that Mark is a billionaire. 사람들은 Mark가 억만장자라고 말한다.

→ **It is said that** Mark is a billionaire. Mark는 억만장자라고 말해진다.

→ Mark **is said** to be a billionaire.

❸ by 이외의 전치사를 쓰는 수동태

행위자를 나타낼 때 보통 by를 쓰지만, 일부 동사들은 다른 전치사를 사용한다.

· be filled with	~로 가득 차다	· be interested in	~에 관심[흥미]이 있다
· be covered with	~로 덮이다	· be tired of	~에 싫증나다[지치다]
· be crowded with	~로 붐비다	· be known to	~에게 알려져 있다
· be satisfied with	~에 만족하다	· be known for	~로 알려져 있다[유명하다]
· be disappointed with[in]	~에 실망하다	· be made of	~로 만들어지다 (물리적 변화)
· be surprised at[by]	~에 놀라다	· be made from	~로 만들어지다 (화학적 변화)

The jar **is filled with** colorful candles. 그 병은 형형색색의 양초로 가득 차 있다.

My sister **is interested in** animals. 내 여동생은 동물에 관심이 있다.

The city **is known for** its historical buildings. 그 도시는 그곳의 역사적인 건물들로 유명하다.

The bridge **is made of** steel and concrete. 그 다리는 강철과 콘크리트로 만들어졌다.

Most cheese **is made from** cow's milk. 대부분의 치즈는 젖소의 우유로 만들어진다.

Answer Key p.9

괄호 안에서 알맞은 것을 고르시오.

1 The dog is being looked after (the vet, by the vet).

2 The picnic was (put, put off) because it rained.

3 The comedian's jokes were (laughed, laughed at) by the audience.

4 It (reports, is reported) that the actor will star in a new movie.

5 He is said (be, to be) the best soccer player in the country.

6 All the trees are covered (in, with) snow after the heavy snowfall.

7 She was tired (by, of) the noise from upstairs.

다음 문장을 주어진 말로 시작하는 수동태로 바꿔 쓰시오. (단, 「by+행위자」는 생략할 것)

1 People say that Emily is kind.

→ It ________________________________.

→ Emily ________________________________.

2 They believe that John is a good leader.

→ It ________________________________.

→ John ________________________________.

우리말과 일치하도록 괄호 안의 말을 이용하여 문장을 완성하시오.

1 나는 동물 보호소에서 자원봉사하는 것에 관심이 있다. (interest)

→ I __________ __________ __________ volunteering at animal shelters.

2 대부분의 학생들이 그 수업에 만족했다. (satisfy)

→ Most students __________ __________ __________ the class.

3 그 회사는 혁신적인 제품들로 알려져 있다. (know)

→ The company __________ __________ __________ its innovative products.

4 그 서류 가방은 가죽으로 만들어졌다. (make)

→ The briefcase __________ __________ __________ leather.

WRITING FOCUS

A 배열 영작 우리말과 일치하도록 괄호 안의 말을 바르게 배열하시오.

1 그 금붕어는 Eric에 의해 보살펴졌다. (the, taken, goldfish, by, care, was, of, Eric)

→ ______________________________

2 나는 더 이상 비웃음을 당하지 않을 것이다. (I, be, won't, at, anymore, laughed)

→ ______________________________

3 Martin이 그 경주에서 이길 것으로 예상된다. (Martin, is, the, expected, it, win, will, that, race)

→ ______________________________

4 그 식당은 그 도시에서 최고라고 말해진다. (the, best, to, the, said, restaurant, is, be, the, in, city)

→ ______________________________

5 그 책장은 먼지로 덮여 있다. (with, bookshelf, is, the, covered, dust)

→ ______________________________

6 Amy는 그녀의 일에 싫증이 났다. (Amy, was, of, job, tired, her)

→ ______________________________

B 빈칸 완성 우리말과 일치하도록 괄호 안의 말을 이용하여 빈칸에 알맞은 말을 쓰시오.

1 그 보고서는 금요일까지 제출되어야 한다. (must, hand in)

→ The report ________ ________ ________ ________ by Friday.

2 웃음은 최고의 보약이라고 말해진다. (say, be)

→ Laughter ________ ________ ________ ________ the best medicine.

3 그는 올해 졸업할 것으로 예상된다. (expect, graduate)

→ He ________ ________ ________ ________ this year.

4 외계인은 다른 행성에 존재할 수 있다고 믿어진다. (believe)

→ It ________ ________ ________ aliens may exist on other planets.

5 그 쇼핑몰은 손님들로 붐볐다. (crowd)

→ The shopping mall ________ ________ ________ customers.

6 Henry는 그의 새 스마트폰에 만족한다. (satisfy)

→ Henry ________ ________ ________ his new smartphone.

C 문장 완성 우리말과 일치하도록 괄호 안의 말을 이용하여 문장을 완성하시오.

1 그 문제는 곧 처리될 것이다. (will, deal with)

→ The matter ______________________________ soon.

2 Brown 씨는 많은 사람들에게 존경을 받는다. (look up to, many)

→ Mr. Brown ______________________________.

3 Susan은 훌륭한 가수라고 말해진다. (say, that, a great singer)

→ It ______________________________.

4 George가 발표를 할 것으로 예상된다. (expect, give a presentation)

→ George ______________________________.

5 Dylan의 방은 그림들로 가득 차 있다. (fill, paintings)

→ Dylan's room ______________________________.

6 빵은 밀가루로 만들어진다. (make, flour)

→ Bread ______________________________.

D 오류 수정 어법상 틀린 부분을 바르게 고쳐 문장을 다시 쓰시오.

1 The event called off due to the pandemic. (그 행사는 전염병으로 인해 취소되었다.)

→ ______________________________

2 The TV was turned by Chris off. (그 TV는 Chris에 의해 꺼졌다.)

→ ______________________________

3 It believed that they left the country. (그들은 그 나라를 떠났다고 믿어진다.)

→ ______________________________

4 Mark is said being a hardworking man. (Mark는 열심히 일하는 사람이라고 말해진다.)

→ ______________________________

5 Sabrina is interested with Latin music. (Sabrina는 라틴 음악에 관심이 있다.)

→ ______________________________

6 The bag was filled by Christmas gifts. (그 자루는 크리스마스 선물들로 가득 차 있었다.)

→ ______________________________

ACTUAL TEST

문항 수	객관식 8 / 서술형 12
맞은 개수	/ 20

[01-02] 빈칸에 들어갈 말로 알맞은 것은?

01

The room is __________ for the baby's first birthday party.

① decorate ② decorates
③ decorating ④ been decorated
⑤ being decorated

02

The assignment should __________ by next Friday.

① do ② be done
③ be doing ④ have done
⑤ being done

03 우리말과 일치하도록 주어진 말을 배열할 때, 다섯 번째로 오는 단어는?

어젯밤에 폭풍우로 인해 전원이 꺼졌다.
(storm, turned, the, was, off, power, the, by)
→ ______________________________ last night.

① by ② off ③ the
④ storm ⑤ turned

04 빈칸에 들어갈 말이 나머지 넷과 다른 것은?

① The glass is filled ________ ice and soda.
② He was satisfied ________ the test results.
③ The museum is crowded ________ visitors.
④ I was surprised ________ his sudden arrival.
⑤ The garden was covered ________ colorful leaves.

05 우리말을 영어로 바르게 옮긴 것을 모두 고르면?

그녀는 위대한 과학자라고 말해진다.

① She is said be a great scientist.
② She said to be a great scientist.
③ She is said to be a great scientist.
④ It said that she is a great scientist.
⑤ It is said that she is a great scientist.

빈출

06 주어진 문장을 수동태로 바르게 바꾼 것을 모두 고르면?

Ryan gave me a surprise gift.

① I was given a surprise gift by Ryan.
② I was given to a surprise gift by Ryan.
③ A surprise gift was given me by Ryan.
④ A surprise gift was given to me by Ryan.
⑤ A surprise gift was given for me by Ryan.

07 주어진 문장을 수동태로 바꾼 것 중 알맞지 않은 것은?

① Someone left the door open.
→ The door was left open.
② They call J.S. Bach the father of music.
→ J.S. Bach is called the father of music.
③ They allow students to have long hair.
→ Students are allowed to have long hair.
④ My mom made me do the dishes.
→ I was made do the dishes by my mom.
⑤ We saw him walking to the park.
→ He was seen walking to the park by us.

고난도

08 어법상 올바른 문장을 모두 고르면?

ⓐ The pizza is being cooked in the oven.
ⓑ The Olympic Games are held every four years.
ⓒ The ancient Egyptians were built the pyramids.
ⓓ Dinner will be served in the dining room at 6:00 p.m.
ⓔ Bill has been canceled his appointment with the doctor.

① ⓐ, ⓑ ② ⓐ, ⓒ, ⓓ
③ ⓐ, ⓑ, ⓓ ④ ⓑ, ⓓ, ⓔ
⑤ ⓓ, ⓔ

서술형

09 주어진 문장을 수동태로 바꿔 쓰시오.

(1) The earthquake destroyed the buildings.

→ ______________________

(2) All drivers must follow the traffic rules.

→ ______________________

10 우리말과 일치하도록 주어진 말을 활용하여 문장을 완성하시오.

(1) 그 국립 미술관은 많은 사람들에 의해 방문된다.
(the national gallery, visit, many)

→ ______________________

(2) 그 집은 Tom에 의해 청소되고 있다.
(the house, clean)

→ ______________________

11 밑줄 친 부분을 어법에 맞게 고치시오.

(1) They have invited to the party.
(그들은 그 파티에 초대를 받았다.)

→ ______________

(2) My mom was made this sweater for me.
(나의 엄마는 나에게 이 스웨터를 만들어주셨다.)

→ ______________

12 우리말과 일치하도록 주어진 말을 바르게 배열하시오.

나의 할아버지는 모두에게 존경을 받으셨다.
(was, my, looked, by, grandfather, up, everybody, to)

→ ______________________

13 〈보기〉에서 알맞은 말을 골라 문장을 완성하시오. (단, 한 번씩만 쓸 것)

보기	in	for	of	to

(1) I am tired ________ hearing the same song.

(2) My brother is interested ________ photography.

(3) The singer is known ________ her beautiful voice.

14 대화를 읽고, 어법상 틀린 부분을 찾아 바르게 고치시오.

A: It's so hot today. Can you turn on the air conditioner?
B: I'm sorry. It's broken. It will fix tomorrow.

____________ → ____________

15 그림을 보고, 〈조건〉에 맞게 문장을 완성하시오.

조건 1. the cookies, make, them을 순서대로 활용할 것
2. 현재진행형을 사용할 것

→ ______________________

16 다음 문장을 주어진 말로 시작하는 수동태로 바꿔 쓰시오.

The waiter showed us the menu.

(1) We ______________________.

(2) The menu ______________________.

17 주어진 문장을 〈조건〉에 맞게 수동태로 바꿔 쓰시오.

People say that he speaks five languages.

조건 1. He로 시작할 것
2. by people은 생략할 것

→ ______________________

고난도

18 어법상 틀린 문장 2개를 골라 기호를 쓰고, 틀린 부분을 바르게 고치시오.

ⓐ The project has to be finished soon.
ⓑ The file has been deleted by mistake.
ⓒ A new bike was bought to me by my father.
ⓓ The visitors were made to wait outside the building.
ⓔ The cheese should keep in the refrigerator.

(　　) ____________ → ____________

(　　) ____________ → ____________

[19-20] 대화를 읽고, 물음에 답하시오.

A: Hey, did you hear that the science teacher has the flu?
B: Oh, no! He must be in bed now.
A: Yes, he won't be back for a few days.
B: 그분의 수업들은 취소되었니?
A: No, (A) Ms. Taylor is teaching them.
B: That's good. I hope he gets well soon.

*flu 독감

19 밑줄 친 우리말과 일치하도록 주어진 말을 바르게 배열하시오.

his, have, been, classes, canceled

→ ______________________

20 밑줄 친 (A)를 수동태로 바꿔 쓰시오.

→ No, ______________________.

Chapter 04

부정사와 동명사

UNIT 01

to부정사의 용법

GRAMMAR FOCUS

❶ to부정사의 명사적 용법

(1) 주어, 보어, 목적어 역할: to부정사가 명사처럼 쓰여 문장에서 주어, 보어, 목적어 역할을 한다. '~하는 것, ~하기'로 해석한다.

주어	**To drink** this water is not safe. = **It** is not safe **to drink** this water. 가주어 진주어	이 물을 **마시는 것은** 안전하지 않다.
보어	One of his talents is **to mimic** people.	그의 재능 중 하나는 사람들을 **흉내 내는 것이다.**
목적어	She likes **to learn** new languages.	그녀는 새로운 언어를 **배우는 것을** 좋아한다.

(2) 의문사 + to부정사: 문장에서 주어, 보어, 목적어로 쓰일 수 있으며, 「의문사 + 주어 + should + 동사원형」으로 바꿔 쓸 수 있다.

· what to-v	무엇을 ~할지	· who(m) to-v	누가[누구를] ~할지	· where to-v	어디서[어디로] ~할지
· which to-v	어느 것을 ~할지	· when to-v	언제 ~할지	· how to-v	어떻게 ~할지

He didn't know **what to do** first. 그는 무엇을 먼저 해야 할지 몰랐다.
= He didn't know **what he should do** first.

cf. why to-v는 쓰지 않는다.

❷ to부정사의 형용사적 용법

to부정사가 형용사처럼 쓰여 앞에 있는 명사나 대명사를 꾸며준다. '~할, ~하는'으로 해석한다.

(대)명사 + to부정사	Karen has *a job* **to do.**	Karen은 **할** 일이 있다.
(대)명사 + to부정사 + 전치사	I need *a pen* **to write with.**	나는 **쓸** 펜이 필요하다.
-thing/-body/-one + 형용사 + to부정사	I want *something* **cold to drink.**	나는 **차가운 마실** 것을 원한다.

❸ to부정사의 부사적 용법

to부정사가 부사처럼 쓰여 동사, 형용사, 부사를 꾸며준다.

목적 (~하기 위해)	I swim **to stay** healthy. = I swim **in order to[so as to] stay** healthy.	나는 건강을 **유지하기 위해** 수영을 한다.
감정의 원인 (~해서)	I was surprised **to get** his letter.	나는 그의 편지를 **받아서** 놀랐다.
판단의 근거 (~하다니)	He must be angry **to say** that.	그렇게 **말하다니** 그는 화났음에 틀림없다.
결과 (~해서 …하다)	Her son grew up **to be** a doctor.	그의 아들은 자라**서** 의사가 **되었다.**
형용사 수식 (~하기에)	The bag is expensive **to buy.**	그 가방은 **사기에** 비싸다.

Answer Key p.11

괄호 안에서 알맞은 것을 고르시오.

1 (It, That) is essential to drink water in hot weather.

2 His dream is (play, to play) basketball in the NBA.

3 We need to (go, going) grocery shopping today.

4 He didn't know how (pronounce, to pronounce) the word.

5 They found a nice house to (live, live in) near the park.

6 Let's find something (to do fun, fun to do) this weekend.

7 She was surprised (to find, found) her lost keys in her purse.

두 문장의 의미가 같도록 빈칸에 알맞은 말을 쓰시오.

1 She asked me where she should park her car.
→ She asked me __________ __________ __________ her car.

2 He showed me how I should use the photocopier.
→ He showed me __________ __________ __________ the photocopier.

3 Cathy is thinking about what she should buy for her sister's birthday.
→ Cathy is thinking about __________ __________ __________ for her sister's birthday.

〈보기〉에서 알맞은 말을 골라 to부정사를 사용하여 문장을 완성하시오.

보기	be	lift	say	use	win

1 The team practiced hard __________ the game.

2 She was sad __________ goodbye to her friends.

3 He must be strong __________ that heavy box.

4 The boy grew up __________ a famous actor.

5 The new tablet PC is really easy __________.

WRITING FOCUS

A 배열 영작 우리말과 일치하도록 괄호 안의 말을 바르게 배열하시오.

1 하루 만에 그 책을 다 읽는 것은 쉽지 않다. (it, not, book, easy, is, finish, to, the)

→ ______________________________ in a day.

2 나의 어릴 적 꿈은 전 세계를 여행하는 것이었다. (my, travel, was, childhood, to, dream)

→ ______________________________ around the world.

3 Allen과 그의 친구는 함께 사업을 시작하기로 결정했다. (to, business, start, decided, a, together)

→ Allen and his friend ______________________________.

4 그녀는 저녁 식사 후에 달콤한 먹을 것을 원했다. (eat, after, to, sweet, dinner)

→ She wanted something ______________________________.

5 그는 전기를 절약하기 위해 에어컨을 껐다. (tuned off, he, save, the, to, air conditioner)

→ ______________________________ electricity.

6 Lisa는 그녀의 책상 위에 있는 선물을 발견하고 놀랐다. (Lisa, a, was, present, find, to, surprised)

→ ______________________________ on her desk.

B 빈칸 완성 우리말과 일치하도록 괄호 안의 말을 이용하여 빈칸에 알맞은 말을 쓰시오.

1 매일 식당에서 먹는 것은 돈이 많이 든다. (expensive, eat)

→ It is ________ ________ ________ at restaurants every day.

2 우리 형은 내 과학 숙제를 도와주기로 약속했다. (promise, help)

→ My brother ________ ________ ________ me with my science homework.

3 Nick은 취업 면접에 무엇을 입을지 생각 중이다. (wear)

→ Nick is thinking about ________ ________ ________ to his job interview.

4 나는 내 화학 수업을 위해 써야 할 보고서가 있다. (report, write)

→ I have a ________ ________ ________ for my chemistry class.

5 번지 점프를 하러 가다니 그녀는 용감함에 틀림없다. (brave, go)

→ She must be ________ ________ ________ bungee jumping.

6 그는 자라서 훌륭한 건축가가 되었다. (grow up, be)

→ He ________ ________ ________ ________ a great architect.

C 문장 완성 우리말과 일치하도록 괄호 안의 말을 이용하여 문장을 완성하시오. (단, to부정사를 사용할 것)

1 외국어를 배우는 것은 어렵다. (difficult, learn a foreign language)

→ It is ______________________________.

2 그의 목표는 올림픽에서 금메달을 따는 것이다. (goal, win a gold medal)

→ ______________________________ at the Olympics.

3 나는 올해 어디로 휴가를 갈지 아직 결정하지 못했다. (go on vacation, this year)

→ I haven't decided ______________________________ yet.

4 우리는 앉을 의자 두 개가 필요하다. (chairs, sit on)

→ We need ______________________________.

5 당신은 마음을 평온하게 하기 위해 명상을 할 수 있다. (meditate, calm your mind)

→ You can ______________________________.

6 그 탁자는 나 혼자서도 조립하기 쉬웠다. (table, easy, assemble)

→ ______________________________ on my own.

D 오류 수정 필요한 곳에 to를 넣어 문장을 다시 쓰시오.

1 It is wonderful have close friends.

→ ______________________________

2 The most important thing is have a positive attitude.

→ ______________________________

3 My dad promised buy me a new cellphone.

→ ______________________________

4 I don't know how solve this problem.

→ ______________________________

5 I went to the library borrow some books.

→ ______________________________

6 You need something warm wear for camping.

→ ______________________________

UNIT 02

to부정사의 의미상 주어와 부정, 주요 구문

GRAMMAR FOCUS

❶ to부정사의 의미상 주어와 부정

(1) **to부정사의 의미상 주어:** to부정사의 행위의 주체는 to부정사 앞에 「for + 목적격」으로 나타낸다. 단, 사람의 성격이나 성품을 나타내는 형용사가 오면 「of + 목적격」을 쓴다.

for + 목적격	It is *important* **for him** to study English.	**그가** 영어를 공부하는 것은 중요하다.
of + 목적격	It was *rude* **of her** to ignore him.	**그녀가** 그를 무시한 것은 무례했다.

cf. 「of + 목적격」을 쓰는 형용사: kind, nice, wise, clever, polite, rude, careless, foolish, thoughtful, generous 등

(2) **to부정사의 부정:** to부정사 앞에 not을 붙인다.

I decided **not to go** to the concert. 나는 그 콘서트에 **가지 않기로** 결정했다.

He wakes up early **not to skip** breakfast. 그는 아침을 **거르지 않기 위해** 일찍 일어난다.

❷ too ~ to, enough to

too + 형용사/부사 + to부정사 = so + 형용사/부사 + that + 주어 + can't + 동사원형 너무 ~해서 …할 수 없다	He is **too young to drive** a car. = He is **so young that he can't drive** a car. 그는 너무 어려서 차를 운전할 수 없다.
	This shirt is **too big for me to wear.** = This shirt is **so big that** I **can't wear** it. 이 셔츠는 너무 커서 내가 입을 수 없다.
형용사/부사 + enough + to부정사 = so + 형용사/부사 + that + 주어 + can + 동사원형 ~할 만큼 충분히 …하다	You are **tall enough to play** basketball. = You are **so tall that you can** play basketball. 너는 농구를 할 수 있을 만큼 충분히 키가 크다.
	The house was **cheap enough for us to buy.** = The house was **so cheap that** we **could buy** it. 그 집은 우리가 살 수 있을 만큼 충분히 저렴했다.

cf. to부정사의 의미상 주어가 있는 경우에는 의미상 주어가 that절의 주어가 된다. that절에서 동사의 목적어가 필요한 경우에는 목적어를 쓰는 것에 유의한다.

❸ seem to

seem + to부정사 = It seems that + 주어 + 동사 ~처럼 보인다, ~인 것 같다	He **seems to be** busy these days. = **It seems that he is** busy these days. 그는 요즘 바쁜 것처럼 보인다.

plus to부정사의 시제가 문장의 시제보다 앞선 과거일 때는 「to + have p.p.」 형태로 쓴다.

He seems **to have been** busy last week. 그는 지난주에 바빴던 것처럼 보인다.

= It seems that he **was** busy last week.

Answer Key p.12

괄호 안의 말을 이용하여 문장을 완성하시오.

1 It is difficult ____________ to speak in public. (I)

2 It is nice ____________ to give me a birthday card. (you)

3 It is natural ____________ to bark at strangers. (dogs)

4 It was careless ____________ to break the dishes. (she)

5 It is boring ____________ to stay at home on a rainy day. (Jack)

6 It is wise ____________ to save some money for the future. (they)

밑줄 친 부분을 어법에 맞게 고치시오.

1 It is important <u>of you</u> to listen carefully.

2 It was thoughtful <u>of they</u> to bring a gift.

3 John promised <u>to not be</u> late again.

4 The hike took <u>so long</u> to complete before dark.

5 The phone call was <u>enough loud</u> to hear the conversation.

6 The ice cream was so melted that I <u>can't eat</u> it.

두 문장의 의미가 같도록 빈칸에 알맞은 말을 쓰시오.

1 The coffee was so hot that I couldn't drink it.

→ The coffee was ________ ________ ________ ________ ________ ________.

2 The weather was so warm that we could swim in the sea.

→ The weather was ________ ________ ________ ________ ________ ________ in the sea.

3 It seems that the old man knows everything.

→ The old man ________ ________ ________ everything.

4 It seems that she lost her phone somewhere.

→ She seems to ________ ________ her phone somewhere.

WRITING FOCUS

A 배열 영작 우리말과 일치하도록 괄호 안의 말을 바르게 배열하시오.

1 그가 그 어르신에게 자신의 자리를 양보한 것은 친절했다. (it, kind, to, him, of, give up, was, his seat)

→ ______________________________ to the elderly man.

2 내가 그 일을 5시까지 끝내는 것은 불가능하다. (me, impossible, it, finish, is, the, for, to, work)

→ ______________________________ by 5 o'clock.

3 이 소파는 너무 작아서 우리 셋이 앉을 수 없다. (to, small, three of us, sit on, too, for)

→ This sofa is ______________________________.

4 그는 그 문제를 풀 수 있을 만큼 충분히 똑똑하다. (to, the, enough, problem, smart, solve)

→ He is ______________________________.

5 그 식당은 항상 붐비는 것처럼 보인다. (seems, the, it, that, is, restaurant)

→ ______________________________ always crowded.

6 그녀는 예술에 재능이 있는 것처럼 보인다. (seems, she, to, talented, be)

→ ______________________________ at art.

B 빈칸 완성 우리말과 일치하도록 괄호 안의 말을 이용하여 빈칸에 알맞은 말을 쓰시오.

1 우리가 다른 문화들을 이해하는 것은 필요하다. (necessary, understand)

→ It is ________ ________ ________ ________ ________ other cultures.

2 그가 자신의 우산을 잃어버린 것은 부주의했다. (careless, lose)

→ It was ________ ________ ________ ________ ________ his umbrella.

3 나의 할아버지는 외롭지 않기 위해 개 한 마리를 사셨다. (lonely)

→ My grandfather bought a dog ________ ________ ________ ________.

4 그 영화는 너무 무서워서 혼자 볼 수 없다. (scary, watch)

→ The movie is ________ ________ ________ ________ alone.

5 그녀는 그 경주에서 우승할 수 있을 만큼 충분히 빠르다. (fast, win)

→ She is ________ ________ ________ ________ the race.

6 집에 아무도 없는 것처럼 보인다. (seem, be)

→ No one ________ ________ ________ at home.

Answer Key p.12

C 문장 완성 우리말과 일치하도록 괄호 안의 말을 이용하여 문장을 완성하시오. (단, to부정사를 사용할 것)

1 그가 화를 내는 것은 드물다. (unusual, get angry)

→ It is ________________________________.

2 네가 나를 배웅해 준 것은 친절했다. (nice, see me off)

→ It was ________________________________.

3 Fred는 그 경주에 참가하지 않기로 결정했다. (participate in, race)

→ Fred decided ________________________________.

4 그 집은 너무 작아서 다섯 명이 살 수 없다. (small, people, live in)

→ The house is ________________________________.

5 너는 그 선거에서 투표할 수 있을 만큼 충분히 나이가 들었다. (enough, old, vote)

→ ________________________________ in the election.

6 그녀는 오늘 기분이 좋지 않은 것처럼 보인다. (seem, to, in a bad mood)

→ ________________________________ today.

D 오류 수정 어법상 틀린 부분을 바르게 고쳐 문장을 다시 쓰시오.

1 It was foolish for him to say that. (그가 그렇게 말한 것은 어리석었다.)

→ ________________________________

2 It is important to not bother a guided dog. (안내견을 괴롭히지 않는 것은 중요하다.)

→ ________________________________

3 Linda is very busy to cook dinner. (Linda는 너무 바빠서 저녁을 요리할 수 없다.)

→ ________________________________

4 He is enough tall to go on the ride. (그는 그 놀이기구를 탈 수 있을 만큼 충분히 키가 크다.)

→ ________________________________

5 The package is too heavy that I can't lift it. (그 소포는 너무 무거워서 내가 그것을 들 수 없다.)

→ ________________________________

6 Mary seems to finish her homework. (Mary는 숙제를 끝낸 것처럼 보인다.)

→ ________________________________

UNIT 03

다양한 형태의 목적격보어

GRAMMAR FOCUS

1 to부정사 목적격보어

want, tell, ask, advise, expect, allow, enable, encourage, persuade, order, warn 등의 동사는 목적격보어로 to부정사가 온다.

I	**want**	you	**to pass** the test.	나는 네가 그 시험에 합격하기를 원한다.
My mom	**told**	me	**to turn** off the TV.	엄마는 나에게 TV를 끄라고 말씀하셨다.

He **asked** them **to wait** in line. 그는 그들에게 줄을 서라고 요청했다.

I **expect** him **to come** early. 나는 그가 일찍 올 것으로 예상한다.

Dad **allowed** us **to go** camping. 아빠는 우리가 캠핑을 가는 것을 허락해 주셨다.

She **encouraged** me **to keep** trying. 그녀는 내가 계속 노력하도록 격려했다.

The man **ordered** them **to stop**. 그 남자는 그들에게 멈추라고 명령했다.

cf. help는 목적격보어로 to부정사와 원형부정사를 둘 다 취할 수 있다.

My teacher helped me (**to**) **memorize** the words. 나의 선생님은 내가 그 단어들을 암기하는 것을 도와주셨다.

2 원형부정사 목적격보어

(1) 지각동사: 지각동사 see, hear, feel, smell 등은 목적격보어로 원형부정사가 온다.

We	**saw**	him	**enter** the house.	우리는 그가 집에 들어가는 것을 보았다.
I	**heard**	someone	**knock** on the door.	나는 누군가가 문을 두드리는 소리를 들었다.

cf. 지각동사는 목적격보어로 분사도 쓸 수 있다.

She **felt** the ground **shaking**. 그녀는 땅이 흔들리고 있는 것을 느꼈다.

I **heard** my name **called**. 나는 내 이름이 불려지는 소리를 들었다.

(2) 사역동사: '~가 …하게 하다'의 의미를 갖는 사역동사 make, have, let은 목적격보어로 원형부정사가 온다. 단, get이 사역동사로 쓰일 때는 목적격보어로 to부정사가 온다.

She	**made**	us	**clean** our room.	그녀는 우리에게 방을 청소하도록 시켰다.
He	**had**	the secretary	**type** the report.	그는 비서에게 그 보고서를 입력하게 했다.
John	**let**	me	**drive** his car.	John은 내가 그의 차를 운전하게 허락했다.
I	**got**	him	**to go** to the dentist.	나는 그를 (설득하여) 치과에 가게 했다.

plus 목적어와 목적격보어가 수동의 관계일 때는 「have/get + 목적어 + 과거분사」를 쓴다.

Susan **had** her house **painted** (by someone). Susan은 그녀의 집에 페인트칠을 했다.

I **got** my wallet **stolen** (by someone). 나는 내 지갑을 도난당했다.

Answer Key p.13

괄호 안에서 알맞은 것을 고르시오.

1 I want you (reading, to read) this book.

2 The doctor advised him (gets, to get) plenty of rest.

3 Carol felt the rain (fall, fell) on her head.

4 I heard the girls (singing, to sing) a beautiful song.

5 My parents make me (do, to do) my homework before dinner.

6 The students got the teacher (postpone, to postpone) the exam.

7 My uncle has his car (wash, washed) once a month.

밑줄 친 동사를 괄호 안의 동사로 바꿔 문장을 다시 쓰시오.

1 John asked the repairman to fix the computer. (have)

→ John ____.

2 The police told everyone to leave the building. (make)

→ The police ____.

3 Mr. Smith never allows his kids to watch TV after 8:00 p.m. (let)

→ Mr. Smith never ____.

4 Sue persuaded her husband to give up smoking. (get)

→ Sue ____.

괄호 안의 말을 이용하여 문장을 완성하시오.

1 She encouraged the students ______________ the class project. (finish)

2 My brother warned me ______________ the file. (not, download)

3 Did you see the accident ______________ last night? (happen)

4 Kevin had the barber ______________ his hair. (cut)

5 Mom made me ______________ back home before 7:00 p.m. (come)

6 James gets his car ______________ regularly. (check)

WRITING FOCUS

A 배열 영작 우리말과 일치하도록 괄호 안의 말을 바르게 배열하시오.

1 나의 부모님은 내가 의사가 되기를 원하신다. (to, me, a, want, doctor, be)

→ My parents ____.

2 그 의사는 간호사에게 환자의 체온을 재 달라고 요청했다. (nurse, to, the, asked, take, doctor, the)

→ ____ the patient's temperature.

3 그 보청기는 나의 할아버지가 더 잘 들으실 수 있도록 도와준다. (hear, my, better, helps, grandfather)

→ The hearing aid ____.

4 경찰은 그 도둑이 지갑을 훔치는 것을 보았다. (a, saw, the, steal, thief, purse)

→ The police ____.

5 나는 누군가가 밖에서 내 이름을 부르는 소리를 들었다. (I, my, heard, name, call, someone).

→ ____ outside.

6 새로 오신 선생님은 우리가 더 열심히 공부하게 만들었다. (harder, us, study, made)

→ The new teacher ____.

B 빈칸 완성 우리말과 일치하도록 괄호 안의 말을 이용하여 빈칸에 알맞은 말을 쓰시오.

1 그는 우리에게 그 가게 앞에 주차하지 말라고 말했다. (tell, park)

→ He __________ __________ __________ __________ __________ in front of the shop.

2 내가 이 상자를 위층으로 옮기는 것을 도와줄 수 있니? (help, move)

→ Can you __________ __________ __________ this box upstairs?

3 Mark는 누군가가 그의 어깨를 만지는 것을 느꼈다. (feel, touch, someone)

→ Mark __________ __________ __________ his shoulder.

4 나의 상사는 내가 2주 동안 휴가 가는 것을 허락해 주었다. (let, go)

→ My boss __________ __________ __________ on vacation for two weeks.

5 나의 엄마는 나에게 설탕을 사 오게 하셨다. (have, buy)

→ My mom __________ __________ __________ some sugar.

6 나는 그것을 제시간에 끝낼 수 없을 것 같다. (get, do, it)

→ I don't think I can __________ __________ __________ on time.

Answer Key p.13

C 문장 완성 우리말과 일치하도록 괄호 안의 말을 이용하여 문장을 완성하시오.

1 그는 자신의 룸메이트에게 TV 소리를 줄이라고 말했다. (tell, roommate, turn down)

→ He ______________________ the TV.

2 나의 부모님은 내가 늦게까지 밖에 있는 것을 허락하지 않으신다. (allow, stay out late)

→ My parents don't ______________________.

3 나의 형은 어제 내가 숙제하는 것을 도와주었다. (help, do one's homework)

→ My brother ______________________ yesterday.

4 우리는 학교 밴드가 무대에서 공연하는 것을 보았다. (see, the school band, perform)

→ We ______________________ on stage.

5 이 노래는 나를 기분 좋게 만든다. (make, feel good)

→ This song ______________________.

6 Sue는 2주마다 그녀의 손톱을 손질한다. (get, nails, do)

→ Sue ______________________ every two weeks.

D 오류 수정 어법상 틀린 부분을 바르게 고쳐 문장을 다시 쓰시오.

1 Ann asked me going shopping with her. (Ann은 나에게 그녀와 함께 쇼핑하러 가자고 부탁했다.)

→ ______________________

2 We expect of him to be a great leader. (우리는 그가 훌륭한 지도자가 될 것으로 기대한다.)

→ ______________________

3 This herbal tea helped me slept well at night. (이 허브차는 내가 밤에 잘 자도록 도와주었다.)

→ ______________________

4 She heard her baby cries in the room. (그녀는 자신의 아기가 방에서 우는 소리를 들었다.)

→ ______________________

5 Mr. Kim had the students to write an essay. (김 선생님은 그 학생들에게 에세이를 쓰게 했다.)

→ ______________________

6 I had my wisdom tooth pull out at the dentist's. (나는 치과에서 내 사랑니를 뽑았다.)

→ ______________________

UNIT

04 동명사

GRAMMAR FOCUS

❶ 동명사의 역할

주어	**Running** is good for your heart.	**달리기는** 심장에 좋다.
보어	My hobby is **collecting** old coins.	내 취미는 옛날 동전을 **수집하는 것이다.**
동사의 목적어	He enjoys **spending** time with his family.	그는 가족과 함께 시간 **보내는 것을** 즐긴다.
전치사의 목적어	We are excited about **watching** the show.	우리는 그 공연을 **보는 것에** 들떠 있다.

plus 동명사의 의미상 주어는 동명사 앞에 소유격을 써서 나타낸다. 동명사의 부정형은 동명사 앞에 not을 붙인다.

Her dancing is beautiful. **그녀가 춤추는 것**은 아름답다.

Ava was sad about **not going** to the amusement park. Ava는 놀이공원에 **가지 못해서** 슬펐다.

❷ 동명사의 관용 표현

· go v-ing	~하러 가다	· look forward to v-ing	~하는 것을 고대하다
· feel like v-ing	~하고 싶다	· be used to v-ing	~하는 것에 익숙하다
· have difficulty v-ing	~하는 데 어려움을 겪다	· cannot help v-ing	~하지 않을 수 없다
· be busy v-ing	~하느라 바쁘다	· It is no use v-ing	~해도 소용없다
· be worth v-ing	~할 가치가 있다	· spend + 시간/돈 + v-ing	~하는 데 시간/돈을 쓰다

I'm **looking forward to visiting** my family. 나는 내 가족을 방문하는 것을 고대하고 있다.

She **is used to driving** a big car. 그녀는 큰 차를 운전하는 것에 익숙하다.

❸ 동명사 vs. to부정사

동명사를 목적어로 취하는 동사	enjoy, mind, avoid, keep, practice, finish, stop, quit, give up, consider, postpone, put off 등			
to부정사를 목적어로 취하는 동사	want, would like, wish, hope, expect, need, decide, plan, promise, agree, refuse, fail, afford, pretend 등			
둘 다 목적어로 취하는 동사	like, love, hate, dislike, start, begin, continue 등			
둘 다 목적어로 취하되 의미가 달라지는 동사	remember v-ing	~한 것을 기억하다	regret v-ing	~한 것을 후회하다
	remember to-v	~할 것을 기억하다	regret to-v	~해서 유감이다
	forget v-ing	~한 것을 잊다	try v-ing	(시험 삼아) ~해 보다
	forget to-v	~할 것을 잊다	try to-v	~하려고 노력하다

He *avoids* **drinking** coffee in the evening. 그는 저녁에는 커피 마시는 것을 피한다.

She *promised* **to take** care of my dog tomorrow. 그녀는 내일 내 개를 돌봐 주기로 약속했다.

Most people *hate* **working[to work]** on weekends. 대부분의 사람들은 주말에 일하는 것을 싫어한다.

I *remember* **returning** the book to the library. 나는 도서관에 그 책을 반납한 것을 기억한다.

I *remember* **to return** the book to the library. 나는 도서관에 그 책을 반납해야 할 것을 기억한다.

cf. 「stop + to부정사」에 쓰인 to부정사는 부사적 용법으로, 목적(~하기 위해)을 나타낸다.

He *stopped* **talking** with her. 그는 그녀와 **이야기하는 것을** 멈추었다.

He *stopped* **to talk** with her. 그는 그녀와 **이야기하기 위해** 멈춰 섰다.

Answer Key p.13

괄호 안에서 알맞은 것을 고르시오.

1 (Eat, Eating) too many sweets is bad for your teeth.

2 One of her duties at home is (clean, cleaning) her room.

3 Jin and her husband are tired of (living, to live) in a big city.

4 Jerry didn't mind (I, my) being late for the meeting.

5 I am considering (not going, going not) to that party.

6 Angela is still not used to (wear, wearing) glasses.

우리말과 일치하도록 괄호 안의 말을 이용하여 문장을 완성하시오.

1 나는 오늘 저녁에는 아무것도 하고 싶지 않다. (feel, do)

→ I don't ________ ________ ________ anything this evening.

2 그녀는 오늘 아침 눈 속을 걷는 데 어려움을 겪었다. (difficulty, walk)

→ She ________ ________ ________ in the snow this morning.

3 나는 너와 네 여동생을 보는 것을 고대하고 있어. (forward, see)

→ I am ________ ________ ________ ________ you and your sister.

4 그의 농담이 너무 웃겨서 나는 웃지 않을 수 없었다. (help, laugh)

→ Because his joke was so funny, I ________ ________ ________.

괄호 안의 말을 이용하여 문장을 완성하시오.

1 Jessica keeps ________ her passwords. (forget)

2 Karen hopes ________ a job before she graduates. (find)

3 He can't afford ________ a new car. (buy)

4 I remember ________ to the beach last summer. (go)

5 Don't forget ________ the plants twice a week. (water)

6 The mechanic tried ________ my car for two hours, but he failed. (fix)

7 They stopped ________ to take a break. (work)

WRITING FOCUS

A 배열 영작 **우리말과 일치하도록 괄호 안의 말을 바르게 배열하시오.**

1 내 취미는 시와 단편 소설을 읽는 것이다. (and, is, poetry, short stories, reading)

→ My hobby ______________________________.

2 나의 형은 겨울에 스키 타러 가는 것을 즐긴다. (enjoys, skiing, in, going, winter)

→ My brother ______________________________.

3 그녀는 나와 함께 영화를 보러 가는 것에 관심이 없었다. (going, with, the, to, movies, me)

→ She was not interested in ______________________________.

4 그 환자는 숨쉬는 데 어려움을 겪고 있었다. (was, breathing, difficulty, having)

→ The patient ______________________________.

5 제가 이 편지 번역하는 것을 도와주시겠어요? (do, helping, you, me, mind, translate)

→ ______________________________ this letter?

6 그는 종종 가스 잠그는 것을 잊는다. (the, gas, to, forgets, turn off)

→ He often ______________________________.

B 빈칸 완성 **우리말과 일치하도록 괄호 안의 말을 이용하여 빈칸에 알맞은 말을 쓰시오.**

1 나에게 그 문제에 대한 진실을 말해 줘서 고마워. (tell)

→ Thank you for __________ __________ the truth about the problem.

2 그는 체중을 줄이기 위해 토요일마다 등산을 간다. (go, hike)

→ He __________ __________ on Saturdays to lose weight.

3 그들은 부엌에서 저녁 식사를 준비하느라 바쁘다. (busy, prepare)

→ They __________ __________ __________ dinner in the kitchen.

4 그들은 다음 주 회의를 취소하는 것에 동의했다. (agree, cancel)

→ They __________ __________ __________ next week's meeting.

5 Jenny는 열흘 전에 도서관에서 일하는 것을 그만두었다. (quit, work)

→ Jenny __________ __________ at the library ten days ago.

6 그들은 자신의 아이들에게 크리스마스 선물을 사 줄 여유가 없었다. (can, afford, buy)

→ They __________ __________ __________ __________ their kids Christmas gifts.

Answer Key p.14

C 문장 완성 우리말과 일치하도록 괄호 안의 말을 이용하여 문장을 완성하시오.

1 나는 다음 달에 체육관에 등록하려고 생각 중이다. (think of, sign up)

→ ________________ for the gym next month.

2 그녀는 자신의 친구들과 눈을 마주치는 것을 피했다. (avoid, make eye contact)

→ ________________ with her friends.

3 그들은 모닥불 주위에서 함께 노래를 부르기 시작했다. (start, sing together)

→ ________________ around the campfire.

4 그는 초인종이 울렸을 때 식사 하는 것을 멈추었다. (stop, eat)

→ ________________ when the doorbell rang.

5 우리는 바닷가에 살지 않기 때문에 배를 사도 소용이 없다. (it, use, buy a boat)

→ ________________ because we don't live by the sea.

6 그 강의는 너무 지루해서 나는 하품을 하지 않을 수 없었다. (help, yawn)

→ The lecture was so boring that ________________.

D 오류 수정 어법상 틀린 부분을 바르게 고쳐 문장을 다시 쓰시오.

1 The workers don't mind to work at night.

→ ________________

2 He left the party without say goodbye.

→ ________________

3 I am tired of she complaining.

→ ________________

4 His problem is coming not to class on time.

→ ________________

5 They are looking forward to go to Paris next week.

→ ________________

6 I remember to travel abroad for the first time.

→ ________________

ACTUAL TEST

문항 수	객관식 8 / 서술형 12
맞은 개수	/ 20

01 밑줄 친 부분의 쓰임이 나머지 넷과 다른 것은?

① It is important to be kind to others.
② It is challenging to learn a new language.
③ It is used to protect your skin from the sun.
④ It was exciting for me to see a shooting star.
⑤ It was not easy for us to climb the mountain.

02 밑줄 친 부분이 어법상 어색한 것은?

① I don't know what to do next.
② Let's decide where to go for lunch.
③ He taught me how to play the guitar.
④ They didn't know why to do the work.
⑤ I asked her when to start the meeting.

03 어법상 올바른 문장을 모두 고르면?

① Is there a chair to sit on?
② He needed someone to talk.
③ I want delicious something to eat.
④ She has two hamsters to take care of.
⑤ They are looking for a nice hotel to stay.

빈출

04 〈보기〉의 밑줄 친 부분과 쓰임이 같은 것은?

보기 I have a question to ask you.

① She was glad to pass the exam.
② This song is fun and easy to sing.
③ He has little time to sleep these days.
④ Her dream is to be a fashion designer.
⑤ They left home early to avoid the traffic.

05 빈칸에 들어갈 말로 알맞지 않은 것은?

It was ________ of him to talk about the matter.

① wise ② rude ③ foolish
④ generous ⑤ necessary

빈출 고난도

06 두 문장의 의미가 같도록 할 때, 바르게 바꾼 것은?

① He is so busy that he can't take a break.
→ He is busy enough to take a break.
② She is so tired that she can't stay awake.
→ She is too tired not to stay awake.
③ I was too surprised to believe it.
→ I was so surprised that I can't believe it.
④ The shoes are very big, so I can't wear them.
→ The shoes are too big for me to wear.
⑤ He is so talented that he can play any instrument.
→ He is enough talented to play any instrument.

고난도

07 어법상 올바른 문장의 개수는?

ⓐ He had his car fixed yesterday.
ⓑ I want of you to pass the exam.
ⓒ We saw the girl singing on stage.
ⓓ He helped me to move the furniture.
ⓔ What made you changing your mind?
ⓕ She asked me helped her with the box.
ⓖ She got her kids to eat the vegetables.

① 2개 ② 3개 ③ 4개
④ 5개 ⑤ 6개

08 다음 중 어법상 어색한 것은?

① I feel like eating ice cream.
② Bill used to studying at night.
③ This book is worth reading twice.
④ Jim spent five hours writing his essay.
⑤ She can't help crying during sad movies.

서술형

09 주어진 문장과 의미가 같도록 빈칸에 알맞은 말을 쓰시오.

I didn't know how to prepare for the job interview.

→ I didn't know ________ ________ ________ ________ for the interview.

[10-11] 우리말과 일치하도록 주어진 말을 바르게 배열하시오.

10

Tim은 함께 놀 친구를 찾고 있다.
(Tim, a, looking, with, friend, for, play, is, to)

→ ________________________

11

그녀는 그 기차를 놓치지 않기 위해 서둘렀다.
(miss, she, to, train, hurried, not, the)

→ ________________________

12 우리말과 일치하도록 〈보기〉에서 필요한 단어들만 골라 배열하여 문장을 완성하시오.

(1) 그녀가 그 책을 이해하는 것은 어렵다.

보기 it is of for difficult she her to understand

→ ________________________ the book.

(2) 그가 그 노부인을 도운 것은 친절했다.

보기 it was of for to he him help kind

→ ________________________ the old lady.

13 주어진 문장과 의미가 같도록 바꿔 쓸 때, 어법상 틀린 부분을 찾아 바르게 고치시오.

Emma plays the piano well enough to perform in concerts.
→ Emma plays the piano well so that she can perform in concerts.

________________ → ________________

14 주어진 말을 사용하여 두 문장을 한 문장으로 연결하시오.

- The laptop is very expensive.
- I can't buy it.

(1) ________________________
(so, that)

(2) ________________________
(too, for)

15 우리말과 일치하도록 주어진 말을 활용하여 문장을 완성하시오.

(1) 그는 우리에게 잠시 기다리라고 말했다. (tell, wait)

→ He ____________________ for a minute.

(2) 그녀는 나에게 그 꽃에 물을 주게 했다. (have, water)

→ She ____________________ the flowers.

16 그림을 보고, 〈조건〉에 맞게 문장을 완성하시오.

조건
1. 사역동사 make를 활용할 것
2. 과거시제를 사용할 것
3. 6단어를 추가하여 문장을 완성할 것

→ My mom ____________________________
____________________________________.

17 괄호 안에서 알맞은 말을 골라 빈칸에 쓰시오.

(1) The doctor advised him (rest / to rest) at home.

(2) I saw David (walking / walked) his dog in the park.

(3) Jane got her phone (repair / repaired).

(1) __________ (2) __________ (3) __________

18 빈칸에 들어갈 말을 〈보기〉에서 골라 알맞은 형태로 쓰시오.

보기	bring	play	study

(1) I remember __________ hide-and-seek with my friends when I was young.

(2) Ann forgot __________ her umbrella, so she had to borrow one.

(3) Ray regrets not __________ for the science test.

[19-20] 대화를 읽고, 물음에 답하시오.

A: You look excited today. What's going on?
B: I'm going to see my favorite band's concert tonight.
A: ⓐLet me guess. BTA?
B: That's right.
A: ______________________________________?
(easy, the, it, concert ticket, was, to, get)
B: ⓑIt was almost impossible getting it, but ⓒI kept trying.
A: Great! Where there's a will, there's a way.
B: Thanks. ⓓI'm really looking forward to see the performance.

19 괄호 안에 주어진 말을 바르게 배열하여 문장을 완성하시오.

→ ______________________________________?

20 어법상 틀린 문장 2개를 찾아 기호를 쓰고, 틀린 부분을 바르게 고치시오.

(   ) ______________ → ______________

(   ) ______________ → ______________

Chapter 05

분사와 분사구문

UNIT 01 현재분사와 과거분사
UNIT 02 분사구문
UNIT 03 주의해야 할 분사구문

UNIT 01

현재분사와 과거분사

GRAMMAR FOCUS

❶ 분사의 종류

현재분사	동사원형 + **-ing**	능동(~하는) 진행(~하고 있는)	**surprising** news **falling** leaves	**놀라운** 소식 **떨어지는** 나뭇잎들
과거분사	동사원형 + **-ed**, 불규칙 과거분사	수동(~된) 완료(~한)	**surprised** people **fallen** leaves	**놀란** 사람들 **떨어진** 나뭇잎들

❷ 분사의 쓰임

(1) **명사 수식**: 분사가 명사를 단독으로 수식할 때는 주로 명사 앞에 오며, 다른 어구와 함께 쓰여 길어질 때는 명사 뒤에서 수식한다.

Look at the **smiling** baby over there. 저기 웃고 있는 아기를 봐.

The baby **smiling** at me is very cute. 나를 보고 웃고 있는 아기는 매우 귀엽다.

(2) **보어 역할**: 분사는 주격보어와 목적격보어로 쓰일 수 있다.

He looked very **depressed.** 그는 매우 우울해 보였다. 〈주격보어〉

Jane found her son **hiding** in the closet. Jane은 그녀의 아들이 옷장 안에 숨어 있는 것을 발견했다. 〈목적격보어〉

(3) **동사구에서 쓰이는 분사**: 현재분사는 진행형에, 과거분사는 완료형과 수동태에서 사용된다.

The dog **is sleeping** in front of the house. 그 개는 집 앞에서 자고 있다. 〈진행형: be동사 + 현재분사〉

He **hasn't finished** his homework yet. 그는 아직 숙제를 끝내지 못했다. 〈완료형: have/has/had + 과거분사〉

The driver **was injured** in the accident. 운전자는 그 사고에서 부상을 당했다. 〈수동태: be동사 + 과거분사〉

❸ 감정을 나타내는 분사

감정과 관련된 타동사는 분사형으로 자주 쓰인다. 감정을 일으키는 원인이면 현재분사를, 감정을 느끼는 주체이면 과거분사를 사용한다.

- exciting(흥미진진한) – excited(신이 난)
- interesting(흥미로운) – interested(흥미를 느끼는)
- boring(지루한) – bored(지루해하는)
- tiring(피곤하게 하는) – tired(피곤한)
- exhausting(지치게 하는) – exhausted(지친)
- surprising(놀라운) – surprised(놀란)
- satisfying(만족스러운) – satisfied(만족한)
- disappointing(실망스러운) – disappointed(실망한)
- confusing(혼동스러운) – confused(혼동한)
- amusing(재미있는) – amused(재미를 느끼는)

The class *bores* the students. 그 수업은 학생들을 지루하게 한다.

→ It is a **boring** class. 그것은 **지루한** 수업이다.

→ They are **bored** students. 그들은 **지루해하는** 학생들이다.

Answer Key p.15

괄호 안에서 알맞은 것을 고르시오.

1 I ate a (boiling, boiled) egg and salad for breakfast.

2 He raked up the (falling, fallen) leaves in the garden.

3 The tall boy (waving, waved) at me is my brother.

4 They found the picture (stealing, stolen) from the gallery.

5 I heard someone (typing, typed) on the keyboard in the room.

6 We saw a strange car (parking, parked) in front of our house.

밑줄 친 부분을 어법에 맞게 고치시오.

1 It is dangerous to drink polluting water.

2 I watched an interested TV program about birds.

3 The students wait for the tour bus look very happy.

4 Mike hasn't checked the emails send to him yet.

5 The magician showed us some amazed tricks with cards.

6 The confusing student raised his hand to ask a question.

〈보기〉에서 알맞은 말을 골라 분사 형태로 바꿔 문장을 완성하시오.

보기	disappoint	excite	satisfy	tire

1 농구는 관람하기에 매우 흥미진진한 스포츠이다.

→ Basketball is a very __________ sport to watch.

2 대다수 사람들이 그 선거 결과에 만족했다.

→ A majority of people were __________ with the election results.

3 우리가 어젯밤에 본 영화는 매우 실망스러웠다.

→ The movie we saw last night was very __________.

4 그 피곤한 학생은 그의 숙제를 하는 동안 잠이 들었다.

→ The __________ student fell asleep while doing his homework.

WRITING FOCUS

A 배열 영작 우리말과 일치하도록 괄호 안의 말을 바르게 배열하시오.

1 실크로 만들어진 그 셔츠는 비쌌다. (shirt, made, the, silk, of)

→ ______________________________ was expensive.

2 통화하는 여자는 이 건물의 주인이다. (woman, phone, the, on, the, talking)

→ ______________________________ is the owner of this building.

3 그는 영어로 쓰인 소설 읽는 것을 즐긴다. (in, novels, written, English)

→ He enjoys reading ______________________________.

4 기차를 기다리는 승객들은 연착으로 인해 짜증이 났다. (passengers, the, waiting, train, for, the)

→ ______________________________ were annoyed by the delay.

5 우리는 그녀가 길을 건너는 것을 보았다. (her, the, saw, street, crossing)

→ We ______________________________.

6 나는 스티커 사진 부스에서 내 사진을 찍었다. (my, taken, picture, had)

→ I ______________________________ in the sticker photo booth.

B 빈칸 완성 우리말과 일치하도록 괄호 안의 말을 이용하여 빈칸에 알맞은 말을 쓰시오.

1 구르는 돌에는 이끼가 끼지 않는다. (roll, stone)

→ A __________ __________ gathers no moss.

2 몇몇 항공편이 추운 날씨 때문에 취소되었다. (freeze, weather)

→ Some flights have been canceled due to the __________ __________.

3 도서관에서 공부하는 학생들이 많이 있다. (students, study)

→ There are many __________ __________ in the library.

4 그 밴드는 재활용 재료로 만든 악기로 음악을 연주했다. (instruments, make)

→ The band played music with __________ __________ of recycled materials.

5 Lucy는 바닥에 물이 엎질러진 것을 발견했다. (spill)

→ Lucy found water __________ on the floor.

6 그들은 자신의 아들이 식당 안을 뛰어다니게 내버려두었다. (run around)

→ They left their son __________ __________ in the restaurant.

C 문장 완성 우리말과 일치하도록 괄호 안의 말을 이용하여 문장을 완성하시오. (단, 분사를 사용할 것)

1 그 채소들을 끓는 물에 넣어라. (boil, water)

→ Put the vegetables into ________________________________.

2 그에게는 Patrick이라는 이름의 개가 있다. (a dog, name)

→ He has ________________________________.

3 나는 내 영어 성적에 실망했다. (feel, disappoint)

→ ________________________________ with my English grade.

4 이 건물 앞에 주차된 차는 내 차이다. (car, park, in front of this building)

→ ________________________________ is my car.

5 자신의 이름이 불리는 것을 들으면 손을 들으세요. (when, hear, your name, call)

→ Raise your hand ________________________________.

6 새해 첫날에 나는 바다 위로 해가 떠오르는 것을 구경했다. (watch, the sun, rise)

→ On New Year's Day, ________________________________ over the sea.

D 오류 수정 어법상 틀린 부분을 바르게 고쳐 문장을 다시 쓰시오.

1 The movie was so bored that I fell asleep. (그 영화는 너무 지루해서 나는 잠이 들었다.)

→ ________________________________

2 Who is that boy talk to Mina? (미나와 이야기하고 있는 저 남자아이는 누구니?)

→ ________________________________

3 Climbing Mt. Everest is exhausted. (에베레스트 산을 오르는 것은 고된 일이다.)

→ ________________________________

4 She was very surprising to see us again. (그녀는 우리를 다시 봐서 매우 놀랐다.)

→ ________________________________

5 What is the main language speaking in India? (인도에서 사용되는 주요 언어는 무엇입니까?)

→ ________________________________

6 He found the front door lock. (그는 현관문이 잠긴 것을 발견했다.)

→ ________________________________

UNIT 02 분사구문

GRAMMAR FOCUS

❶ 분사구문

분사구문은 부사절을 부사구로 바꾼 것을 말한다. 분사구문은 부사절과 주절의 주어가 같은 경우, 부사절의 접속사와 주어를 생략하고 동사를 -ing 형태로 바꾸어 만든다.

① 부사절의 접속사 생략 ② 부사절의 주어 생략 (주절의 주어와 같은 경우) ③ 부사절의 동사를 현재분사로 전환 (주절의 시제와 같은 경우)	~~If~~ ~~you~~ **take** subway line one, you can get to City Hall. ① ② ③ → **Taking** subway line one, you can get to City Hall. 1호선을 타면 너는 시청에 갈 수 있다.

plus 1. 분사구문의 부정은 분사 앞에 not을 붙인다.

Because I didn't feel well, I left the party early. 몸이 좋지 않아서 나는 파티에서 일찍 나왔다.

→ Not **feeling** well, I left the party early.

2. 부사절의 동사가 be동사일 때 분사구문의 being은 생략 가능하다. 단, 진행형인 경우에는 현재분사만 남긴다.

As he was a talented singer, he won the competition. 재능 있는 가수였기 때문에 그는 그 대회에서 우승했다.

→ (Being) A talented singer, he won the competition.

While my sister was watching a movie, she fell asleep. 영화를 보는 동안 내 여동생은 잠이 들었다.

→ (~~Being~~) **Watching** a movie, my sister fell asleep.

❷ 분사구문의 의미

시간 (~할 때, ~ 후에) when, before, after 등	**Hearing** the news, I was shocked. (→ When **I heard** the news, I was shocked.) 그 소식을 들었을 때 나는 충격을 받았다.
동시동작 (~하면서) while, as 등	**Watching** a movie, they ate popcorn. (→ While **they were watching** a movie, they ate popcorn.) 영화를 보면서 그들은 팝콘을 먹었다.
이유 (~ 때문에, ~ 해서) because, as, since 등	**Feeing** cold, Jane drank some hot tea. (→ Because **she felt** cold, Jane drank some hot tea.) 추워서 Jane은 뜨거운 차를 마셨다.
조건 (~하면) if	**Turning** to the left, you will find the restaurant. (→ If **you turn** to the left, you will find the restaurant.) 왼쪽으로 돌면 당신은 그 식당을 찾을 것입니다.
양보 (~이지만) although, though 등	**Being** very smart, he made a big mistake. (→ Although **he is** very smart, he made a big mistake.) 매우 영리했지만 그는 큰 실수를 저질렀다.

plus 의미를 명확하게 나타내기 위해 분사구문의 접속사를 생략하지 않기도 한다.

After **graduating** from university, he had to get a job. 대학을 졸업한 후 그는 직장을 구해야 했다.

Answer Key p.16

괄호 안에서 알맞은 것을 고르시오.

1 (Feeling, Felt) tired, I went to bed early.

2 (Prepare, Preparing) dinner, she cut her finger.

3 (Be, Being) very tall, he became a basketball player.

4 (Taking, To take) this medicine, you will feel better.

5 (Not wanting, Wanting not) to wake him up, I left the house quietly.

6 (Built, Building) a sandcastle, the children were sitting on the beach.

다음 문장을 분사구문으로 바꿔 쓰시오.

1 When he drives to work, he listens to the radio.

→ ____________________, he listens to the radio.

2 Because I didn't know his phone number, I wasn't able to contact him.

→ ____________________, I wasn't able to contact him.

3 Since she was kind and friendly, she was popular with her classmates.

→ ____________________, she was popular with her classmates.

4 While I was cleaning my room, I found some old photos.

→ ____________________, I found some old photos.

우리말과 일치하도록 괄호 안의 말을 이용하여 문장을 완성하시오.

1 매일 운동을 하기 때문에 그는 몸 상태가 좋다. (work out)

→ __________ __________ every day, he is in good shape.

2 그 차가 더 이상 필요하지 않아서 나는 그것을 팔기로 결심했다. (need)

→ __________ __________ the car anymore, I decided to sell it.

3 그는 비가 그치기를 기다리면서 건물 로비에 서 있었다. (wait)

→ He stood in the lobby of the building __________ for the rain to stop.

4 한 블록을 더 가면 왼쪽에 은행이 보일 것입니다. (go)

→ __________ one more block, you will see the bank on your left.

WRITING FOCUS

A 배열 영작 우리말과 일치하도록 괄호 안의 말을 바르게 배열하시오.

1 지난주에 아이스하키를 하다가 그는 무릎을 다쳤다. (he, playing, hurt, ice hockey, last week)

→ ______________________________ his knee.

2 할 일이 없었기 때문에 그 아이들은 지루했다. (the, nothing, children, to, having, do, were)

→ ______________________________ bored.

3 겨우 다섯 살이었지만 모차르트는 피아노를 칠 수 있었다. (only, being, Mozart, five years old, could)

→ ______________________________ play the piano.

4 수업에 늦고 싶지 않아서 그는 학교로 달려가기 시작했다. (he, wanting, started, to, not, for, be, class, late)

→ ______________________________ running to school.

5 좀 더 연습한다면 너는 노래를 더 잘하게 될 거야. (more, you, practice, having, will)

→ ______________________________ sing better.

6 백화점에서 쇼핑을 하다가 나는 바닥에서 지갑을 보았다. (I, the, shopping, saw, department store, at)

→ ______________________________ a purse on the floor.

B 빈칸 완성 우리말과 일치하도록 괄호 안의 말을 이용하여 빈칸에 알맞은 말을 쓰시오.

1 학교에서 집으로 걸어오다가 Cathy는 길 잃은 개를 보았다. (walk, home)

→ __________ __________ from school, Cathy saw a stray dog.

2 오븐에서 피자를 꺼내다가 그녀는 화상을 입었다. (take, a pizza)

→ __________ __________ __________ out of the oven, she burned herself.

3 이 소설을 읽는다면 너는 그 작가가 얼마나 훌륭한지 알게 될 것이다. (read, this novel)

→ __________ __________ __________, you will find out how great the writer is.

4 연세가 아주 많으시지만 나의 할아버지는 매일 운동을 하신다. (very old)

→ __________ __________ __________, my grandfather exercises every day.

5 Greg은 소파에서 TV를 보다가 잠이 들었다. (watch TV)

→ Greg fell asleep __________ __________ on the sofa.

6 그녀에게 뭐라고 말해야 할지 몰라서 그는 침묵을 지켰다. (know)

→ __________ __________ what to say to her, he remained silent.

C 문장 완성 우리말과 일치하도록 괄호 안의 말을 이용하여 문장을 완성하시오. (단, 분사구문을 사용할 것)

1 문을 열었을 때 나는 그 방이 풍선으로 장식된 것을 발견했다. (open, the door)

→ ____________________, I found the room decorated with balloons.

2 음악을 듣고 있어서 그녀는 초인종이 울리는 것을 듣지 못했다. (listen to, music)

→ ____________________, she didn't hear the doorbell ring.

3 덥고 목이 말라서 그는 차가운 물 한 잔을 마셨다. (hot and thirsty)

→ ____________________, he drank a cold glass of water.

4 우리 동아리에 가입하면 너는 재미있는 일이 많을 거야. (join, our club)

→ ____________________, you will have a lot of fun.

5 집에 음식이 없었기 때문에 우리는 외식을 하기로 결정했다. (have, no food, at home)

→ ____________________, we decided to eat out.

6 휴가를 위한 충분한 돈이 없어서 그는 여행 가는 것을 포기했다. (have, enough money)

→ ____________________ for a holiday, he gave up going on a trip.

D 오류 수정 밑줄 친 부분을 바르게 고쳐 문장을 다시 쓰시오. (단, 분사구문을 사용할 것)

1 Parked my car, I hit the one behind me. (내 차를 주차하다가 나는 내 뒤에 있던 차를 들이받았다.)

→ ____________________

2 Not felt well, he stayed in bed. (몸이 좋지 않았기 때문에 그는 침대에 있었다.)

→ ____________________

3 Hurry up, we won't be late for the concert. (서두르면 우리는 콘서트에 늦지 않을 거야.)

→ ____________________

4 Having not any homework, I played computer games. (숙제가 없었기 때문에 나는 컴퓨터 게임을 했다.)

→ ____________________

5 She was in New York worked at a travel agency. (그녀는 여행사에서 근무하면서 뉴욕에 있었다.)

→ ____________________

6 Although live next door, we rarely see each other. (옆집에 살지만 우리는 서로를 거의 보지 못한다.)

→ ____________________

UNIT 03

주의해야 할 분사구문

GRAMMAR FOCUS

1 주의해야 할 분사구문

(1) 완료형 분사구문

부사절의 시제가 주절의 시제보다 앞설 때 분사구문은 「having + p.p.」 형태로 쓴다.

As I had missed the bus, I had to wait for the next one. 버스를 놓쳐서 나는 다음 버스를 기다려야 했다.

→ **Having missed** the bus, I had to wait for the next one.

(2) 수동형 분사구문

부사절이 수동태인 경우, 분사구문의 being이나 having been은 주로 생략하고 과거분사로 시작한다.

As the item was delivered by ship, it arrived late. 선박으로 배송되었기 때문에 그 물건은 늦게 도착했다.

→ **(Being) Delivered** by ship, the item arrived late.

As he had been injured, he couldn't play in the game. 부상을 당했기 때문에 그는 경기에서 뛰지 못했다.

→ **(Having been) Injured**, he couldn't play in the game.

(3) 주어가 있는 분사구문

부사절과 주절의 주어가 다른 경우에는 분사 앞에 부사절의 주어를 써준다.

As it was Sunday, the stores were not open. 일요일이었기 때문에 상점들은 문을 열지 않았다.

→ It **being** Sunday, the stores were not open.

As my car was broken down, I took the bus to work. 내 차가 고장 났기 때문에 나는 버스를 타고 출근했다.

→ My car **broken** down, I took the bus to work.

2 with + 목적어 + 분사

부대상황을 나타내며 '~하면서, ~한[된] 채로'라고 해석한다. 이때 목적어와 분사가 능동의 관계이면 현재분사를 쓰고, 수동의 관계이면 과거분사를 쓴다.

She rode her bike **with her hair blowing** in the wind. 그녀는 바람에 머리카락을 날리면서 자전거를 탔다.

He sat in the rocking chair **with his legs crossed.** 그는 다리를 꼰 채로 흔들의자에 앉아 있었다.

3 독립분사구문

부사절과 주절의 주어가 다르더라도 막연한 일반적인 주어라면 생략하고 분사구문을 만들 수 있다.

· Generally speaking	일반적으로 말하면	· Frankly speaking	솔직히 말하면
· Strictly speaking	엄밀히 말하면	· Judging from	~로 판단해 보면
· Roughly speaking	대강 말하면	· Considering	~을 고려하면

Strictly speaking, penguins are not unique to Antarctica. 엄밀히 말하면 펭귄은 남극에만 있는 것이 아니다.

Judging from his voice, he is in his 30s. 그의 목소리로 판단해 보면 그는 30대이다.

Answer Key p.16

괄호 안에서 알맞은 것을 고르시오.

1 (Baking, Having baked) the cake, she served it at the party.

2 (Making, Made) of glass, the vase can be easily broken.

3 (Being, It being) a rainy day, we decided to stay indoors.

4 Janet was crying in her room with the door (locking, locked).

5 My mom told me not to brush my teeth with the tap (run, running).

6 (Considering, To consider) all the evidence, the rumor is probably true.

다음 문장을 분사구문으로 바꿔 쓰시오. (단, 접속사를 쓰지 말 것)

1 Because Mary had spent all the money, she couldn't buy the dress.

→ ______________________________, Mary couldn't buy the dress.

2 Because I had not seen him for ages, I didn't recognize him.

→ ______________________________, I didn't recognize him.

3 Although I was tired, I kept studying for the exam.

→ ______________________________, I kept studying for the exam.

4 Since it was a small suitcase, the boy could carry it easily.

→ ______________________________, the boy could carry it easily.

EXERCISE C

우리말과 일치하도록 괄호 안의 말을 이용하여 문장을 완성하시오.

1 호텔에 도착한 후에 우리는 짐을 풀기 시작했다. (arrive)

→ __________ __________ at the hotel, we started unpacking.

2 파란색으로 칠해져서 우리의 새로운 집은 멋져 보인다. (paint)

→ __________ blue, our new house looks wonderful.

3 그녀는 두 눈을 반짝이면서 내 말을 들었다. (shine)

→ She listened to me with her eyes __________.

4 솔직히 말하면 나는 그의 제안이 현실적이지 않다고 생각한다. (frankly, speak)

→ __________ __________, I don't think his suggestion is practical.

WRITING FOCUS

A 배열 영작 **우리말과 일치하도록 괄호 안의 말을 바르게 배열하시오.**

1 숙제를 마치고 나는 내 친구와 영화를 보러 나갔다. (I, finished, homework, having, my, went out)
→ ______________________ to a movie with my friend.

2 그곳에 여러 번 가 봐서 나는 그 도시에 대해 많이 알고 있다. (I, having, there, been, know, many times)
→ ______________________ a lot about the city.

3 전구로 장식되어서 그 집은 아름다워 보였다. (the, decorated, house, lights, with, looked)
→ ______________________ beautiful.

4 불이 꺼져서 우리는 아무것도 볼 수 없었다. (the, gone out, lights, we, see, having, couldn't)
→ ______________________ anything.

5 비가 조금 내리는 따뜻한 날이었다. (with, little, a, falling, rain)
→ It was a warm day ______________________.

6 그의 얼굴 표정으로 판단해 보면 그는 불안한 것 같다. (judging, look, from, the)
→ ______________________ on his face, he seems nervous.

B 빈칸 완성 **우리말과 일치하도록 괄호 안의 말을 이용하여 빈칸에 알맞은 말을 쓰시오.**

1 몇 시간 동안 쉬지 않고 공부했기 때문에 그는 완전히 지쳤다. (study)
→ ________ ________ for hours without a break, he was completely exhausted.

2 충분한 돈을 저축했기 때문에 우리는 휴가를 갈 수 있다. (save)
→ ________ ________ enough money, we can go on vacation.

3 서비스 센터에서 수리를 받아서 그 컴퓨터는 잘 작동하고 있다. (fix)
→ ________ at the service center, the computer is working well.

4 휴일이었기 때문에 대부분의 상점이 문을 닫았다. (it, a holiday)
→ ________ ________ ________ ________, most of the shops were closed.

5 그녀는 눈을 감은 채로 그 노래를 불렀다. (her eyes, close)
→ She sang the song ________ ________ ________ ________.

6 솔직히 말하면 나는 정치에 관심이 없다. (frankly, speak)
→ ________ ________, I'm not interested in politics.

Answer Key p.17

C 문장 완성 우리말과 일치하도록 괄호 안의 말을 이용하여 문장을 완성하시오. (단, 분사구문을 사용할 것)

1 밤에 잘 잤더니 나는 아침에 일찍 일어났다. (sleep well, during the night)

→ ______________________________, I woke up early in the morning.

2 내 여권을 분실했기 때문에 나는 새것을 신청해야 한다. (lose, my passport)

→ ______________________________, I have to apply for a new one.

3 도심에 위치하고 있어서 그 식당은 관광객들에게 인기가 많다. (locate, in the city center)

→ ______________________________, the restaurant is popular with tourists.

4 화산 폭발에 대한 경고를 받은 후 사람들은 마을을 떠났다. (warn of, the eruption)

→ ______________________________, people left the town.

5 그는 팔짱을 낀 채로 나를 보고 있었다. (his arms, cross)

→ He was looking at me ______________________________.

6 그의 나이를 고려하면 소년은 성숙하다. (consider, his age)

→ ______________________________, the boy is mature.

D 문장 전환 다음 문장을 분사구문으로 바꿔 쓰시오. (단, 접속사를 쓰지 말 것)

1 After he had turned off the lights, he went to bed.

→ ______________________________, he went to bed.

2 Because he hadn't slept for two days, he wasn't able to concentrate.

→ ______________________________, he wasn't able to concentrate.

3 Since the safe is made of steel, it is very heavy.

→ ______________________________, the safe is very heavy.

4 As I had been interested in astronomy since childhood, I bought a telescope.

→ ______________________________, I bought a telescope.

5 As it was a stormy day, the field trip was canceled.

→ ______________________________, the field trip was canceled.

6 After the sun had set, we headed for home.

→ ______________________________, we headed for home.

ACTUAL TEST

문항 수	객관식 8 / 서술형 12
맞은 개수	/ 20

01 빈칸에 들어갈 말이 순서대로 짝지어진 것은?

- Look at the girl ________ on the floor.
- The car ________ outside is my father's.
- My uncle works at a company ________ computers.

① cried – parked – made
② crying – parking – made
③ cried – parking – making
④ crying – parked – making
⑤ crying – parking – making

02 밑줄 친 부분의 쓰임이 나머지 넷과 다른 것은?

① The laughing children look happy.
② The chef is cooking a delicious meal.
③ I felt my phone vibrating in my pocket.
④ She enjoys walking her dog in the park.
⑤ The boy playing the drums is my brother.

03 밑줄 친 부분이 어법상 틀린 것은?

① The story was really touching.
② His job was tiring and often stressful.
③ The chair made of wood is comfortable.
④ The frozen lake looked like a giant mirror.
⑤ We visited a castle building 100 years ago.

04 괄호 안의 동사를 알맞은 형태로 바꿀 때, 형태가 나머지 넷과 다른 것은?

① I heard some (shock) news yesterday.
② The math questions are really (confuse).
③ The movie was (bore) from start to finish.
④ She is very (excite) about her trip to Europe.
⑤ Jack found himself in an (embarrass) situation.

05 두 문장의 의미가 같도록 할 때, 빈칸에 들어갈 말로 알맞은 것은?

As I didn't want to get lost, I used a map.
= ____________ to get lost, I used a map.

① Wanting
② Not wanting
③ Wanting not
④ Didn't wanting
⑤ Being not want

빈출

06 밑줄 친 부분을 분사구문으로 바르게 바꾼 것은?

① Because I felt sick, I went to the doctor.
→ Felt sick
② As the girl was left alone, she felt lonely.
→ Leaving alone
③ While I was reading a book, I fell asleep.
→ Being read a book
④ Since I had met her before, I greeted her.
→ Having met her before
⑤ If it is fine tomorrow, we will go hiking.
→ Being fine tomorrow

고난도

07 어법상 올바른 문장을 모두 고르면?

ⓐ There are two people waited for a bus.
ⓑ I love the pictures painted by Van Gogh.
ⓒ Invited to the party, Tiffany bought a new dress.
ⓓ I went to bed with the lights turning on.
ⓔ Generally spoken, people retire in their 60s.

① ⓐ, ⓑ
② ⓐ, ⓑ, ⓒ
③ ⓑ, ⓒ
④ ⓑ, ⓒ, ⓓ
⑤ ⓑ, ⓓ, ⓔ

08 밑줄 친 ⓐ~ⓔ에 대한 설명으로 틀린 것은?

ⓐ Studying hard, you'll pass the exam.
ⓑ Loved by her friends, she never feels alone.
ⓒ When walking in the park, I listen to music.
ⓓ Having slept many hours, he felt tired.
ⓔ It being a cloudy night, I couldn't see the moon.

① ⓐ는 조건을 나타내는 분사구문이다.
② ⓑ는 분사구문 앞에 Being이 생략된 형태이다.
③ ⓒ에서 When은 시간의 의미를 명확히 나타내기 위해 쓰였다.
④ ⓓ는 '많은 시간을 잤기 때문에'로 해석된다.
⑤ ⓔ는 부사절과 주절의 주어가 다르므로 부사절의 주어인 It이 쓰였다.

서술형

09 주어진 말을 알맞은 형태로 써서 문장을 완성하시오.

(1) Who is the man ________ by the window? (sit)

(2) The ________ wallet was found in the subway station. (steal)

10 주어진 말을 활용하여 대화를 완성하시오.

A: How was your dinner at the new restaurant?
B: The food was good, but the service was very ________. (disappoint)

[11-12] 밑줄 친 부분을 분사구문으로 바꿔 쓰시오. (단, 접속사를 쓰지 말 것)

11

Because I didn't know the way, I had to ask someone.

→ ____________________, I had to ask someone.

12

When I was asked the question, I didn't know what to say.

→ ____________________, I didn't know what to say.

[13-14] 밑줄 친 부분을 부사절로 바꿔 쓰시오.

13

Turing left, you will see the library on your right.

→ ____________________, you will see the library on your right.

14

Interested in the book, he didn't buy it.

→ ____________________, he didn't buy it.

15 그림을 보고, 주어진 말을 활용하여 문장을 완성하시오.

He is standing in front of the painting ________ ________________________. (with, arms, cross)

16 우리말과 일치하도록 주어진 말을 활용하여 문장을 완성하시오.

(1) 요즘 바쁘기 때문에 나는 체육관에 갈 수 없다. (busy)

→ __________ __________ these days, I can't go to the gym.

(2) 그 영화를 전에 봤기 때문에 그녀는 결말을 알고 있었다. (see, the movie)

→ __________ __________ __________ __________ before, she knew the ending.

17 우리말과 일치하도록 주어진 말을 활용하여 지시에 맞게 문장을 완성하시오.

> 차로 출근하는 동안 그는 교통사고를 목격했다.
> (drive to work)

(1) 접속사 while을 사용해서 부사절로 쓸 것

→ ______________________________, he saw a car accident.

(2) 분사구문으로 쓸 것

→ ______________________________, he saw a car accident.

18 우리말과 일치하도록 주어진 말을 바르게 배열하시오.

> 날씨가 좋아서 우리는 강가를 산책하기로 했다.
> (nice, the, being, weather)

→ ______________________________, we decided to take a walk by the river.

19 어법상 <u>틀린</u> 부분을 찾아 바르게 고치시오.

> Judged from his accent, he may be from a different country.
> (그의 억양으로 판단해 보면 그는 다른 나라 출신일지도 모른다.)

______________ → ______________

고난도

20 밑줄 친 부분이 어법상 <u>틀린</u> 문장 <u>2개</u>를 골라 기호를 쓰고, 밑줄 친 부분을 바르게 고치시오.

> ⓐ <u>Having lived</u> in London, I know many great places to visit.
> ⓑ <u>Bitten</u> by a mosquito, my arm started itching.
> ⓒ <u>Having not</u> any homework, I played with my friends.
> ⓓ Elizabeth took a lot of photos, <u>explored</u> the city.

(　　) → ______________

(　　) → ______________

Chapter 06

비교

UNIT
01 원급, 비교급, 최상급

GRAMMAR FOCUS

1 원급 비교

'~만큼 …한/하게'의 의미로 동등한 두 대상을 비교할 때 쓴다.

as + 형용사/부사의 원급 + as ~만큼 …한/하게	The movie is **as exciting as** the book. 그 영화는 책만큼 흥미진진하다. He knows about computers **as much as** I do. 그는 나만큼 많이 컴퓨터에 대해 알고 있다.
not as + 원급 + as ~만큼 …하지 않은/않게	My test score is **not as good as** yours. 내 시험 점수는 네 것만큼 좋지 않다.

2 비교급 비교

'~보다 더 …한/하게'의 의미로 두 대상을 비교할 때 쓴다.

비교급 + than ~보다 더 …한/하게	The horse is **bigger than** the zebra. 말은 얼룩말보다 더 크다. The final exam was **more difficult than** the midterm exam. 기말고사는 중간고사보다 더 어려웠다.
much[even, still, far, a lot] + 비교급 + than ~보다 훨씬 더 …한/하게	My new computer is **much faster than** my old one. 내 새 컴퓨터는 내 예전 것보다 훨씬 더 빠르다. The restaurant is **even more expensive than** I expected. 그 식당은 내가 예상했던 것보다 훨씬 더 비싸다.

cf. '~보다 덜 …한/하게'는 「less + 원급 + than」 형태로 쓴다.

The festival was **less crowded than** last year. 그 축제는 작년보다 덜 붐볐다.

He speaks English **less fluently than** his brother. 그는 자신의 형보다 영어를 덜 유창하게 말한다.

3 최상급 비교

'가장 ~한/하게'의 의미로 셋 이상을 비교할 때 쓴다. 최상급 뒤에는 주로 「in + 장소/단체」, 「of + 숫자/기간」 형태로 비교의 범위를 나타낸다.

the + 최상급(+ in/of) (~에서) 가장 …한/하게	She is **the most talented** musician *in* the band. 그녀는 그 밴드에서 가장 재능 있는 뮤지션이다. Today is **the coldest** day *of* the year. 오늘은 올해 중 가장 추운 날이다.
the + 최상급(+ that) + 주어 + have ever p.p. 지금까지 ~한 것 중 가장 …한	This is **the best** pizza **(that) I have ever eaten.** 이것은 내가 지금까지 먹어 본 것 중 최고의 피자이다.
one of the + 최상급 + 복수명사 가장 ~한 … 중 하나	The peacock is **one of the most beautiful** birds. 공작새는 가장 아름다운 새 중 하나이다.

Answer Key p.18

괄호 안에서 알맞은 것을 고르시오.

1 Brazil is not as (big, bigger) as Canada.

2 My brother swims (well, better) than me.

3 My phone battery lasts less (long, longer) than it used to.

4 The weather today is (much, very) warmer than last week.

5 Sidney is the (large, largest) city in Australia.

6 Anthony is the (nicer, nicest) person I've ever met.

7 Ron is one of the smartest (student, students) in my class.

두 문장의 의미가 같도록 빈칸에 알맞은 말을 쓰시오.

1 Tom is 180cm tall. His father is 180cm tall, too. (tall)

→ Tom is ________ ________ ________ his father.

2 For me, learning English is not as difficult as learning Chinese. (difficult)

→ For me, learning Chinese is ________ ________ ________ learning English.

3 Sam runs 100m in 15 seconds. Mike runs 100m in 18 seconds. Jerry runs 100m in 20 seconds. (fast)

→ Sam is ________ ________ ________ the three.

괄호 안의 말을 알맞은 형태로 바꿔 문장을 완성하시오.

1 K2는 에베레스트 산만큼 높지 않다. (high)

→ K2 is ________ ________ ________ ________ Mount Everest.

2 테니스는 한국에서 축구보다 덜 인기 있다. (popular)

→ Tennis is ________ ________ ________ soccer in Korea.

3 그것은 내가 지금까지 본 것 중 최악의 영화이다. (bad, movie, see)

→ It is ________ ________ ________ I ________ ________ ________.

4 〈모나리자〉는 역사상 가장 유명한 그림 중 하나이다. (famous, painting)

→ The *Mona Lisa* is ________ ________ ________ ________ ________ ________ in history.

WRITING FOCUS

A 배열 영작 **우리말과 일치하도록 괄호 안의 말을 바르게 배열하시오.**

1 그녀는 나만큼 독서를 즐긴다. (as, reading, do, enjoys, I, much, as)

→ She ____.

2 그는 평소만큼 상냥하지 않았다. (wasn't, usually, he, friendly, as, as, is)

→ He ____.

3 그 가게는 내가 생각했던 것보다 훨씬 더 멀리 떨어져 있다. (is, farther, I, much, away, than, thought)

→ The store ____.

4 이것은 그 마을에서 가장 역사적인 건물이다. (the, historical, most, town, the, building, in)

→ This is ____.

5 홍해는 세계에서 가장 염도가 높은 바다 중 하나이다. (the, one, saltiest, world, of, in, the, seas)

→ The Red Sea is ____.

6 이것은 내가 지금까지 본 것 중 가장 아름다운 일몰이다. (I've, the, seen, sunset, ever, most, beautiful)

→ This is ____.

B 빈칸 완성 **우리말과 일치하도록 괄호 안의 말을 이용하여 빈칸에 알맞은 말을 쓰시오.**

1 그 의자는 그 식탁만큼 비싸다. (expensive)

→ The chair is ________ ________ ________ the table.

2 이 호텔 방은 내가 기대했던 것만큼 넓지 않다. (spacious)

→ This hotel room is ________ ________ ________ ________ I expected.

3 우리 형은 나보다 더 빨리 배운다. (quickly)

→ My brother learns ________ ________ ________ me.

4 이것은 내가 가진 가장 큰 가방이다. (big, bag)

→ This is ________ ________ ________ I have.

5 그는 그 팀에서 가장 훌륭한 선수 중 한 명이다. (good, player)

→ He is ________ ________ ________ ________ ________ on the team.

6 이것은 내가 지금까지 맛본 것 중 가장 맛있는 케이크이다. (delicious, taste)

→ This is ________ ________ ________ cake I've ________ ________.

C 문장 완성 우리말과 일치하도록 괄호 안의 말을 이용하여 문장을 완성하시오.

1 그녀의 신곡은 그녀의 이전 곡만큼 인기가 있다. (popular, last song)

→ Her new song is ______________________________.

2 그 문제는 내가 생각했던 것만큼 심각하지는 않다. (serious, thought)

→ The problem is ______________________________.

3 건강은 돈과 재산보다 더 중요하다. (important, money, wealth)

→ Health is ______________________________.

4 수학이 나에게는 영어보다 훨씬 더 어렵다. (difficult, English)

→ Math is ______________________________ for me.

5 오늘은 이번 달 중 가장 바쁜 날이다. (busy, day, the month)

→ Today is ______________________________.

6 전화기는 역사상 가장 위대한 발명품 중 하나이다. (great, invention, in history)

→ The telephone is ______________________________.

D 오류 수정 어법상 틀린 부분을 바르게 고쳐 문장을 다시 쓰시오.

1 She drinks tea so much as she drinks water.

→ ______________________________

2 The blue dress is not as prettier as the pink one.

→ ______________________________

3 This hotel is cheap than the one we stayed at the last time.

→ ______________________________

4 Peter's sister is very younger than him.

→ ______________________________

5 That was funniest joke I've ever heard.

→ ______________________________

6 The Eiffel Tower is one of the most famous landmark in Paris.

→ ______________________________

UNIT
02 여러 가지 비교 표현

GRAMMAR FOCUS

❶ 원급을 이용한 표현

(1) 배수사 + as + 원급 + as: '~의 몇 배만큼 …한/하게'의 의미로 「배수사 + 비교급 + than」으로 바꿔 쓸 수 있다.

This river is	**three times**	**as long as**	that one.	이 강은 저 강의 세 배만큼 길다.
		longer than		이 강은 저 강보다 세 배 더 길다.

cf. '~의 절반만큼 …한/하게'는 「half as + 원급 + as」로 나타낸다.

The used car is **half as expensive as** the new car. 그 중고차는 새 차의 절반 가격이다.

She ate only **half as much as** I did. 그녀는 내가 먹은 것의 절반만큼만 먹었다.

(2) as + 원급 + as possible: '가능한 한 ~한/하게'의 의미로 「as + 원급 + as + 주어 + can[could]」으로 바꿔 쓸 수 있다.

He left for the airport	**as early as possible.**	그는 가능한 한 일찍 공항으로 떠났다.
	as early as he could.	

❷ 비교급을 이용한 표현

(1) 비교급 + and + 비교급: '점점 더 ~한/하게'

The weather is getting	**hotter and hotter.**	날씨가 점점 더 더워지고 있다.
She became	**more and more famous.**	그녀는 점점 더 유명해졌다.

(2) the + 비교급 ~, the + 비교급 …: '더 ~할수록 더 …하다'

The more	he earns,	**the more**	he spends.	더 많이 벌수록 그는 더 많이 쓴다.
The deeper	you dive,	**the darker**	it becomes.	더 깊이 잠수할수록 더 어두워진다.

cf. 「the + 비교급 ~, the + 비교급 …」은 접속사 as를 사용해서 바꿔 쓸 수 있다.

→ **As** he earns **more**, he spends **more**.

→ **As** you dive **deeper**, it becomes **darker**.

❸ 원급과 비교급을 이용한 최상급 표현

the + 최상급	Ann is **the smartest student** in the class. Ann은 그 반에서 가장 똑똑한 학생이다.
= 비교급 + than any other + 단수명사	= Ann is **smarter than any other** student in the class. Ann은 그 반에서 다른 어떤 학생보다 더 똑똑하다.
= 부정 주어 ~ as + 원급 + as	= **No other student** in the class is **as smart as** Ann. 그 반의 다른 어떤 학생도 Ann만큼 똑똑하지 않다.
= 부정 주어 ~ 비교급 + than	= **No other student** in the class is **smarter than** Ann. 그 반의 다른 어떤 학생도 Ann보다 더 똑똑하지 않다.

Answer Key p.19

괄호 안에서 알맞은 것을 고르시오.

1 I need to finish this project as soon as (can, possible).

2 She ran as far as she (can, could) in the marathon.

3 The new building is (three times taller, taller three times) than the old one.

4 Traffic is getting (heavy and heavy, heavier and heavier).

5 The more you exercise, the (less, little) stressed you feel.

6 Seoul is larger than any other (city, cities) in Korea.

7 Nothing is (beautiful, more beautiful) than nature itself.

두 문장의 의미가 같도록 빈칸에 알맞은 말을 쓰시오.

1 To pass the exam, he studied as hard as he could.

→ To pass the exam, he studied ________ ________ ________ ________.

2 John is 16 years old. His sister is 8 years old.

→ John is ________ ________ ________ ________ his sister.

3 The large pizza is three times as big as the small one.

→ The large pizza is three times ________ ________ the small one.

4 As you read more, you become smarter.

→ ________ ________ you read, ________ ________ you become.

〈보기〉의 문장과 의미가 같도록 빈칸에 알맞은 말을 쓰시오.

보기 Antarctica is the coldest continent on the Earth.

1 Antarctica is ________ ________ ________ ________ ________ on the Earth.

2 No other continent on the Earth is ________ ________ ________ Antarctica.

3 No other continent on the Earth is ________ ________ Antarctica.

WRITING FOCUS

A 배열 영작 우리말과 일치하도록 괄호 안의 말을 바르게 배열하시오.

1 그녀는 그 버스를 타기 위해 가능한 한 빨리 달렸다. (fast, she, as, could, ran, she, as)

→ ______________________________ to catch the bus.

2 그 사전은 그 잡지보다 세 배 더 두껍다. (the, magazine, three, is, than, thicker, times)

→ The dictionary ______________________________.

3 유가는 점점 더 비싸지고 있다. (getting, higher, and, are, higher)

→ Oil prices ______________________________.

4 더 많이 들을수록 더 적게 말한다. (the, listen, you, more, you, less, the, speak)

→ ______________________________

5 망고는 다른 어떤 과일보다 더 달콤하다. (mangos, sweeter, other, are, any, fruit, than)

→ ______________________________

6 그 반의 어느 소년도 Roy보다 키가 더 크지 않다. (boy, in, than, the, Roy, no, class, is, taller, other)

→ ______________________________

B 빈칸 완성 우리말과 일치하도록 괄호 안의 말을 이용하여 빈칸에 알맞은 말을 쓰시오.

1 가능한 한 빨리 제 이메일에 회신해 주세요. (soon)

→ Please respond to my email ________ ________ ________ ________.

2 그의 가방은 내 가방의 두 배만큼 무겁다. (heavy)

→ His bag is ________ ________ ________ ________ my bag.

3 온라인 쇼핑은 점점 더 인기를 얻고 있다. (popular)

→ Online shopping is getting ________ ________ ________ ________.

4 더 열심히 노력할수록 그는 더 적은 실수를 했다. (hard, few, mistake)

→ ________ ________ he tried, ________ ________ ________ he made.

5 다른 어떤 계절도 겨울만큼 춥지 않다. (cold)

→ No other season ________ ________ ________ ________ winter.

6 목성은 태양계에서 다른 어떤 행성보다 더 크다. (planet)

→ Jupiter is bigger than ________ ________ ________ in the solar system.

Answer Key p.19

C 문장 완성 두 문장의 의미가 같도록 빈칸에 알맞은 말을 쓰시오. (괄호 안에 주어진 구문을 사용할 것)

1 He painted the picture as realistically as possible. (as+원급+as+주어+can)

→ He painted the picture ______________________.

2 The diamond ring is ten times as expensive as the gold ring. (배수사+비교급+than)

→ The diamond ring is ______________________.

3 As I talked with him more, I became more tired. (the+비교급 ~, the+비교급 …)

→ ____________ I talked with him, ____________ I became.

4 August is the hottest month in Korea. (비교급)

→ August is ______________________ in Korea.

5 Heracles was the strongest man in the world. (as+원급+as)

→ ____________ in the world was ____________ Heracles.

6 Australia is the smallest continent in the world. (비교급)

→ ____________ in the world is ____________ Australia.

D 오류 수정 밑줄 친 부분을 바르게 고쳐 문장을 다시 쓰시오.

1 I try to exercise as often as <u>can</u>.

→ ______________________

2 The building is <u>taller three times</u> than the house.

→ ______________________

3 She is becoming <u>fluenter and fluenter</u> in English.

→ ______________________

4 The more you eat, <u>you become fatter</u>.

→ ______________________

5 The tree is older than <u>any other trees</u> in the garden.

→ ______________________

6 No other metal <u>is not</u> as useful as iron.

→ ______________________

ACTUAL TEST

문항 수	객관식 8 / 서술형 12
맞은 개수	/ 20

[01-02] 빈칸에 들어갈 말로 알맞은 것을 고르시오.

01

My smartphone is as __________ as yours.

① new ② newer
③ newest ④ more new
⑤ the most new

02

That was __________ exam I've ever taken.

① difficult ② more difficult
③ most difficult ④ the more difficult
⑤ the most difficult

03 빈칸에 들어갈 말로 알맞지 않은 것은?

The noise from the construction site is __________ worse than usual.

① far ② very ③ a lot
④ even ⑤ much

빈출

04 표의 내용과 일치하는 것을 2개 고르면?

	John	Tom	Mike
Age	16	18	17
Height	175cm	183cm	173cm
Weight	63kg	65kg	68kg

① John is as old as Tom.
② Tom is not as tall as Mike.
③ Tom is heavier than John.
④ Mike is shorter than John.
⑤ Mike is the youngest of the three.

고난도

05 두 문장의 의미가 서로 다른 것은?

① Jane's hair is not as long as Emily's hair.
= Emily's hair is shorter than Jane's hair.
② I know a lot about cars. Liam knows more about them.
= I don't know about cars as much as Liam.
③ The red hat is $30. The blue hat is $15.
= The red hat is twice as expensive as the blue hat.
④ Rachel is 22 years old. Amy is 11 years old.
= Amy is half as old as Rachel.
⑤ Learning English is difficult, but learning Arabic is more difficult.
= Learning English is not as difficult as learning Arabic.

06 문장의 의미가 나머지 넷과 다른 것은?

① Sam is the most diligent student in the class.
② No other student in the class is as diligent as Sam.
③ No other student in the class is more diligent than Sam.
④ Sam is more diligent than any other student in the class.
⑤ Sam is not as diligent as the other students in the class.

07 다음 중 어법상 올바른 것은?

① David ran as fast as he possible.
② The music is getting loud and loud.
③ The more you have, the much you want.
④ Jupiter is about 11 times as big as Earth.
⑤ Bob's sister is much more younger than him.

08 어법상 올바른 문장의 개수는?

ⓐ She carried the vase as carefully as possible.
ⓑ This coffee is twice as strong as that one.
ⓒ As the day went on, the weather got worse and worse.
ⓓ The more electricity you use, your bill will be higher.
ⓔ February is shorter than any other months.

① 1개 ② 2개 ③ 3개
④ 4개 ⑤ 5개

서술형

09 빈칸에 들어갈 말을 〈보기〉에서 골라 알맞은 형태로 쓰시오. (단, 한 번씩만 쓸 것)

보기	large	funny	sweet

(1) The cake tastes as __________ as honey.

(2) The movie is __________ than the book.

(3) The Pacific Ocean is the __________ ocean on the Earth.

10 어법상 <u>틀린</u> 부분을 찾아 바르게 고치시오.

(1) The actor is not as taller as he looks on TV.

__________ → __________

(2) He is one of the most famous pianist in the world.

__________ → __________

11 주어진 문장과 의미가 같도록 빈칸에 알맞은 말을 쓰시오.

She spoke to me as slowly as possible.

→ She spoke to me __________ __________ __________ __________ __________.

12 주어진 정보와 괄호 안의 말을 활용하여 문장을 완성하시오.

(1) The peach is 250g. The melon weighs 500g.

→ The melon weighs __________ __________ __________ __________ the peach. (heavy, as)

(2) Jill studied for one hour. Jack studied for three hours.

→ Jack studied __________ __________ __________ __________ Jill. (long, than)

[13-14] 주어진 문장과 의미가 같도록 〈조건〉에 맞게 바꿔 쓰시오.

13

Lily can sing better than Ethan.

조건 「as+원급+as」를 사용할 것

→ Ethan can't sing __________________.

14

As I go to bed later, I feel more tired.

조건 「the+비교급 ~, the+비교급 …」을 사용할 것

→ __________________

15 다음 가격표를 보고, 〈조건〉에 맞게 문장을 완성하시오.

$1	$1.50	$3	$7

조건 괄호 안의 말과 expensive를 활용할 것

(1) The eraser is ___________ ___________ ___________ the notebook. (less)

(2) The notebook is ___________ ___________ ___________ ___________ the ruler. (as)

(3) The pencil sharpener is ___________ ___________ ___________ any other ___________. (item)

16 우리말과 일치하도록 주어진 말을 활용하여 문장을 완성하시오.

(1) 11월에는 날씨가 점점 더 추워진다. (cold)

→ The weather gets ______________________ ________________ in November.

(2) 면접을 기다리면서 그녀는 점점 더 초조해졌다. (nervous)

→ As she waited for her interview, she got ______________________________________.

17 주어진 문장과 의미가 같도록 지시에 맞게 바꿔 쓰시오.

Peter is the best player on the team.

(1) 비교급을 사용할 것

→ Peter is ___________ ___________ ___________ ___________ ___________ on the team.

(2) 원급을 사용할 것

→ ___________ ___________ ___________ on the team is ___________ ___________ ___________ Peter.

18 어법상 <u>틀린</u> 문장 <u>2개</u>를 골라 기호를 쓰고, 틀린 부분을 바르게 고치시오.

ⓐ The longer I live in this city, the better I like it.
ⓑ The more friends I have, the little lonely I feel.
ⓒ The older we grow, the more wise we become.
ⓓ The faster you run, the earlier you will finish the race.

(　　) ________________ → ________________
(　　) ________________ → ________________

[19-20] 대화를 읽고, 물음에 답하시오.

A: I'm learning to cook. <u>더 많이 연습할수록 나는 더 잘하게 돼.</u>
B: That's great. <u>네가 지금까지 만든 것 중 최고의 요리는 무엇이니?</u>
A: Definitely the lasagna. Everyone loved it.

고난도

19 밑줄 친 우리말과 일치하도록 〈조건〉에 맞게 문장을 완성하시오.

조건 practice, become을 활용할 것

→ The ___________ ___________ ___________, the ___________ ___________ ___________.

20 밑줄 친 우리말과 일치하도록 주어진 말을 바르게 배열하시오.

best, have, what, ever, the, you, dish, is, made

→ ______________________________________

Chapter 07

접속사

UNIT 01 부사절 접속사

GRAMMAR FOCUS

❶ 시간, 조건을 나타내는 접속사

when	~할 때	**When** I entered the classroom, no one was there. 내가 교실에 들어갔을 때 거기에는 아무도 없었다.
while	~하는 동안	**While** I was cooking dinner, my phone rang. 내가 저녁을 요리하는 동안, 내 전화기가 울렸다. *during + 명사(구): ~ 동안
as	~할 때, ~하면서	**As** he got up, he hit his head against the shelf. 그는 일어나면서 선반에 머리를 부딪쳤다.
since	~ 이후로	Andy has had several jobs **since** he left college. Andy는 대학을 졸업한 이후로 여러 직업을 가졌다.
until, till	~할 때까지	I can't watch TV **until** I finish my homework. 나는 숙제를 마칠 때까지 TV를 볼 수 없다.
as soon as	~하자마자	Jane called me **as soon as** she arrived at the airport. Jane은 공항에 도착하자마자 내게 전화했다.
if	(만일) ~한다면	You will fail **if** you *don't work* hard. = You will fail **unless** you *work* hard. 너는 열심히 일하지 않으면 실패할 것이다.
unless	(만일) ~하지 않으면	
as long as	~하는 한	The water is fine **as long as** you don't drink it. 그 물은 당신이 그것을 마시지 않는 한 괜찮다.

plus 시간과 조건의 부사절에서는 현재시제로 미래를 나타낸다.

I will wait **until** the price *goes* down. 나는 가격이 내려갈 때까지 기다릴 것이다.

The field trip will be postponed **if** it *rains* tomorrow. 현장 학습은 내일 비가 오면 연기될 것이다.

❷ 이유, 양보, 대조를 나타내는 접속사

because, as, since	~ 때문에	**Because** it rained heavily, we stayed indoors. 비가 많이 왔기 때문에 우리는 실내에 있었다. *because of / due to + 명사(구): ~ 때문에
although, though, even though	비록 ~이지만	**Although** he had a fever, he attended the class. 그는 열이 났지만 그 수업에 참석했다. *despite / in spite of + 명사(구): ~에도 불구하고
while	~ 반면에	Tim likes sports **while** his brother doesn't like them. Tim은 스포츠를 좋아하는 반면에 그의 형은 싫어한다.

❸ 목적을 나타내는 접속사

so that	~하기 위해, ~하도록	I hurried **so that[in order that]** I could catch the train. = I hurried **in order to[so as to]** catch the train. 나는 그 기차를 탈 수 있도록 서둘렀다.

cf. 결과를 나타내는 「so + 형용사/부사 + that ~」 구문과 혼동하지 않도록 주의한다.

She was **so** pleased **that** she jumped up and down. 그녀는 너무 기뻐서 펄쩍펄쩍 뛰었다.

Answer Key p.20

괄호 안에서 알맞은 것을 고르시오.

1 John hurt his arm (if, while) he was playing tennis.

2 (When, Until) she was six, she started reading and writing.

3 My mother dislikes cats (since, unless) she is allergic to cat hair.

4 Before they (travel, will travel) to Africa, they will get vaccinations.

5 The girl burst out laughing (during, while) the conversation.

6 (Because, Because of) the gossip, people wondered what had happened to Nancy.

〈보기〉에서 알맞은 말을 골라 두 문장을 한 문장으로 바꿔 쓰시오. (단, 한 번씩만 쓸 것)

보기	because	if	so that	although

1 You want to stay here. You should follow the rules.

→ ______________________________, you should follow the rules.

2 They don't believe him at all. He lies a lot.

→ They don't believe him at all ______________________________.

3 My computer is old. It works very well.

→ ______________________________, it works very well.

4 He practiced the piano every day. He could improve his skills.

→ He practiced the piano every day ______________________________.

우리말과 일치하도록 빈칸에 알맞은 말을 쓰시오.

1 긴급 상황이 아니면 밤에는 내게 전화하지 마세요.

→ Don't call me at night __________ it's an emergency.

2 그 소년은 우리가 그를 볼 수 없도록 문 뒤에 숨었다.

→ The boy hid behind the door __________ __________ we could not see him.

3 오랜 기다림에도 불구하고, 그는 자신의 형에게서 아무 소식도 듣지 못했다.

→ __________ the long wait, he didn't hear anything from his brother.

WRITING FOCUS

A 배열 영작 우리말과 일치하도록 괄호 안의 말을 바르게 배열하시오.

1 나는 점심을 먹는 동안 짧은 동영상 한 편을 보았다. (I, while, having, was, lunch)

→ ______________________________, I watched a short video clip.

2 당신이 답을 찾자마자 저에게 알려주세요. (as, you, the, soon, find out, as, answer)

→ ______________________________, please let me know.

3 그는 충분한 수면을 취하지 못했기 때문에 하루 종일 졸렸다. (enough, he, get, because, sleep, didn't)

→ ______________________________, he felt sleepy all day long.

4 그녀는 지쳐 있었지만 자신의 숙제를 끝내야만 했다. (even, exhausted, she, though, felt)

→ ______________________________, she had to finish her homework.

5 나는 (그것을) 기억할 수 있도록 그의 주소를 적어두었다. (I, remember, that, could, so, it)

→ I wrote down his address ______________________________.

6 나는 시끄러운 음악 때문에 그의 말을 거의 들을 수 없었다. (because, the, music, of, loud)

→ I could hardly hear him ______________________________.

B 빈칸 완성 우리말과 일치하도록 빈칸에 알맞은 말을 쓰시오.

1 그들은 초등학교 때부터 가장 친한 친구이다.

→ They have been best friends __________ they were in elementary school.

2 우리는 Chris가 도착할 때까지 파티를 시작하지 않을 것이다.

→ We won't start the party __________ Chris arrives.

3 나는 할 일이 많지 않다면 7시에는 거기에 있을 거야.

→ I will be there at 7 o'clock __________ I have a lot to do.

4 너는 조용히 있는 한 방에 있어도 된다.

→ __________ __________ __________ you keep quiet, you can stay in the room.

5 그는 재능이 있음에도 불구하고 너무 게을러서 성공할 수 없다.

→ __________ __________ he is talented, he is too lazy to succeed.

6 그는 그 음악을 더 잘 들을 수 있도록 볼륨을 높였다.

→ He turned up the volume __________ __________ he could hear the music better.

Answer Key p.21

C 문장 완성 우리말과 일치하도록 괄호 안의 말을 이용하여 문장을 완성하시오.

1 당신이 도움이 필요한 사람들을 도울 때 보상을 기대해서는 안 된다. (help, people in need)

→ ______________________________, you should not expect a reward.

2 Andrew는 나이가 들면서 시력이 나빠지기 시작했다. (grow older)

→ ______________________________, his vision began to fail.

3 Nora는 (그것이) 회복될 때까지 그 새를 돌봐주었다. (it, recover)

→ Nora took care of the bird ______________________________.

4 나는 배가 고팠기 때문에 감자칩 한 봉지를 샀다. (feel hungry)

→ ______________________________, I bought a bag of potato chips.

5 그는 집에서 일할 수 있도록 컴퓨터를 설치했다. (work from home)

→ He set up the computer ______________________________.

6 그 호텔은 너무 비싸서 우리는 다른 곳을 예약했다. (expensive, book)

→ The hotel was ______________________________ another one.

D 오류 수정 밑줄 친 부분을 바르게 고쳐 문장을 다시 쓰시오.

1 Because it was 4:00 a.m., he couldn't sleep.

→ ______________________________

2 Come here as long as you finish work.

→ ______________________________

3 When you will come back from the trip, I won't be here.

→ ______________________________

4 John had worked for the same company since he retired.

→ ______________________________

5 It rained heavily so that the streets were flooded.

→ ______________________________

6 I spent most of my time at home while the winter break.

→ ______________________________

UNIT
02 상관접속사, 명사절 접속사

GRAMMAR FOCUS

① 상관접속사

상관접속사는 두 개 이상의 단어가 짝을 이루어 쓰이는 접속사이다. 상관접속사가 주어로 쓰인 경우 both *A* and *B*는 항상 복수 취급하고, 나머지는 동사를 B에 일치시킨다.

both *A* and *B* A와 B 둘 다	**Both** *soccer* **and** *basketball* **are** team sports. 축구와 농구 둘 다 팀 스포츠이다.
either *A* or *B* A나 B 둘 중 하나	**Either** you **or** *Mike* **has** to stay and take care of the kids. 너나 Mike 둘 중 한 명이 남아서 그 아이들을 돌봐야 한다.
neither *A* nor *B* A도 B도 아닌	**Neither** she **nor** *her children* **speak** English. 그녀도 그녀의 아이들도 영어를 하지 않는다.
not only *A* but also *B* = *B* as well as *A* A뿐만 아니라 B도	**Not only** John **but also** *his brothers* **are** good athletes. = *His brothers* **as well as** John **are** good athletes. John뿐만 아니라 그의 형제들도 훌륭한 운동선수이다.

② 명사절 접속사

(1) 접속사 that: 접속사 that이 이끄는 명사절은 문장에서 주어, 보어, 목적어 역할을 한다. 주어로 쓰인 that절은 주로 가주어 it으로 대신하고, 목적어로 쓰인 that절에서 that은 생략할 수 있다.

That Jill survived the tsunami was unbelievable. Jill이 그 쓰나미에서 살아남았다는 것은 믿을 수 없었다. 〈주어〉

(= It was unbelievable **that Jill survived the tsunami**.)

The point is **that we should act responsibly.** 요점은 우리가 책임감 있게 행동해야 한다는 것이다. 〈보어〉

I think (that) **he has good leadership qualities.** 나는 그가 훌륭한 리더십 자질을 가지고 있다고 생각한다. 〈목적어〉

(2) 간접의문문: 의문문이 다른 문장 안에 쓰인 것으로, 의문사나 if[whether]가 접속사 역할을 한다.

의문사가 있는 경우 **「의문사 + 주어 + 동사」**	I don't know. + *Why is she* crying? → I don't know **why she is** crying. 나는 그녀가 왜 울고 있는지 모른다.
의문사가 주어인 경우 **「의문사 + 동사」**	Tell me. + *Who broke* the vase? → Tell me **who broke** the vase. 누가 그 화병을 깼는지 나에게 말해줘.
의문사가 없는 경우 **「if[whether] + 주어 + 동사」**	I wonder. + *Does he speak* Korean? → I wonder **if[whether] he speaks** Korean. 나는 그가 한국어를 하는지 궁금하다.

cf. 주절의 동사가 think, believe, guess, imagine, suppose 등인 경우 의문사를 맨 앞에 쓴다.

Do you think? + What should I do? → **What** *do you think* **I should** do?

plus 다음과 같은 경우에는 whether 대신 if를 쓸 수 없다.

- **Whether** he will succeed is uncertain. 〈주어일 때〉
- He was worried *about* **whether** he could get there on time. 〈전치사의 목적어일 때〉
- I visited him to see **whether** *or not* he was okay. 〈or not 바로 앞〉
- I don't know **whether** *to* laugh or cry. 〈to부정사 앞〉 *whether to-v: ~해야 할지

우리말과 일치하도록 빈칸에 알맞은 말을 쓰시오.

1 우리는 휴가를 위해 제주나 부산 둘 중 한 곳에 갈 것이다.

→ We will go to __________ Jeju __________ Busan for our vacation.

2 Amy는 학교에 다닐 뿐만 아니라 파트타임으로도 일한다.

→ Amy __________ __________ goes to school __________ __________ has a part time job.

3 Alex와 Ryan 둘 다 그 축구 팀에 있다.

→ __________ Alex __________ Ryan __________ on the football team.

4 운전자도 승객들도 부상을 입지 않았다.

→ __________ the driver __________ the passengers __________ injured.

EXERCISE
B

다음 문장에서 that[That]이 들어갈 곳에 V로 표시하시오.

1 Her problem is she lacks confidence.

2 It is a fact smoking is harmful to health.

3 He quickly realized he was on the wrong bus.

4 They are getting married is not surprising at all.

EXERCISE
C

다음 두 문장을 한 문장으로 바꿔 쓰시오.

1 I don't know. + What is his name?

→ ____

2 She wants to know. + Why did he leave for America?

→ ____

3 Let's see. + What is on the menu today?

→ ____

4 I wonder. + Does anyone live in that house?

→ ____

5 Do you think? + Who is the best player on the team?

→ ____

WRITING FOCUS

A 배열 영작 우리말과 일치하도록 괄호 안의 말을 바르게 배열하시오.

1 그의 삶과 그의 작품 둘 다 그 학생들에게 영감을 주었다. (his life, his work, both, inspired, and)

→ ______________________________ the students.

2 당신은 그 컴퓨터를 상점이나 온라인 중 한 곳에서 살 수 있다. (shop, either, a, or, at, online)

→ You can buy the computer ______________________________.

3 이 가방은 예쁠 뿐만 아니라 실용적이다. (only, pretty, functional, not, also, is, but)

→ This bag ______________________________.

4 Jack은 자신이 큰 위험에 처해 있다는 것을 알았다. (in, was, he, that, great, knew, danger)

→ Jack ______________________________.

5 제가 어디서 택시를 탈 수 있는지 아세요? (where, a, can, I, taxi, take)

→ Do you know ______________________________?

6 내가 그 이름을 정확하게 발음하고 있는지 잘 모르겠다. (am, if, name, I, the, pronouncing)

→ I'm not sure ______________________________ correctly.

B 빈칸 완성 우리말과 일치하도록 괄호 안의 말을 이용하여 빈칸에 알맞은 말을 쓰시오.

1 커피와 차 둘 다 인기 있는 음료이다. (coffee, tea)

→ ________ ________ ________ ________ ________ popular beverages.

2 그녀는 그것을 부정하지도 인정하지도 않았다. (deny, admit)

→ She ________ ________ ________ ________ it.

3 그녀는 오늘 밤에 늦게 도착할 가능성이 있다. (possible)

→ ________ ________ ________ ________ she will arrive late tonight.

4 우리는 그가 무엇을 하고 있는지 궁금했다. (what, doing)

→ We were curious about ________ ________ ________ ________.

5 나는 그에게 그 수업에 참석할지 물어보았다. (would, attend)

→ I asked him ________ ________ ________ ________ the class.

6 너는 누가 창문을 깼다고 생각하니? (think, break)

→ ________ ________ ________ ________ ________ the window?

Answer Key p.21

C 문장 완성 우리말과 일치하도록 괄호 안의 말을 이용하여 문장을 완성하시오.

1 이 방은 서재와 침실로 둘 다 사용된다. (a study room, a bedroom)

→ This room serves as ______________________________.

2 그에 대한 나의 첫인상은 좋지도 나쁘지도 않았다. (good, bad)

→ My first impression of him was ______________________________.

3 당신은 자신뿐만 아니라 다른 사람들도 생각해야 한다. (others, yourself, well)

→ You should think of ______________________________.

4 나는 그가 1년 더 여기에 머물 것이라고 생각한다. (stay, one more year)

→ I think ______________________________.

5 나는 이 근처에 문구점이 있는지 궁금하다. (there, a stationery store)

→ I wonder ______________________________ near here.

6 많은 학생들이 무슨 일이 일어나고 있는지 보려고 뛰어나갔다. (what, happening)

→ Lots of students ran out to see ______________________________.

D 오류 수정 밑줄 친 부분을 바르게 고쳐 문장을 다시 쓰시오.

1 Both he and I <u>am</u> going to join the drama club.

→ ______________________________

2 Either Joseph or Mary <u>have to</u> take responsibility for it.

→ ______________________________

3 You as well as Jake <u>deserves</u> to win the prize.

→ ______________________________

4 I wonder why <u>did Mark change</u> his mind.

→ ______________________________

5 <u>If</u> we can go there depends on the cost.

→ ______________________________

6 <u>Do you think who</u> the right person for the job is?

→ ______________________________

ACTUAL TEST

문항 수	객관식 8 / 서술형 12
맞은 개수	/ 20

01 빈칸에 공통으로 들어갈 말은?

• I bought a pair of jeans ________ they were on sale.
• It has been two years ________ my family moved to this city.

① if ② since ③ when
④ unless ⑤ although

02 밑줄 친 접속사의 쓰임이 어색한 것은?

① I will wait until you finish your work.
② I met Joe while I was walking to school.
③ Unless you don't eat, you will be hungry.
④ Although I missed the bus, I arrived on time.
⑤ James ran home as soon as he got the message.

03 문장의 의미가 나머지 넷과 다른 것은?

① I got up early so as to see the sunrise.
② I got up early in order to see the sunrise.
③ I got up so early that I could see the sunrise.
④ I got up early so that I could see the sunrise.
⑤ I got up early in order that I could see the sunrise.

빈출

04 밑줄 친 부분이 어법상 올바른 것은?

① Neither you nor he speak Spanish.
② Both he and I am going to the library.
③ Either Tim or Sue has to water the plants.
④ Not only she but also he are good at math.
⑤ He as well as you need to listen to the teacher.

05 밑줄 친 부분의 쓰임이 나머지 넷과 다른 것은?

① That the Earth is round is true.
② I think that Rosa is a good singer.
③ I know that girl wearing the blue hat.
④ It is strange that he hasn't arrived yet.
⑤ The good news is that we all passed the test.

빈출

06 두 문장을 한 문장으로 바르게 바꾼 것은?

① I don't know. + How old is she?
→ I don't know how she is old.
② Tell me. + Who took my umbrella?
→ Tell me who took my umbrella.
③ Do you know? + Where did she go?
→ Do you know where did she go?
④ Do you think? + When will the rain stop?
→ Do you think when the rain will stop?
⑤ I wonder. + Is the store open on Sundays?
→ I wonder the store is open on Sundays.

07 빈칸에 if[If]를 쓸 수 있는 것은?

① I wonder ________ or not she likes Korean food.
② We are curious about ________ the rumor is true.
③ He asked me ________ I would join the book club.
④ ________ you succeed or fail depends on your efforts.
⑤ I didn't know ________ to order pizza or pasta for dinner.

고난도

08 빈칸 ⓐ~ⓔ에 들어갈 말로 어색한 것은?

- The package will arrive either tomorrow ___ⓐ___ the day after.
- The problem is ___ⓑ___ the printer is out of ink.
- I don't know ___ⓒ___ or not it will rain this weekend.
- You must do this ___ⓓ___ you don't want to.
- I exercise every day ___ⓔ___ stay healthy.

① ⓐ – or
② ⓑ – that
③ ⓒ – whether
④ ⓓ – if
⑤ ⓔ – in order to

서술형

09 〈보기〉에서 알맞은 말을 골라 문장을 완성하시오. (단, 한 번씩만 쓸 것)

보기 although since while

(1) The phone rang twice __________ we were having dinner.

(2) She wore sunglasses __________ the sun was shining brightly.

(3) He managed to finish the race __________ his leg was hurt.

10 어법상 틀린 부분을 찾아 바르게 고치시오.

(1) When he will arrive, we will start the meeting.

__________ → __________

(2) We will go on a picnic if the weather will be good.

__________ → __________

[11-12] 주어진 문장과 의미가 같도록 빈칸에 알맞은 말을 쓰시오.

11

You cannot enter if you don't have a ticket.

→ You cannot enter __________ __________ __________ a ticket.

12

I saved money in order to buy a new laptop.

→ I saved money __________ __________ __________ __________ __________ a new laptop.

[13-14] 우리말과 일치하도록 〈보기〉에서 필요한 단어들만 골라 배열하여 문장을 완성하시오.

13

그 책은 유익하지도 재미있지도 않았다.

보기 was either neither or nor informative interesting

→ The book ____________________.

14

나는 그녀가 꽃을 좋아하는지 궁금하다.

보기 I she wonder if that does like likes flowers

→ ____________________

15 학생들의 취미 활동을 나타낸 표를 보고, 상관접속사를 사용하여 문장을 완성하시오.

	Amy	Leo	Jane	Alex
swimming	O			O
taking pictures		O	O	
playing tennis	O			
reading books			O	

(1) Amy enjoys ___________ ___________ swimming ___________ ___________ playing tennis.

(2) ___________ Leo ___________ Jane enjoy taking pictures.

(3) ___________ Leo ___________ Alex enjoys reading books.

16 우리말과 일치하도록 〈조건〉에 맞게 문장을 완성하시오.

우리는 시간이 소중하다는 것을 깨달아야 한다.

조건 1. should, realize, time, valuable을 사용할 것
2. 총 7단어로 쓸 것

→ ______________________________
____

17 두 문장을 간접의문문을 사용하여 한 문장으로 바꿔 쓰시오.

(1) Do you know? + How does she go to work?

→ ______________________________

(2) Tom wants to know. + Was the test easy?

→ ______________________________

18 괄호 안에서 알맞은 말을 골라 빈칸에 쓰시오.

(1) (While / During) he was driving, he listened to the radio.
(2) He continued to play (although / despite) his injury.
(3) I was late for work (because / due to) my alarm clock didn't work.

(1) ___________ (2) ___________ (3) ___________

19 밑줄 친 우리말과 일치하도록 〈조건〉에 맞게 문장을 완성하시오.

A: Why are you coughing so much?
B: <u>미세먼지 때문에 기침하는 것 같아.</u>
A: You should try wearing a mask when you go outside.

조건 of, the fine dust를 사용할 것

→ I think I'm coughing ___________ ___________ ___________ ___________ ___________.

고난도

20 어법상 <u>틀린</u> 문장을 찾아 기호를 쓰고 바르게 고쳐 문장을 다시 쓰시오.

A: Hey, Brian. Do you want to watch a movie tonight?
B: Well, ⓐ<u>I'm not sure if I can go or not.</u>
A: Why?
B: I need to finish my science report first. ⓑ<u>I'll let you know as soon as I finish it.</u>
A: Okay, ⓒ<u>I'll wait until you're done.</u> ⓓ<u>Do you think how long it will take?</u>
B: About an hour, I guess.

(   ) → ______________________________

Chapter 08

관계사

UNIT 01 관계대명사

UNIT 02 관계부사, 복합관계사

UNIT 03 주의해야 할 관계사 용법

UNIT
01 관계대명사

GRAMMAR FOCUS

1 주격, 목적격, 소유격 관계대명사

관계대명사는 접속사와 대명사의 역할을 하며, 관계대명사가 이끄는 절은 형용사절로 앞에 있는 명사(선행사)를 꾸며준다.

(1) **주격 관계대명사:** 관계대명사절에서 주어 역할을 하며, 선행사에 따라 who, which, that을 쓴다.

사람	**who, that**	I hate people. + **They** always complain. → I hate people **who**[**that**] always complain. 나는 항상 불평하는 사람들이 싫다.
사물, 동물	**which, that**	The books are mine. + **They** are on the table. → The books **which**[**that**] are on the table are mine. 탁자 위에 있는 책들은 나의 것이다.

cf. 1. 주격 관계대명사절의 동사는 선행사의 수에 일치시킨다.

Yesterday, I met *a man* **who** speaks five languages. 어제 나는 5개 국어를 구사하는 남자를 만났다.
└ speak (×)

2. 선행사가 주어인 경우, 문장의 동사는 선행사의 수에 일치시킨다.

The people **who** live next door are very friendly. 옆집에 사는 사람들은 매우 상냥하다.
└ is (×)

(2) **목적격 관계대명사:** 관계대명사절에서 목적어 역할을 하며, 선행사에 따라 who(m), which, that을 쓴다.

사람	**who(m), that**	She is the woman. + I met **her** in Spain. → She is the woman **who(m)**[**that**] I met in Spain. 그녀는 내가 스페인에서 만났던 여자이다.
사물, 동물	**which, that**	The game ended in a tie. + We watched **it**. → The game **which**[**that**] we watched ended in a tie. 우리가 본 경기는 무승부로 끝났다.

cf. 주격, 목적격 관계대명사의 선행사가 〈사람 + 사물(동물)〉인 경우에는 관계대명사 that을 쓴다.

(3) **소유격 관계대명사:** 관계대명사절에서 소유격 역할을 하며, 선행사의 종류에 관계없이 항상 whose를 쓴다.

사람, 사물, 동물	**whose**	I met a woman. + **Her** husband is a writer. → I met a woman **whose** husband is a writer. 나는 남편이 작가인 여자를 만났다.
		The house is empty. + **Its** window is broken. → The house **whose** window is broken is empty. 창문이 깨진 그 집은 비어 있다.

2 관계대명사 what

선행사를 포함하는 관계대명사로 the thing that[which]로 바꿔 쓸 수 있으며, '~하는 것'으로 해석한다. what이 이끄는 절은 명사절로 문장에서 주어, 보어, 목적어 역할을 한다.

What she said made him smile. 그녀가 말한 것은 그를 웃게 했다. 〈주어〉

This is **what** I want for my birthday. 이것이 내가 내 생일에 원하는 것이다. 〈보어〉

He forgot **what** he needed to buy at the grocery store. 그는 식료품점에서 사야 할 것을 잊어버렸다. 〈목적어〉

Answer Key p.23

괄호 안에서 알맞은 것을 고르시오.

1 He rescued the boy (who, which) fell into the river.

2 She is a writer (which, whose) books are best sellers.

3 The coat (whom, which) I bought yesterday was expensive.

4 This is the person (which, that) I introduced to you the other day.

5 (What, That) she said yesterday made me angry.

6 The only thing (what, that) he wanted was his family's happiness.

두 문장을 관계대명사를 사용하여 한 문장으로 쓰시오.

1 I don't like movies. They have lots of violent scenes.

→ I don't like movies ______________________.

2 The singer canceled her concert. I wanted to see her.

→ The singer ______________________.

3 She teaches students. Their native language is not English.

→ She teaches students ______________________.

4 Look at the man and the dog. They are playing with a ball together.

→ Look at the man and the dog ______________________.

우리말과 일치하도록 빈칸에 알맞은 관계대명사를 쓰시오.

1 나는 취미가 암벽 등반인 친구가 있다.

→ I have a friend ________ hobby is rock climbing.

2 그 벤치에 놓여 있는 스마트폰은 Andrew의 것이다.

→ The smartphone ________ is lying on the bench is Andrew's.

3 미술에 관심이 있는 많은 사람들이 그 그림들을 보러 왔다.

→ Many people ________ were interested in art came to see the paintings.

4 Angela는 항상 내가 말하는 것에 동의하지 않는다.

→ Angela always disagrees with ________ I say.

WRITING FOCUS

A 배열 영작 우리말과 일치하도록 괄호 안의 말을 바르게 배열하시오.

1 파리에서 태어났거나 사는 사람을 파리지앵이라고 부른다. (people, in, were, live, who, born, or, Paris)

→ ______________________________ are called Parisians.

2 그는 그 캠프장에서 일어나는 모든 일에 책임이 있다. (at, that, the, everything, campsite, happens)

→ He is responsible for ______________________________.

3 그녀가 결혼한 남자는 유머 감각이 좋다. (that, man, she, the, married, has)

→ ______________________________ a good sense of humor.

4 나는 영어 발음이 완벽한 언니가 있다. (a, English pronunciation, perfect, whose, sister, is)

→ I have ______________________________.

5 나는 네가 방금 말한 것을 이해할 수 없어. (said, you, what, just)

→ I don't understand ______________________________.

6 그 아이에게 필요한 것은 애정 어린 보살핌이다. (needs, the, what, is, child)

→ ______________________________ loving care.

B 빈칸 완성 우리말과 일치하도록 괄호 안의 말을 이용하여 빈칸을 완성하시오.

1 지휘자는 오케스트라의 연주를 지휘하는 사람이다. (direct)

→ A conductor is a person __________ __________ an orchestra's performance.

2 네가 방문하고 싶은 세 나라의 이름을 나에게 말해줘. (want)

→ Tell me the names of three countries __________ __________ __________ to visit.

3 나는 UN에서 일하고자 하는 바람을 가진 학생을 만났다. (desire)

→ I met a student __________ __________ __________ to work for the UN.

4 백과사전은 여러 주제들에 대한 정보를 담고 있는 책이다. (contain)

→ An encyclopedia is a book __________ __________ information on many subjects.

5 우리를 태우고 가던 버스가 도중에 고장 났다. (take)

→ The bus __________ __________ __________ us broke down on the way.

6 내가 나의 선생님에 대해 가장 좋아하는 것은 그분의 부드러운 목소리이다. (like)

→ __________ __________ __________ most about my teacher is her soft voice.

C 문장 완성 우리말과 일치하도록 괄호 안의 말을 이용하여 문장을 완성하시오.

1 이것은 내가 내 이웃에게 받은 햄스터이다. (the hamster, get, from my neighbor)

→ This is ______________________________.

2 작곡가는 음악을 만드는 사람이다. (person, write music)

→ A composer is ______________________________.

3 네가 추천한 그 영화는 아주 감동적이었어. (the movie, recommend)

→ ______________________________ was so touching.

4 너를 놀라게 할 좋은 소식 몇 가지를 네게 말해줄게. (some good news, surprise, will)

→ I'll tell you ______________________________.

5 내가 그 영화에서 가장 좋아했던 것은 음악이었다. (like, most, about the movie)

→ ______________________________ was the music.

6 사고로 부모님이 돌아가신 그 소년은 그의 삼촌 집으로 보내졌다. (parents, die, in the accident)

→ The boy ______________________________ was sent to his uncle's.

D 오류 수정 어법상 틀린 부분을 바르게 고쳐 문장을 다시 쓰시오.

1 The man whom is standing over there is my father.

→ ______________________________

2 I can't find the book whose I borrowed from you.

→ ______________________________

3 We helped the people that houses were destroyed by the hurricane.

→ ______________________________

4 All the students who received the medal was proud.

→ ______________________________

5 This is the poem which my brother wrote it.

→ ______________________________

6 Mary couldn't believe that she heard.

→ ______________________________

UNIT 02

관계부사, 복합관계사

GRAMMAR FOCUS

❶ 관계부사

관계부사는 접속사와 부사의 역할을 하며, 관계부사가 이끄는 절도 형용사절로 선행사를 수식한다. 관계부사는 선행사의 종류에 따라 when, where, why, how를 쓰고, 「전치사 + 관계대명사」로 바꿔 쓸 수 있다.

선행사	관계부사	예문
시간 (the time, the day 등)	**when**	I remember the day. + We first met **on the day.** → I remember the day **when[on which]** we first met. 나는 우리가 처음 만난 날을 기억한다.
장소 (the place, the city 등)	**where**	This is the town. + I was born **in the town.** → This is the town **where[in which]** I was born. 이곳은 내가 태어난 마을이다.
이유 (the reason)	**why**	I don't know the reason. + He is angry **for the reason.** → I don't know the reason **why[for which]** he is angry. 나는 그가 화난 이유를 모른다.
방법 (the way)	**how**	I wonder the way. + He solved the problem **in the way.** → I wonder **how[the way]** he solved the problem. → I wonder the way **in which** he solved the problem. 나는 그가 그 문제를 푼 방법이 궁금하다.

cf. 관계부사 how는 선행사 the way와 함께 쓸 수 없으며, 둘 중 하나만 써야 한다.

I wonder **the way how** he solved the problem. (×)

plus 선행사가 time, place, reason 등 일반적인 경우, 선행사나 관계부사 중 하나를 생략할 수 있다.

This is **the place where** I hid the key. 이곳이 내가 열쇠를 숨긴 곳이다.

= This is **where** I hid the key. / This is **the place** I hid the key.

❷ 복합관계사

(1) 복합관계대명사: 「관계대명사 + -ever」의 형태로, 명사절 또는 양보의 부사절을 이끈다.

복합관계대명사	예문	의미
whoever	**Whoever** comes with you is welcome. **Whoever** calls me, just take a message.	(anyone who: ~하는 누구든지) (no matter who: 누가 ~할지라도)
whatever	She can do **whatever** she wants. Don't believe him, **whatever** he says.	(anything that: ~하는 무엇이든지) (no matter what: 무엇을[이] ~할지라도)
whichever	You can have **whichever** you like. **Whichever** you choose, it will be good.	(anything that: ~하는 어느 것이든지) (no matter which: 어느 것을[이] ~할지라도)

(2) 복합관계부사: 「관계부사 + -ever」의 형태로, 시간, 장소의 부사절 또는 양보의 부사절을 이끈다.

복합관계부사	예문	의미
whenever	I listen to music **whenever** I feel sad. Call me **whenever** you arrive.	(at any time (that): ~할 때마다) (no matter when: 언제 ~하더라도)
wherever	Sit **wherever** you like. **Wherever** he is, he thinks of her.	(at any place (that): ~하는 곳 어디든지) (no matter where: 어디에(서) ~하더라도)
however	**However hard** it is, don't give up. *어순 주의: 「however + 형용사 / 부사 + 주어 + 동사」	(no matter how: 아무리 ~하더라도)

Answer Key p.24

괄호 안에서 알맞은 것을 고르시오.

1 The town (that, where) he grew up was very small.

2 Fall is the season (when, where) trees begin to lose their leaves.

3 He showed me (how, the way how) the machine works.

4 We didn't know the reason (how, why) the car made a strange noise.

5 July and August are the months (at which, during which) many people go on vacation.

6 This is the house (for which, in which) Mozart was born and lived with his family.

두 문장을 관계부사를 사용하여 한 문장으로 쓰시오.

1 The hotel was nice. We stayed at the hotel.

→ ______________________________

2 I like the way. She sings that song in the way.

→ ______________________________

3 Do you know the reason? He missed the bus for the reason.

→ ______________________________

4 The time was late. We arrived home at the time.

→ ______________________________

빈칸에 알맞은 말을 〈보기〉에서 골라 쓰시오. (단, 한 번씩만 쓸 것)

보기	whoever	whatever	whichever	wherever	whenever	however

1 __________ my mom cooks is delicious.

2 __________ comes first will get the best seats.

3 Tim makes friends quickly __________ he goes.

4 You can ask me __________ you have a question.

5 __________ much he tried, he couldn't find a job.

6 The game will be exciting __________ team wins.

WRITING FOCUS

A 배열 영작 우리말과 일치하도록 괄호 안의 말을 바르게 배열하시오.

1 2021년은 그가 고등학교를 졸업한 때이다. (he, the, graduated, when, from, year, high school)

→ 2021 was ______________________________.

2 제가 등산화를 살 수 있는 가게가 있나요? (where, a, buy, shop, can, I, hiking boots)

→ Is there ______________________________?

3 그 식당이 붐비는 이유는 그곳의 맛있는 음식 때문이다. (the, why, restaurant, the, is, reason, crowded)

→ ______________________________ is its delicious food.

4 그녀는 내가 거실을 재배치한 방식을 마음에 들어 했다. (the, rearranged, way, the, I, living room)

→ She liked ______________________________.

5 나는 이 책을 원하는 누구에게나 줄 것이다. (this, whoever, book, wants, give, to, it)

→ I will ______________________________.

6 아무리 바빠도 그는 매일 아침 운동을 하려고 노력한다. (he, however, is, busy)

→ ______________________________, he tries to work out every morning.

B 빈칸 완성 우리말과 일치하도록 괄호 안의 말을 이용하여 빈칸을 완성하시오.

1 그는 나에게 자신이 집에 돌아올 시간을 말해 주지 않았다. (time)

→ He didn't tell me ________ ________ ________ he would come back home.

2 잘츠부르크는 〈사운드 오브 뮤직〉이 촬영된 도시이다. (city)

→ Salzburg is ________ ________ ________ *The Sound of Music* was filmed.

3 너는 네가 혼난 이유를 아니? (reason)

→ Do you know ________ ________ ________ you were scolded?

4 엄마는 나에게 김치 만드는 방법을 보여주셨다. (way)

→ My mom showed me ________ ________ ________ made *kimchi*.

5 인터넷은 우리가 어디에 있더라도 다른 사람들과 연락을 유지하도록 도와준다. (be)

→ The Internet helps us to keep in touch with others ________ ________ ________.

6 당신이 어느 쪽 길을 택하더라도 당신은 목적지에 도착할 것이다. (way, take)

→ ________ ________ ________ ________, you will reach your destination.

C 문장 완성 우리말과 일치하도록 괄호 안의 말과 알맞은 관계사를 이용하여 문장을 완성하시오.

1 우리가 수영하러 갔던 날은 더웠다. (go for a swim)

→ ______________________ was hot.

2 내가 공부했던 학교에는 훌륭한 선생님들이 계셨다. (study)

→ ______________________ had great teachers.

3 그녀는 자신이 늦은 이유를 설명할 수 없었다. (late)

→ She couldn't explain the reason ______________________.

4 Anna는 나에게 그녀가 수제 양초를 만든 방법을 보여 주었다. (homemade candles)

→ Anna showed me ______________________.

5 그는 매우 부유해서 자신이 원하는 무엇이든지 살 수 있다. (want)

→ He is so rich that he can buy ______________________.

6 당신은 (그곳이) 필요할 때마다 그 회의실을 사용할 수 있습니다. (need, it)

→ You can use the meeting room ______________________.

D 오류 수정 밑줄 친 부분을 바르게 고쳐 문장을 다시 쓰시오.

1 June is the month where I was born.

→ ______________________

2 This is the place that I last saw him.

→ ______________________

3 This is the house when they lived two years ago.

→ ______________________

4 Technology has changed the way how we live.

→ ______________________

5 Whatever broke the window will have to pay for it.

→ ______________________

6 However it is cold, he always goes swimming.

→ ______________________

UNIT 03

주의해야 할 관계사 용법

GRAMMAR FOCUS

❶ 관계대명사의 생략

「주격 관계대명사 + be동사」와 목적격 관계대명사는 문장에서 생략할 수 있다.

The man (**who was**) sitting behind me was Ben. 내 뒤에 앉아 있던 남자는 Ben이었다. 〈주격 관계대명사 + be동사〉

The popcorn (**which**) I made was too salty. 내가 만든 팝콘은 너무 짰다. 〈목적격 관계대명사〉

❷ 전치사 + 관계대명사

관계대명사가 전치사의 목적어일 때, 전치사는 관계대명사 앞이나 관계대명사절 끝에 올 수 있다. 단, 전치사가 관계대명사 앞에 올 경우에는 목적격인 whom과 which만 쓸 수 있으며, 이때는 관계대명사를 생략할 수 없다.

I met a man. + I used to work **with him**.

→	I met a man	with **whom** I used to work. **who**(m) I used to work with. **that** I used to work with. I used to work with.	나는 함께 일했던 남자를 만났다.

Here is the key. + You were looking for **the key**.

→	Here is the key	for **which** you were looking. **which** you were looking for. **that** you were looking for. you were looking for.	네가 찾고 있던 열쇠가 여기 있다.

plus 「전치사 + 관계대명사」가 시간이나 장소를 의미할 때는 관계부사 when, where로 바꿔 쓸 수 있다.

Do you know the date **on which** (= when) they will arrive? 너는 그들이 도착할 날짜를 알고 있니?

This is the office **at which** (= where) my father works. 이곳은 우리 아버지가 일하시는 사무실이다.

❸ 관계사의 계속적 용법

선행사에 대한 부가 정보를 제공할 때 쓰며, 이 경우 관계사 앞에 콤마(,)를 붙인다. 계속적 용법에 쓰이는 관계사는 생략할 수 없으며, that은 계속적 용법에 쓸 수 없다.

제한적 용법	I called my friend **who lives in Boston**. 나는 보스턴에 사는 내 친구에게 전화했다. 〈필수 정보〉
계속적 용법	I called my sister Irene, **who(= and she) lives in Boston**. 나는 내 여동생 Irene에게 전화했는데, 그녀는 보스턴에 산다. 〈부가 정보〉

plus which는 앞 문장 전체를 선행사로 취할 수 있으며, 이 경우 which 앞에 콤마(,)를 쓴다.

We don't need to move now. + **That** is great.

→ We don't need to move now, **which**(= **and that**) is great.

우리는 이제 이사할 필요가 없는데, 그것은 정말 잘된 일이다.

Answer Key p.24

다음 문장에서 생략할 수 있는 부분을 괄호로 묶으시오. (없으면 X 표시할 것)

1 The girl who is wearing a yellow dress is my sister.

2 A vehicle is a thing that is used for transporting people or goods on land.

3 Yesterday, I saw someone who looks like you at the mall.

4 My father bought the car that he had wanted to buy.

5 She painted her room blue, which is her favorite color.

6 Korea and Japan were the first countries that co-hosted the World Cup.

두 문장이 같은 의미가 되도록 바꿔 쓰시오. (단, 「전치사+관계대명사」 형태로 쓸 것)

1 Do you know the girl that John is talking to?

→ Do you know the girl ________________________________?

2 The painting that she is looking at is beautiful.

→ The painting ________________________________ is beautiful.

3 The chair that he was sitting on was old but cozy.

→ The chair ________________________________ was old but cozy.

4 The people who we were waiting for were late.

→ The people ________________________________ were late.

우리말과 같은 뜻이 되도록 빈칸에 알맞은 관계대명사를 쓰시오.

1 그는 딸이 한 명 있는데, 그녀는 영어뿐만 아니라 중국어도 할 수 있다.

→ He has a daughter, __________ can speak Chinese as well as English.

2 그 피자는 내가 20분 전에 주문했는데, 벌써 도착했다.

→ The pizza, __________ I ordered 20 minutes ago, has already arrived.

3 우리 가족은 동해안에 갔는데, 거기서 일출을 구경했다.

→ My family went to the east coast, __________ we watched the sunrise.

4 올 겨울에는 눈이 많이 왔는데, 그것은 농사짓기에 좋다.

→ It snowed a lot this winter, __________ is good for farming.

WRITING FOCUS

A 배열 영작 우리말과 일치하도록 괄호 안의 말을 바르게 배열하시오.

1 너는 Jenny와 이야기하고 있는 남자를 아니? (to, man, talking, the, Jenny)

→ Do you know ______________________________?

2 아침 7시에 맞추어져 있던 자명종이 울리지 않았다. (alarm clock, for, set, the, 7:00 a.m.)

→ ______________________________ didn't go off.

3 내가 투표한 후보는 선거에서 우승하지 못했다. (candidate, for, voted, the, I, that)

→ ______________________________ didn't win the election.

4 이것이 네가 어제 나에게 말했던 책이니? (you, about, the, told, book, me, yesterday)

→ Is this ______________________________?

5 그녀는 새로운 도시로 이사했는데, 그곳에서 그녀는 일자리를 찾았다. (found, where, a, she, job)

→ She moved to a new city, ______________________________.

6 Bill은 장학금을 받았는데, 그것은 그를 매우 자랑스럽게 했다. (which, very, him, made, proud)

→ Bill received a scholarship, ______________________________.

B 빈칸 완성 우리말과 일치하도록 괄호 안의 말을 이용하여 빈칸을 완성하시오.

1 너는 기타를 연주하고 있는 저 음악가를 아니? (the guitar)

→ Do you know that musician ________ ________ ________?

2 그녀에 대해 네가 좋아하는 다섯 가지를 나에게 말해 줘. (thing, like)

→ Tell me ________ ________ ________ ________ about her.

3 너와 함께 콘서트에 갔던 친구는 누구니? (the friend, with)

→ Who is ________ ________ ________ ________ you went to the concert?

4 우리가 휴가를 보낸 섬은 아름다웠다. (the island, on)

→ ________ ________ ________ ________ we spent our vacation was beautiful.

5 내 친구 John은 시드니에 사는데, 지난달에 나를 보기 위해 왔다. (live)

→ My friend John, ________ ________ in Sydney, came to see me last month.

6 Peggy는 매일 걸어서 학교에 가는데, 그것은 그녀를 건강하게 유지시켜 준다. (keep)

→ Peggy walks to school every day, ________ ________ her healthy.

Answer Key p.25

C 문장 완성 우리말과 일치하도록 괄호 안의 말을 이용하여 문장을 완성하시오.

1 Chris는 그 프로젝트를 책임지는 사람이다. (responsible for, the project)

→ Chris is the man ______________________.

2 어제 우리가 본 영화는 훌륭했다. (see, yesterday)

→ The movie ______________________ was great.

3 그녀가 함께 춤을 추고 있는 남자는 그녀의 아버지이다. (dance)

→ The man with ______________________ is her father.

4 내 친구가 뛰었던 축구 경기는 흥미진진했다. (play)

→ The soccer game in ______________________ was exciting.

5 이 아이는 내 남동생인데, 그는 음악에 뛰어난 재능을 갖고 있다. (great musical talent)

→ This is my brother, ______________________.

6 쥐 한 마리가 교실을 돌아다녔는데, 그것은 충격이었다. (a shock)

→ A mouse ran around the classroom, ______________________.

D 문장 전환 두 문장의 의미가 같도록 빈칸에 알맞은 말을 쓰시오.

1 The dishes which are in the cupboard need to be washed.

→ The dishes ________ ________ ________ need to be washed.

2 The smartphone which I bought last week takes great photos.

→ The smartphone ________ ________ ________ ________ takes great photos.

3 The restaurant at which we had dinner was crowded.

→ The restaurant that ________ ________ ________ ________ was crowded.

4 I met Jane, and she had attended the same school as me.

→ I met Jane, ________ ________ ________ the same school as me.

5 We visited Venice, and there we took a gondola ride.

→ We visited Venice, ________ ________ ________ a gondola ride.

6 He was late for class again, and this made the teacher angry.

→ He was late for class again, ________ made the teacher angry.

ACTUAL TEST

문항 수	객관식 8 / 서술형 12
맞은 개수	/ 20

01 빈칸에 들어갈 말이 순서대로 짝지어진 것은?

> • The man ________ robbed the bank was caught.
> • She threw away the cup ________ handle was broken.

① who – which ② which – that
③ who – whose ④ whom – which
⑤ whom – whose

02 빈칸에 들어갈 말로 알맞은 것은?

> Daniel broke his mom's favorite vase, ________ made her upset.

① who ② that ③ what
④ which ⑤ whose

03 빈칸에 들어갈 말이 나머지 넷과 다른 것은?

① I can't believe ________ you said to me.
② This is ________ I wanted for Christmas.
③ We believe ________ he is telling the truth.
④ Show me ________ you have in your hands.
⑤ He talked about ________ he saw last night.

04 다음 중 어법상 틀린 것은?

① I'll never forget the day when we met.
② This is the bakery where I often buy bread.
③ Nobody knows the reason why he left early.
④ I asked him the way how he deals with stress.
⑤ December 10 is when my little sister was born.

고난도

05 두 문장을 한 문장으로 바꿔 쓸 때, 바르지 않은 것을 2개 고르면?

> • This is the café.
> • We first met at the café.

① This is the café where we first met.
② This is the café at that we first met.
③ This is the café which we first met at.
④ This is the café at which we first met.
⑤ This is the café where we first met at.

빈출 고난도

06 두 문장의 의미가 같도록 할 때, 바르게 바꾼 것은?

① This is the town where I grew up.
→ This is the town in that I grew up.
② Sunday is the day when my dad cooks.
→ Sunday is the day of which my dad cooks.
③ Tell me the reason why she is smiling.
→ Tell me the reason at which she is smiling.
④ Spring is the season when flowers bloom.
→ Spring is the season in which flowers bloom.
⑤ I like how you decorated the room.
→ I like the way which you decorated the room.

07 밑줄 친 부분의 쓰임이 어색한 것은?

① Draw <u>whatever</u> you like on the paper.
② <u>However</u> tired I am, I will finish the work.
③ You can ask for help <u>whenever</u> you need it.
④ <u>Whoever</u> wins the race will receive the trophy.
⑤ I always bring a book with me <u>whenever</u> I go.

고난도

08 어법상 올바른 문장의 개수는?

ⓐ The only thing that I have is ten dollars.
ⓑ The shop didn't have which I wanted to buy.
ⓒ I have a friend who don't use social media.
ⓓ The museum where we visited last week had impressive exhibits.
ⓔ Whoever needs can have these books.
ⓕ My friend Ian, who is a teacher, lives in Vancouver.

① 1개 ② 2개 ③ 3개
④ 4개 ⑤ 5개

서술형

09 〈보기〉에서 알맞은 말을 골라 문장을 완성하시오.

보기	whom	whose	which

(1) We went to a park __________ had a large playground.

(2) Lucy has a Persian cat __________ fur is long and fluffy.

(3) The designer __________ Mike works with is very creative.

10 우리말과 일치하도록 주어진 말을 바르게 배열하시오.

(1) 이것들은 그가 아이슬란드에서 찍은 사진이다.
(took, pictures, are, in, that, these, he, the, Iceland)
→ ____________________

(2) 그들이 원하는 것은 더 나은 교육이다.
(they, a, what, want, better, is, education)
→ ____________________

11 어법상 틀린 부분을 찾아 바르게 고치시오.

(1) My aunt who live in New York will visit us.
__________ → __________

(2) John was the man whose solved the difficult puzzle.
__________ → __________

12 대화를 읽고, 어법상 틀린 부분을 찾아 바르게 고치시오.

A: Excuse me. This is not that I ordered. I wanted spaghetti, not pizza.
B: Oh, I apologize. I'll get you the food you ordered right away.

__________ → __________

13 두 문장을 지시에 맞게 한 문장으로 연결하시오.

• I remember the day.
• I adopted my puppy on the day.

(1) 관계부사를 사용할 것
→ ____________________

(2) 「전치사+관계대명사」를 사용할 것
→ ____________________

14 주어진 문장과 의미가 같도록 빈칸에 알맞은 말을 쓰시오.

(1) Whoever loves to read can join the book club.
→ __________ __________ loves to read can join the book club.

(2) Whatever you do, try your best.
→ __________ __________ __________ you do, try your best.

15 그림을 보고, 〈예시〉와 같이 두 문장을 관계대명사를 사용하여 한 문장으로 바꿔 쓰시오.

> 예시 The girl is sitting on the bench. Her dress is yellow.
> → The girl whose dress is yellow is sitting on the bench.

(1) The boy is talking to his friend. His backpack is blue.

→ ______________________________

(2) The girl is eating ice cream. Her hair is blond.

→ ______________________________

16 우리말과 일치하도록 〈보기〉에서 필요한 단어들만 골라 배열하여 문장을 완성하시오. (중복 사용 가능)

> 보기 this lived built my parents the house which where is

(1) 이곳은 우리 부모님이 지으신 집이다.

→ ______________________________

(2) 이곳은 우리 부모님이 사시던 집이다.

→ ______________________________

17 〈보기〉에서 알맞은 말을 골라 문장을 완성하시오. (단, 한 번씩만 쓸 것)

> 보기 that which where

(1) The pool in __________ we swam was cold.

(2) This is the room __________ we painted last week.

(3) The library __________ I often study is very peaceful.

[18-19] 두 문장을 〈조건〉에 맞게 한 문장으로 연결하시오.

> 조건 관계대명사의 계속적 용법을 사용할 것

18

- This book is about King Sejong.
- He invented Hangeul.

→ ______________________________

19

- The boy won the first prize at the contest.
- That surprised everyone.

→ ______________________________

20 우리말과 일치하도록 주어진 말을 바르게 배열하시오.

> 그 문제가 아무리 어려워도, 그는 그것을 빨리 풀 수 있다. (problem, difficult, however, is, the)

→ ______________________________, he can solve it quickly.

Chapter 09

가정법

UNIT 01

가정법 과거, 가정법 과거완료

GRAMMAR FOCUS

1 가정법 과거

가정법 과거는 현재 사실과 반대되거나 실현 가능성이 희박한 일을 가정할 때 쓴다.

If + 주어 + 동사의 과거형, (만일) ~라면,	주어 + 조동사의 과거형 + 동사원형 …할 텐데
If I **were** you, 내가 너라면,	I **would take** the job offer. 그 일자리 제안을 받아들일 텐데.
If she **had** a car, 그녀가 차를 가지고 있다면,	she **could drive** to work. 운전해서 출근할 수 있을 텐데.
If I **didn't live** so far away, 내가 그렇게 멀리 살지 않는다면,	I **might see** you more often. 너를 더 자주 볼지도 모를 텐데.

cf. 가정법 과거에서 if절의 be동사는 주어의 인칭과 수에 관계없이 were를 주로 사용한다.

plus 현재나 미래에 실현 가능성이 있을 때는 조건문을 쓴다.

If I **have** time, I **will visit** you. 나에게 시간이 있으면 너를 방문할게. 〈조건문: 가능성이 있음〉

If I **had** time, I **would visit** you. 나에게 시간이 있다면 너를 방문할 텐데. 〈가정법 과거: 가능성이 희박함〉

2 가정법 과거완료

가정법 과거완료는 과거 사실과 반대되는 일을 가정할 때 쓴다.

If + 주어 + had p.p., (만일) ~였다면,	주어 + 조동사의 과거형 + have p.p. …했을 텐데
If the weather **had been** good, 날씨가 좋았다면,	we **would have gone** for a walk. 우리는 산책을 하러 갔을 텐데.
If she **had studied** harder, 그녀가 더 열심히 공부했다면,	she **could have passed** the test. 그 시험에 통과했을 텐데.
If he **had listened** to me, 그가 내 말을 들었다면,	he **might not have made** a mistake. 실수를 하지 않았을지도 모를 텐데.

3 가정법의 문장 전환

가정법은 이유의 접속사(because, as, since 등)를 사용하여 직설법으로 바꿔 쓸 수 있다. 가정법을 직설법으로 바꿀 때는 긍정은 부정으로, 부정은 긍정으로 바꾼다. 시제는 가정법 과거는 현재형으로, 가정법 과거완료는 과거형으로 바꾼다.

가정법 과거 → 직설법 현재	If I **had** more money, I **could travel** around the world. → As I **don't have** more money, I **can't travel** around the world.
가정법 과거완료 → 직설법 과거	If he **had been** more careful, he **wouldn't have lost** his wallet. → As he **wasn't** more careful, he **lost** his wallet.

Answer Key p.26

괄호 안에서 알맞은 것을 고르시오.

1 If it (is, were) sunny tomorrow, we will go to the zoo.

2 If I (am, were) you, I wouldn't make that decision.

3 If you don't hurry, you (will miss, would miss) the train.

4 If I knew how to swim, I (will go, would go) to the beach with you.

5 If you (called, had called) me, I would have come to help you.

6 If I had seen you at school, I (would greet, would have greeted) you.

괄호 안의 말을 알맞은 형태로 바꿔 문장을 완성하시오.

1 If he ______________ more friends, he would not be lonely. (have)

2 If the boy ______________ taller, he could ride the roller coaster. (be)

3 If I knew her address, I ____________________ her a card. (will, send)

4 If the tent ______________ bigger, all of us could have slept in it. (be)

5 I ____________________ you at the party if I had arrived earlier. (will, see)

6 Nick would have adopted a puppy if his mom ______________ it. (allow)

두 문장의 의미가 같도록 빈칸에 알맞은 말을 쓰시오.

1 As we don't have a garden, we don't grow our own vegetables.

→ If we __________ a garden, we __________ __________ our own vegetables.

2 Because it is raining, we cannot go for a walk.

→ If it __________ __________ raining, we __________ __________ for a walk.

3 Because I didn't set the alarm, I woke up late.

→ If I __________ __________ the alarm, I __________ __________ __________ __________ up late.

4 Since the library was closed, we couldn't borrow books.

→ If the library __________ __________ __________ closed, we __________ __________ __________ books.

WRITING FOCUS

A 배열 영작 우리말과 일치하도록 괄호 안의 말을 바르게 배열하시오.

1 내가 너라면, 그의 제안을 거절할 텐데. (I, you, refuse, were, I, would)

→ If ____________________, ____________________ his offer.

2 나에게 차가 있다면, 너를 태워다 줄 텐데. (I, car, had, would, I, give, a)

→ If ____________________, ____________________ you a ride.

3 모든 사람들이 친절하다면, 세상은 더 좋은 곳이 될 텐데. (the, everyone, kind, world, be, were, would)

→ If ____________________, ____________________ a better place.

4 그가 돈을 저축했다면, 새 차를 살 수 있었을 텐데. (could, had, money, saved, bought, have)

→ If he ____________________, he ____________________ a new car.

5 우리가 미리 전화를 했다면, 줄을 서지 않았을 텐데. (had, called, have, wouldn't, waited, ahead)

→ If we ____________________, we ____________________ in line.

6 내가 그것을 먹지 않았다면, 배가 아프지 않았을 텐데. (wouldn't, hadn't, it, had, eaten, have)

→ If I ____________________, I ____________________ a stomachache.

B 빈칸 완성 우리말과 일치하도록 괄호 안의 말을 이용하여 빈칸을 완성하시오.

1 내가 더 젊다면, 내 꿈을 이룰 수 있을 텐데. (be)

→ If I __________ younger, I could make my dream come true.

2 내가 그녀를 더 자주 본다면, 그녀가 그립지 않을 텐데. (see)

→ If I __________ her more often, I wouldn't miss her.

3 나에게 그 책이 있다면 너에게 빌려 줄 텐데. (lend)

→ If I had the book, I __________ __________ it to you.

4 내가 너였다면, 그렇게 하지 않았을 텐데. (be, do)

→ If I __________ __________ you, I wouldn't have done that.

5 내가 그 라벨을 읽었다면, 그 스웨터를 뜨거운 물에 빨지 않았을 텐데. (read)

→ If I __________ __________ the label, I wouldn't have washed the sweater in hot water.

6 도로가 얼지 않았다면, 그 사고가 나지 않았을 텐데. (happen)

→ If the road hadn't been icy, the accident __________ __________ __________.

C 문장 전환 다음 직설법 문장을 가정법 문장으로 바꿔 쓰시오.

1 Because this ring is expensive, I can't buy it.

→ If this ring ______________ expensive, I ______________ it.

2 As you don't visit your grandparents more often, they are not happy.

→ If you ______________ your grandparents more often, they ______________ happy.

3 Since he isn't fluent in English, he can't participate in the English contest.

→ If he ______________ fluent in English, he ______________ in the English contest.

4 Because I didn't study harder, I couldn't pass the exam.

→ If I ______________ harder, I ______________ the exam.

5 As I didn't know the solution to the problem, I didn't tell you.

→ If I ______________ the solution to the problem, I ______________ you.

6 As I was not in your situation, I didn't ask for help.

→ If I ______________ in your situation, I ______________ for help.

D 오류 수정 밑줄 친 부분을 바르게 고쳐 문장을 다시 쓰시오.

1 What will you do if you had one million dollars?

→ ____

2 We could have a snowball fight if there is snow.

→ ____

3 If I were a teacher, I won't give students tests.

→ ____

4 If it didn't rain, we would have gone to the park.

→ ____

5 If you had taken care of your health, you might avoid getting sick.

→ ____

6 If he went to bed earlier, he wouldn't have been so tired.

→ ____

UNIT 02

I wish 가정법, as if 가정법

GRAMMAR FOCUS

1 I wish 가정법

「I wish + 가정법 과거」는 현재나 미래에 이룰 수 없는 일에 대한 아쉬움을 표현한다. 「I wish + 가정법 과거완료」는 과거에 이루지 못한 일에 대한 아쉬움을 표현한다.

I wish + 가정법 과거 ~라면 좋을 텐데	I wish I **were** on vacation now. (→ I'm sorry that I **am not** on vacation now.) 내가 지금 휴가 중이면 좋을 텐데.
	I wish I **had** an older brother or sister. (→ I'm sorry that I **don't have** an older brother or sister.) 나에게 오빠나 언니가 있으면 좋을 텐데.
I wish + 가정법 과거완료 ~했더라면 좋을 텐데	I wish I **had been** more careful with my belongings. (→ I'm sorry that I **wasn't** more careful with my belongings.) 내 소지품을 좀 더 조심했더라면 좋을 텐데.
	I wish I **had gone** to the concert last night. (→ I'm sorry that I **didn't go** to the concert last night.) 어젯밤에 그 콘서트에 갔더라면 좋을 텐데.

2 as if 가정법

as if 가정법은 실제로는 그렇지 않지만 그런 것처럼 가정할 때 쓴다. 「as if + 가정법 과거」는 현재 사실에 반대되는 일을 가정할 때 쓰며, 「as if + 가정법 과거완료」는 과거 사실에 반대되는 일을 가정할 때 쓴다.

as if + 가정법 과거 마치 ~인 것처럼	She speaks **as if** she **were** an expert on the topic. (→ In fact, she **isn't** an expert on the topic.) 그녀는 마치 그 주제에 대해 전문가인 것처럼 말한다.
as if + 가정법 과거완료 마치 ~였던 것처럼	He acts **as if** nothing **had happened** to him. (→ In fact, something **happened** to him.) 그는 마치 자신에게 아무 일도 일어나지 않았던 것처럼 행동한다.

plus as if 가정법은 주절의 시제와 관계없이, 주절과 같은 시점이면 과거형을, 주절보다 앞선 시점이면 과거완료를 쓴다.

He **talked** as if he **liked** me. 그는 마치 나를 좋아하는 것처럼 말했다.

He **talked** as if he **had liked** me. 그는 마치 나를 좋아했던 것처럼 말했다.

Answer Key p.27

괄호 안에서 알맞은 것을 고르시오.

1 It is raining right now. I wish it (isn't, weren't) raining.

2 I wish he (drove, had driven) more carefully yesterday.

3 My brother sometimes talks as if he (is, were) my father.

4 Steve acts as if he (didn't hear, hadn't heard) the news.

5 I wish I (talked, had talked) about the problem before it got worse.

6 My father lost his job last year. I wish my father (didn't lose, hadn't lost) his job.

두 문장의 의미가 같도록 빈칸에 알맞은 말을 쓰시오.

1 I'm sorry that I don't have enough time to exercise.

→ I wish I ______________ enough time to exercise.

2 I'm sorry that I didn't listen to my parents' advice.

→ I wish I ______________ to my parents' advice.

3 In fact, I am not a child.

→ She talks to me as if I ______________ a child.

4 In fact, he didn't see a UFO flying in the sky.

→ He talks as if he ______________ a UFO flying in the sky.

우리말과 일치하도록 괄호 안의 말을 이용하여 문장을 완성하시오.

1 날씨가 너무 추워. 이렇게 춥지 않다면 좋을 텐데. (be)

→ The weather is too cold. I wish it __________ so cold.

2 그는 마치 그 비밀을 알고 있는 것처럼 행동한다. (know)

→ He acts as if he __________ the secret.

3 그녀가 옷에 그렇게 많은 돈을 쓰지 않았더라면 좋을 텐데. (spend)

→ I wish she __________ __________ so much money on clothes.

4 그들은 마치 자신들이 유럽을 여행했던 것처럼 말한다. (travel)

→ They talk as if they __________ __________ to Europe.

WRITING FOCUS

A 배열 영작 우리말과 일치하도록 괄호 안의 말을 바르게 배열하시오.

1 나에게 우산이 있으면 좋을 텐데. (umbrella, I, had, I, wish, an)

→ ______________________________

2 내가 내 친구 Lisa보다 더 키가 크면 좋을 텐데. (I, taller, were, my friend Lisa, wish, I, than)

→ ______________________________

3 내가 차를 운전하는 것을 배웠다면 좋을 텐데. (leaned, I, car, had, a, to, wish, I, drive)

→ ______________________________

4 내 남동생은 마치 자신이 어린 아기인 것처럼 행동한다. (he, as, baby, if, a, were, little)

→ My brother acts ______________________________.

5 그는 마치 자신이 태국에 가 본 것처럼 말한다. (he, to, been, if, had, as, Thailand)

→ He talks ______________________________.

6 그녀는 마치 유령이라도 본 것처럼 보였다. (seen, a, she, if, had, ghost, as)

→ She looked ______________________________.

B 빈칸 완성 우리말과 일치하도록 괄호 안의 말을 이용하여 빈칸에 알맞은 말을 쓰시오.

1 그가 새해 전야를 축하하기 위해 여기 있다면 좋을 텐데. (be)

→ I wish he __________ here to celebrate New Year's Eve.

2 내가 추운 나라에 살지 않는다면 좋을 텐데. (live)

→ I wish I __________ __________ in a cold country.

3 내가 어렸을 때 영어 공부하는 것을 즐겼다면 좋을 텐데. (enjoy)

→ I wish I __________ __________ studying English when I was little.

4 Brian은 마치 자신이 부자인 것처럼 행동한다. (be)

→ Brian acts as if he __________ rich.

5 그는 마치 자신이 그 상을 탔던 것처럼 말한다. (win)

→ He talks as if he __________ __________ the award.

6 그녀는 마치 가장 재미있는 농담을 들은 것처럼 웃었다. (hear)

→ She laughed as if she __________ __________ the funniest joke.

Answer Key p.27

C 문장 완성 우리말과 일치하도록 괄호 안의 말을 이용하여 가정법 문장을 완성하시오.

1 내가 더 외향적이고 사교적이면 좋을 텐데. (more outgoing, sociable)

→ I wish ______________________________.

2 내가 매일 아침 일찍 일어나지 않아도 되면 좋을 텐데. (have to, wake up early)

→ I wish ______________________________ every morning.

3 우리가 더 일찍 예약을 했다면 좋을 텐데. (make a reservation)

→ I wish ______________________________ earlier.

4 그는 마치 자신은 그 결과에 신경 쓰지 않는 것처럼 말한다. (care about, the results)

→ He talks as if ______________________________.

5 나는 마치 내 아버지가 내 졸업식에 계신 것처럼 느껴진다. (at my graduation)

→ I feel as if ______________________________.

6 그들은 마치 자신들이 복권에라도 당첨된 것처럼 기뻐했다. (win, the lottery)

→ They were happy as if ______________________________.

D 문장 전환 어법상 틀린 부분을 바르게 고쳐 문장을 다시 쓰시오.

1 I wish I know more about computers. (내가 컴퓨터에 대해 더 많이 알면 좋을 텐데.)

→ ______________________________

2 I wish I were kinder to him. (내가 그에게 더 친절했다면 좋을 텐데.)

→ ______________________________

3 I wish I didn't lose my cellphone. (내가 내 휴대폰을 잃어버리지 않았다면 좋을 텐데.)

→ ______________________________

4 She acts as if she is a famous celebrity. (그녀는 마치 자신이 유명 연예인인 것처럼 행동한다.)

→ ______________________________

5 I feel as if I am walking on clouds. (나는 마치 구름 위를 걷고 있는 것처럼 느껴진다.)

→ ______________________________

6 She talks as if she has read the book. (그녀는 마치 자신이 그 책을 읽어본 것처럼 말한다.)

→ ______________________________

UNIT
03 주의해야 할 가정법

GRAMMAR FOCUS

❶ 혼합 가정법

if절에는 가정법 과거완료를 쓰고 주절에는 가정법 과거를 쓰는 형태이다. 과거 사실과 반대되는 일이 현재에 미칠 영향에 대해 말할 때 쓴다.

If + 주어 + had + p.p., (만일) ~였다면,	주어 + 조동사의 과거형 + 동사원형 …할 텐데
If I **had taken** the medicine, 내가 그 약을 먹었다면,	I **would feel** better now. 지금은 몸 상태가 더 좋을 텐데.

If I **had studied** English harder, I **could speak** English fluently now.
(→ As I **didn't study** English harder, I **don't speak** English fluently now.)
내가 영어를 더 열심히 공부했다면, 지금 영어를 유창하게 말할 수 있을 텐데.

If I **hadn't stayed** up late last night, I **wouldn't be** tired now.
(→ As I **stayed** up late last night, I **am** tired now.)
내가 어젯밤에 늦게까지 깨어 있지 않았다면, 지금 피곤하지 않을 텐데.

❷ Without[But for]

가정법의 if절을 대신하는 구문으로, 주절이 가정법 과거이면 '~이 없다면', 주절이 가정법 과거완료이면 '~이 없었다면'으로 해석한다.

Without[But for] ~, **가정법 과거** ~이 없다면, …할 텐데	**Without** sunlight, plants **could not grow**. = **But for** sunlight, plants could not grow. = **If it were not for** sunlight, plants could not grow. 햇빛이 없다면, 식물들은 자랄 수 없을 텐데.
Without[But for] ~, **가정법 과거완료** ~이 없었다면, …했을 텐데	**Without** your help, I **would have failed**. = **But for** your help, I would have failed. = **If it had not been for** your help, I would have failed. 너의 도움이 없었다면, 나는 실패했을 텐데.

❸ 가정법에서 접속사 if의 생략

가정법 과거 문장에서 if절의 동사가 were일 때 if를 생략하고 주어와 동사의 위치를 바꿔 쓸 수 있다.
가정법 과거완료 문장에서는 had가 주어 앞에 온다.

If + 주어 + were ~ = Were + 주어 ~	**If I were** in a good mood, I would go to the party with you. = **Were I** in a good mood, I would go to the party with you. 내가 기분이 좋다면, 너와 함께 그 파티에 갈 텐데. *가정법 과거 문장에서 if절에 일반동사가 쓰인 경우에는 if를 생략하지 않음
If + 주어 + had + p.p. ~ = Had + 주어 + p.p. ~	**If I had been** at Sam's place, I could have seen you. = **Had I been** at Sam's place, I could have seen you. 내가 Sam의 집에 있었다면, 너를 볼 수 있었을 텐데.

Answer Key p.28

괄호 안에서 알맞은 것을 고르시오.

1 If I had exercised regularly, I would (be, have been) healthier now.

2 If he (finished, had finished) his homework, he could play now.

3 Without water, no life could (exist, have existed) on the Earth.

4 (Without, But) for the heavy traffic, we would have arrived on time.

5 (Am I, Were I) a millionaire, I might quit my job and start a business.

6 (Had I known, Known I had) your phone number, I would have called you.

우리말과 일치하도록 괄호 안의 말을 이용하여 문장을 완성하시오.

1 그녀가 그 기차를 탔다면, 지금쯤 부산에 있을 텐데. (take, be)

→ If she __________ __________ the train, she __________ __________ in Busan by now.

2 내가 그 기회를 놓쳤다면, 지금 후회하고 있을 텐데. (miss, regret)

→ If I __________ __________ the opportunity, I __________ __________ it now.

3 우리가 이 집을 사지 않았다면, 다른 곳에서 살 텐데. (buy, live)

→ If we __________ __________ this house, we __________ __________ somewhere else.

두 문장의 의미가 같도록 빈칸에 알맞은 말을 쓰시오.

1 If it were not for technology, our lives would be less convenient.

→ __________ technology, our lives would be less convenient.

2 If it had not been for her advice, I would have made a mistake.

→ __________ __________ her advice, I would have made a mistake.

3 If I were the leader of the club, I would have more meetings.

→ __________ __________ the leader of the club, I would have more meetings.

4 If he had been careful, he wouldn't have fallen down.

→ __________ __________ __________ careful, he wouldn't have fallen down.

WRITING FOCUS

A 배열 영작 우리말과 일치하도록 괄호 안의 말을 바르게 배열하시오.

1 그가 더 열심히 공부했다면, 지금은 의사가 되어 있을 텐데. (would, studied, be, harder, had)

→ If he ____________________, he ____________________ a doctor now.

2 내가 스페인어를 배웠다면, 그와 이야기할 수 있을 텐데. (had, could, learned, talk, Spanish)

→ If I ____________________, I ____________________ with him.

3 이메일이 없다면, 그에게 연락하는 것이 어려울 텐데. (if, were, it, for, not, email)

→ ____, it would be hard to contact him.

4 너의 도움이 없었다면, 나는 포기했을 텐데. (if, for, it, been, had, your, not, help)

→ ____, I would have given up.

5 밖이 더 따뜻하다면, 우리는 산책하러 갈 텐데. (it, warmer, were, outside)

→ ____, we would go for a walk.

6 내가 그 책을 읽었다면, 그의 질문에 대답할 수 있었을 텐데. (read, I, the, had, book)

→ ____, I could have answered his question.

B 빈칸 완성 우리말과 일치하도록 괄호 안의 말을 이용하여 빈칸에 알맞은 말을 쓰시오.

1 네가 어젯밤에 창문을 닫았다면, 방이 이렇게 춥지 않을 텐데. (close)

→ If you __________ __________ the window last night, the room wouldn't be this cold.

2 우리가 꽃을 심었다면, 정원은 지금 더 아름다울 텐데. (plant)

→ If we __________ __________ flowers, the garden would be more beautiful now.

3 고소 공포증이 없다면, 나는 번지 점프를 해볼 텐데. (try)

→ __________ my fear of heights, I __________ __________ bungee jumping.

4 그의 강의가 없었다면, 나는 그 시험에 합격할 수 없었을 텐데. (pass)

→ __________ __________ his lecture, I __________ __________ __________ the test.

5 내가 다이어트 중이 아니라면, 케이크 한 조각을 더 먹을 텐데. (be)

→ __________ __________ not on a diet, I would have another slice of cake.

6 우리가 더 일찍 도착했다면, 더 좋은 자리를 찾을 수 있었을 텐데. (arrive)

→ __________ __________ __________ earlier, we could have found better seats.

C 문장 전환 두 문장의 의미가 같도록 가정법을 사용해서 문장을 완성하시오.

1 I ate breakfast, so I am not hungry now.
→ If I __________ breakfast, I __________ hungry now.

2 As we didn't check the map, we are lost now.
→ If we __________ the map, we __________ lost now.

3 Without the supercomputer, they couldn't forecast the weather.
→ If it __________, they couldn't forecast the weather.

4 But for his hard work, he wouldn't have won the award.
→ If it __________, he wouldn't have won the award.

5 Were I you, I would get a job after graduation.
→ If __________, I would get a job after graduation.

6 Had I heard about his troubles, I would have helped him.
→ If __________ about his troubles, I would have helped him.

D 오류 수정 밑줄 친 부분을 바르게 고쳐 문장을 다시 쓰시오.

1 If I had taken the chance, I would have been in a better position now.
→ If I had taken the chance, __________.

2 If we bought some food, we wouldn't be hungry now.
→ __________, we wouldn't be hungry now.

3 Without for music, our lives would be boring.
→ __________, our lives would be boring.

4 If it had not been for the Internet, it would be inconvenient to find information.
→ __________, it would be inconvenient to find information.

5 If it were not for the storm, we could have gone camping.
→ __________, we could have gone camping.

6 Have I been you, I would have made a different decision.
→ __________, I would have made a different decision.

ACTUAL TEST

문항 수	객관식 8 / 서술형 12
맞은 개수	/ 20

[01-03] 빈칸에 들어갈 말로 알맞은 것을 고르시오.

01

If I __________ a famous singer, I would tour the world.

① am ② were
③ will be ④ have been
⑤ had been

02

If she had studied abroad, she __________ a new language.

① learns ② learned
③ can learn ④ could learn
⑤ could have learned

03

I wish I __________ the shirt when it was on sale. It is too expensive now.

① buy ② bought
③ would buy ④ have bought
⑤ had bought

04 우리말을 영어로 잘못 옮긴 것은?

그의 노력이 없었다면, 우리는 그 작업을 끝낼 수 없었을 텐데.

① Without his effort, we couldn't have finished the task.
② But for his effort, we couldn't have finished the task.
③ Were it not for his effort, we couldn't have finished the task.
④ Had it not been for his effort, we couldn't have finished the task.
⑤ If it had not been for his effort, we couldn't have finished the task.

05 밑줄 친 부분이 어법상 틀린 것은?

① I wish today were my birthday.
② I wish I have a younger brother.
③ She acts as if she didn't know me.
④ He talks as if he had read the book.
⑤ I wish I had gone to the dentist earlier.

06 다음 중 어법상 틀린 것은?

① If it were sunny, we would go to the beach.
② I would see her more often if she lived closer.
③ If I had been you, I would have apologized to Mark.
④ What three wishes would you make if you had a magic lamp?
⑤ If I had learned to cook, I would have enjoyed cooking now.

빈출 고난도

07 주어진 문장을 가정법으로 바꾼 것 중 잘못된 것은?

① I'm not hungry because I ate a sandwich.
→ I were hungry if I hadn't eaten a sandwich.
② There aren't any chairs, so we can't sit down.
→ If there were some chairs, we could sit down.
③ As she arrived late, she couldn't see the movie.
→ If she hadn't arrived late, she could have seen the movie.
④ Mary studied all night, so she is tired now.
→ If Mary hadn't studied all night, she wouldn't be tired now.
⑤ As he didn't wake up early, he missed the sunrise.
→ If he had woken up early, he wouldn't have missed the sunrise.

고난도

08 어법상 올바른 문장을 모두 고르면?

ⓐ I have a stomachache. I wish I hadn't eaten so much.
ⓑ He can play in the game if he hadn't injured his leg.
ⓒ If I had gone to bed earlier, I wouldn't have woken up late.
ⓓ The boy plays with the toy robots as if they are his friends.
ⓔ If you are free tomorrow, will you go shopping with me?
ⓕ Had I known she was in the hospital, I would have visited her.

① ⓐ, ⓑ, ⓓ
② ⓐ, ⓒ, ⓔ, ⓕ
③ ⓑ, ⓒ, ⓔ
④ ⓒ, ⓓ, ⓔ, ⓕ
⑤ ⓒ, ⓔ, ⓕ

서술형

09 우리말과 일치하도록 주어진 말을 활용하여 문장을 완성하시오.

(1) 나에게 타임머신이 있다면, 미래로 여행을 갈 텐데. (have, travel)

→ If I ________ a time machine, I ________ ________ to the future.

(2) 그녀가 나를 초대했다면, 나는 그 파티에 갔을 텐데. (invite, go)

→ If she ________ ________ me, I ________ ________ ________ to the party.

[10-11] 어법상 틀린 부분을 찾아 바르게 고치시오.

10

I like cats, but unfortunately, my mother is allergic to them. If she isn't allergic to them, I could have a cat.

________ → ________

11

Tom fell and got hurt while running down the stairs. If he hadn't run down the stairs, he could avoid injury.

________ → ________

[12-13] 직설법 문장은 가정법으로, 가정법 문장은 직설법으로 바꿔 쓰시오.

12

If today were a holiday, I would not have to go to school.

→ As today ________ ________ a holiday, I ________ ________ ________ to school.

13

As I didn't remember her birthday, she was angry with me.

→ If I ________ ________ her birthday, she ________ ________ ________ ________ angry with me.

14 밑줄 친 우리말과 일치하도록 주어진 말을 활용하여 문장을 완성하시오.

A: If you could have any superpower, what would you want?
B: I would want to have super speed. What about you?
A: If I could, I would want the ability to fly. <u>나에게 그런 능력이 있다면 차 없이도 어디든지 갈 수 있을 텐데.</u> (have, go)

→ If I ________ that ability, I ________ anywhere without a car.

15 그림을 보고, 주어진 말을 활용하여 문장을 완성하시오.

(1) (2)

(1) If we ______________________________,
we would go to the beach every day.
(live, in Hawaii)

(2) If he ______________________________,
he wouldn't have broken his leg.
(be, more careful)

16 주어진 문장과 의미가 같도록 문장을 바꿔 쓰시오.

(1) I'm sorry that I can't fly like a bird.
→ I wish ____________________ like a bird.

(2) I'm sorry that I didn't listen to your advice.
→ I wish ____________________ to your advice.

17 우리말과 일치하도록 〈조건〉에 맞게 문장을 완성하시오.

> 조건 1. as if 가정법을 사용할 것
> 2. (1)은 know, (2)는 be를 활용할 것

(1) 그는 자신이 그 문제에 대한 답을 알고 있는 것처럼 행동한다.
→ He acts ______________________________
the solution to the problem.

(2) 그녀는 마치 자신이 전에 그 나라에 가 본 것처럼 말한다.
→ She talks ______________________________
to the country before.

18 우리말과 일치하도록 주어진 말을 활용하여 문장을 완성하시오.

> 내가 내 휴대폰을 집에 두고 오지 않았다면, 지금 너에게 전화를 할 수 있을 텐데. (leave, call)

→ If I ____________________ my cellphone at home, I ____________________ you now.

[19-20] 주어진 문장과 의미가 같도록 빈칸에 알맞은 말을 쓰시오.

19

> If it had not been for the scholarship, he could not have gone to college.

→ __________ __________ __________,
he could not have gone to college.

20

> If I were you, I would not skip breakfast.

→ __________ __________ __________,
I would not skip breakfast.

Chapter 10

일치, 화법, 강조, 도치

UNIT 01 일치

GRAMMAR FOCUS

1 수의 일치

수의 일치는 주어와 동사의 수를 일치시키는 것을 말한다. 주어가 단수이면 단수 동사, 복수이면 복수 동사를 쓴다.

(1) 단수 취급하는 경우

-thing / -body / -one으로 끝나는 명사	**Everything** in this room **is** mine.
each / every + 단수 명사 each of + 복수 명사	**Every** *student* **has** a book. **Each of** *the students* **has** a book.
the number of + 복수 명사 (~의 수)	**The number of** *students* in the class **is** twenty.
일부 국가명	**the** United States **the** Philippines **the** Netherlands
과목명	mathematics physics social studies
시간, 거리, 금액, 무게가 하나의 단위로 쓰이는 경우	**Twelve hours is** half a day. **Ten dollars is** all I have in my wallet.

(2) 복수 취급하는 경우

(both) *A* and *B*	*Jane* **and** *Amy* **are** my friends.
a number of + 복수 명사 (많은 ~)	**A number of** *students* **are** absent from class today.
the + 형용사 (~한 사람들)	**the** rich **the** poor **the** elderly **the** homeless

cf. 부분을 나타내는 표현(some of, half of, most of 등)은 of 뒤에 오는 명사에 동사의 수를 일치시킨다.

Some of *the books* **are** informative. 그 책들 중 몇 권은 유익하다.

Most of *the furniture* **is** old and dirty. 그 가구의 대부분은 낡고 지저분하다.

2 시제 일치

시제 일치는 주절의 시제에 종속절의 시제를 일치시키는 것을 말한다. 주절의 시제가 현재일 때는 종속절에 모든 시제가 올 수 있다. 주절의 시제가 과거일 때는 종속절에 과거나 과거완료가 쓰인다.

주절: 현재 → 주절: 과거	I *think* that she **is** disappointed. → I *thought* that she **was** disappointed.	나는 그녀가 실망하고 있다고 생각한다. 나는 그녀가 실망하고 있다고 생각했다.
	I *think* that she **was** disappointed. → I *thought* that she **had been** disappointed.	나는 그녀가 실망했다고 생각한다. 나는 그녀가 실망했었다고 생각했다.
	I *think* that she **will** be disappointed. → I *thought* that she **would** be disappointed.	나는 그녀가 실망할 거라고 생각한다. 나는 그녀가 실망할 거라고 생각했다.

plus 시제 일치의 예외: 과학적 사실, 현재의 습관, 속담이나 격언은 주절의 시제에 상관없이 항상 현재시제를 쓰고, 역사적 사실은 항상 과거시제를 쓴다.

Tom *told* me that he **studies** English for two hours every day.
Tom은 나에게 매일 두 시간씩 영어 공부를 한다고 말했다. 〈현재의 습관〉

I *know* that World War I **broke out** in 1914.
나는 제1차 세계 대전이 1914년에 일어났다는 것을 안다. 〈역사적 사실〉

Answer Key p.29

괄호 안에서 알맞은 것을 고르시오.

1 Every student (has to, have to) answer the questions.

2 Each set of test papers (is, are) completely sealed.

3 Six hours (is, are) a long time to drive without a break.

4 Fifty dollars (is, are) a reasonable price for those blue jeans.

5 Mathematics (is, are) the most difficult subject for me.

6 The United States (is, are) the fourth largest country in the world.

7 The homeless (was, were) looking for a place to rest.

8 A number of volunteers (is, are) cleaning up the park.

9 The number of people living in cities (is, are) increasing.

10 Some of the cars on the street (was, were) parked in a tow-away zone.

11 Half of the cake (is, are) for you, and the rest is for me.

12 Both experience and knowledge (is, are) essential for his work.

다음 문장에서 주절의 동사를 과거시제로 바꿀 때, 빈칸에 알맞은 말을 쓰시오.

1 I think that Ethan looks confident in his presentation.

→ I thought that Ethan ______________ confident in his presentation.

2 I expect that my package will arrive soon.

→ I expected that my package ______________ soon.

3 Angela says that she can go hiking with us.

→ Angela said that she ______________ hiking with us.

4 He knows that the human body has about 206 bones.

→ He knew that the human body ______________ about 206 bones.

5 She says that she worked in Paris for two years.

→ She said that she ______________ in Paris for two years.

6 Our teacher teaches us that the Berlin Wall fell in 1989.

→ Our teacher taught us that the Berlin Wall ______________ in 1989.

WRITING FOCUS

A 배열 영작 우리말과 일치하도록 괄호 안의 말을 바르게 배열하시오. (단, 동사를 알맞은 형태로 바꿀 것)

1 모두가 물수건을 제공받을 것이다. (going, everyone, is, be, to, served)

→ ______________________________ a wet towel.

2 그 꽃들 각각 다른 색깔을 가지고 있다. (flowers, of, each, has, the)

→ ______________________________ a different color.

3 물리학은 나에게 가장 흥미로운 과목이다. (physics, the, subject, is, most, interesting)

→ ______________________________ to me.

4 부상자들은 병원으로 이송되었다. (taken, the, were, injured)

→ ______________________________ to the hospital.

5 그 커피의 절반이 탁자 위에 엎질러졌다. (the, half, was, coffee, of, spilled)

→ ______________________________ on the table.

6 Susan은 자신이 한국을 방문한 적이 있다고 말했다. (had, said, she, visited, that, Susan)

→ ______________________________ Korea.

B 빈칸 완성 우리말과 일치하도록 괄호 안의 말을 이용하여 빈칸에 알맞은 말을 쓰시오.

1 책상마다 그 위에 고유 번호가 쓰여 있다. (desk, have)

→ Each ________ ________ its own number written on it.

2 필리핀은 7천 개 이상의 섬으로 이루어져 있다. (consist of)

→ The Philippines ________ ________ more than seven thousand islands.

3 내가 가지고 있던 돈의 대부분은 책과 공책에 쓰였다. (spent)

→ Most of the money I had ________ ________ on books and notebooks.

4 그 야영장의 많은 사람들이 모닥불 주위에 둘러앉아 있다. (sitting)

→ A number of people at the campsite ________ ________ around the campfire.

5 나는 그 시험이 한 시간 이상 걸릴 것이라고 생각했다. (think, take)

→ I ________ that the exam ________ ________ more than an hour.

6 코페르니쿠스는 지구가 태양 주위를 돈다고 믿었다. (believe, move)

→ Copernicus ________ that the Earth ________ around the sun.

C 문장 완성 우리말과 일치하도록 괄호 안의 말을 이용하여 문장을 완성하시오.

1 그 동호회의 모든 회원이 똑같은 티셔츠를 입고 있다. (every, member, wearing)

→ ______________ of the club ______________ the same T-shirt.

2 40분은 조깅을 하기에 적당량의 시간이다. (forty minutes, a proper amount of time)

→ ______________________________ for jogging.

3 냉장고에 있는 음식의 대부분이 상했다. (most of, food, gone bad)

→ ______________ in the fridge ______________.

4 그 도시를 방문하는 관광객들의 수는 증가하고 있다. (number, tourists, increasing)

→ ______________ visiting the city ______________.

5 많은 집들이 어젯밤에 폭풍으로 피해를 입었다. (number, house, damaged)

→ ______________________________ by the storm last night.

6 선생님은 물이 섭씨 100도에서 끓는다고 말씀하셨다. (water, boil, at 100 degrees Celsius)

→ The teacher said that ______________________________.

D 오류 수정 어법상 틀린 부분을 바르게 고쳐 문장을 다시 쓰시오.

1 The Netherlands are known for its windmills and tulips. (네덜란드는 풍차와 튤립으로 알려져 있다.)

→ ______________________________

2 The number of players on a soccer team are eleven. (한 축구 팀의 선수 수는 열한 명이다.)

→ ______________________________

3 Ten dollars are a reasonable price for the hat. (10달러는 그 모자의 적정 가격이다.)

→ ______________________________

4 Every child were given a piece of cake. (모든 아이는 케이크 한 조각을 받았다.)

→ ______________________________

5 I thought that he will be surprised by the news. (나는 그가 그 소식을 듣고 놀랄 것이라고 생각했다.)

→ ______________________________

6 Some of the trees on the roadside was cut down. (길가에 있는 나무들 중 몇 그루가 베어졌다.)

→ ______________________________

UNIT 02 화법

GRAMMAR FOCUS

❶ 직접화법과 간접화법

화법은 누군가의 말을 전달하는 방식으로 직접화법과 간접화법이 있다. 화자가 한 말을 따옴표(" ")를 사용하여 그대로 전달하면 직접화법이고, 따옴표 없이 전달자의 입장에 맞게 바꿔서 전달하면 간접화법이다.

직접화법	Sally said, **"I am** hungry."	Sally가 "나는 배가 고파."라고 말했다.
간접화법	Sally said that **she was** hungry.	Sally가 그녀는 배가 고프다고 말했다.

cf. 직접화법에서 화자의 말이 앞에 나오는 경우에는 화자의 말 뒤에 콤마(,)를 쓰고 주어와 동사의 위치가 바뀐다.

"I am hungry**," said Sally**.

❷ 화법 전환

(1) 평서문의 화법 전환

① 전달 동사를 바꾼다. (say → say, say to → tell)	Sue *said*, "*I like these* shoes." → Sue **said** (**that**) **she liked those** shoes. ① ② ③ ④ ⑤
② 콤마와 인용 부호를 없애고 접속사 that을 쓴다. (that은 생략 가능)	
③ that절의 인칭대명사는 전달자의 입장에 맞게 바꾼다.	Bill *said to* me, "*I saw you yesterday*." → Bill **told** me (**that**) **he had seen me the day before**. ① ② ③ ④ ③ ⑤
④ that절의 동사는 시제 일치의 규칙에 맞게 바꾼다.	
⑤ that절의 지시대명사와 부사는 전달자의 입장과 시제에 맞게 바꾼다.	

cf. 화법 전환에 따른 어구 변화: this → that, these → those, here → there, now → then[at the moment], today → that day, yesterday → the day before[the previous day], tomorrow → the next day[the following day]

(2) 의문문의 화법 전환: 전달 동사를 ask로 바꾸고 의문사나 if[whether]를 사용한다.

의문사가 있는 경우 「ask(+목적어)+의문사+주어+동사」	Henry *said to* Jill, "What *did you buy*?" → Henry **asked** Jill what **she had bought**.
의문사가 없는 경우 「ask(+목적어)+if[whether]+주어+동사」	She *said to* me, "*Do you live here*?" → She **asked** me **if**[**whether**] **I lived there**.

cf. 의문사가 주어인 경우에는 「의문사+동사」의 어순 그대로 쓴다.

He said "*Who took* my umbrella?" → He asked **who had taken** his umbrella.

(3) 명령문의 화법 전환: 전달 동사를 tell, ask, advise, order, warn 등으로 바꾸고 to부정사를 사용한다.

긍정 명령문 「동사+목적어+to부정사」	The teacher *said to* us, "*Open* your books." → The teacher **told** us **to open** our books.
부정 명령문 「동사+목적어+not+to부정사」	She *said to* me, "*Don't eat* all the cookies." → She **asked** me **not to eat** all the cookies.

Answer Key p.30

괄호 안에서 알맞은 것을 고르시오.

1 Ann told me that she (is, was) going to school.

2 Kevin said that he (will, would) see me the next day.

3 A woman asked me what time (it was, was it) then.

4 The doctor asked me how often (did I exercise, I exercised).

5 Sue's brother asked her (that, if) she could lend him some money.

6 My roommate told me (turning off, to turn off) the lights before I left.

밑줄 친 부분을 어법에 맞게 고치시오.

1 John said that he is reading a book.

2 Mary told me she will arrive late due to traffic.

3 I asked the teacher what did the word mean.

4 He asked me that I had some time to talk with him.

5 The librarian told us be quiet in the library.

6 Mr. Green told them don't talk during the exam.

다음 문장을 간접화법으로 바꿔 쓰시오.

1 Matt said to me, "What do you want for lunch?"

→ Matt asked me ________________________________.

2 Jane said, "Who is going to teach us?"

→ Jane asked ________________________________.

3 My sister said to me, "Did you see my favorite hat?"

→ My sister asked me ________________________________.

4 Mom said to my brother, "Please take out the garbage."

→ Mom asked my brother ________________________________.

5 Emily said to me, "Don't touch the hot stove."

→ Emily told me ________________________________.

WRITING FOCUS

A 배열 영작 우리말과 일치하도록 괄호 안의 말을 바르게 배열하시오.

1 Bob은 나에게 제시간에 그곳에 도착할 것이라고 말했다. (Bob, would, he, me, there, told, be, that)

→ ______________________________ on time.

2 Tom은 그의 숙제를 이미 끝냈다고 말했다. (said, Tom, that, already, had, he, finished)

→ ______________________________ his homework.

3 그는 우리에게 시청에 어떻게 갈 수 있는지 물었다. (asked, to, he, how, us, could, he, get)

→ ______________________________ City Hall.

4 그녀는 나에게 근처에 버스 정류장이 있는지 물었다. (there, a, if, she, was, bus stop, me, asked)

→ ______________________________ nearby.

5 Carol은 나에게 잠시만 기다려달라고 부탁했다. (Carol, wait, asked, to, me)

→ ______________________________ for a minute.

6 공원 관리인은 우리에게 잔디 위를 걷지 말라고 말했다. (not, park manager, told, the, to, us, walk)

→ ______________________________ on the grass.

B 빈칸 완성 우리말과 일치하도록 괄호 안의 말을 이용하여 빈칸에 알맞은 말을 쓰시오.

1 기상 캐스터는 그날 비가 올 것이라고 말했다. (be going to)

→ The weatherman said that it ________ ________ ________ rain that day.

2 면접관은 나에게 내 이름이 무엇인지 물었다. (my name)

→ The interviewer asked me ________ ________ ________ ________.

3 엄마는 나에게 누가 방을 청소했는지 물었다. (clean)

→ Mom asked me ________ ________ ________ the room.

4 Kelly는 그 남자에게 그곳에 자신의 차를 주차할 수 있는지 물었다. (can, park)

→ Kelly asked the man ________ ________ ________ ________ her car there.

5 나는 그에게 물 한 잔을 가져다 달라고 부탁했다. (bring)

→ I asked him ________ ________ me a glass of water.

6 나는 내 남동생에게 창문을 닫는 것을 잊지 말라고 말했다. (forget)

→ I told my brother ________ ________ ________ to close the window.

Answer Key p.31

C 문장 완성 우리말과 일치하도록 괄호 안의 말을 이용하여 문장을 완성하시오.

1 그는 나에게 나와 함께 영화를 보러 가고 싶다고 말했다. (want to, go to the movies)

→ He told me that ______________________________ with me.

2 선생님은 나에게 왜 늦었는지 물어보셨다. (late)

→ The teacher asked me ______________________________.

3 그 외국인은 나에게 영어를 말할 수 있는지 물었다. (can, speak English)

→ The foreigner asked me ______________________________.

4 내 친구는 나에게 그의 개를 돌봐 달라고 부탁했다. (take care of, dog)

→ My friend asked me ______________________________.

5 김 선생님은 우리에게 금요일까지 기말 리포트를 제출하라고 말씀하셨다. (hand in, the final report)

→ Mr. Kim told us ______________________________ by Friday.

6 나는 Nick에게 그 모임에 늦지 말라고 말했다. (late, for the meeting)

→ I asked Nick ______________________________.

D 오류 수정 어법상 틀린 부분을 바르게 고쳐 문장을 다시 쓰시오.

1 He said that he will arrive in Seoul the following day.

→ ______________________________

2 Lisa told me that she has been to Paris twice.

→ ______________________________

3 The salesperson asked me which color did I prefer.

→ ______________________________

4 The waiter asked us that we were ready to order.

→ ______________________________

5 Mom asked me help her with the dishes.

→ ______________________________

6 He told his son to not talk with strangers.

→ ______________________________

UNIT 03 강조, 도치

GRAMMAR FOCUS

❶ 강조

(1) do/does/did + 동사원형: 문장에서 동사를 강조하며 '정말 ~하다/했다'로 해석한다.

He *studied* for the exam, but he didn't do well.

→ He **did study** for the exam, but he didn't do well. 그는 그 시험을 위해 정말 공부를 했지만 잘하지 못했다.

(2) It is/was ~ that ...: 강조하는 부분을 It is/was와 that 사이에 넣고 '…한 것은 바로 ~이다/였다'로 해석한다.

강조하는 부분	Tom(①) found a wallet(②) in a taxi(③) yesterday(④).
① 주어 강조	→ **It was** *Tom* **that** found a wallet in a taxi yesterday. 어제 택시에서 지갑을 찾은 사람은 바로 Tom이었다.
② 목적어 강조	→ **It was** *a wallet* **that** Tom found in a taxi yesterday. Tom이 어제 택시에서 찾은 것은 바로 지갑이었다.
③ 부사(구) 강조	→ **It was** *in a taxi* **that** Tom found a wallet yesterday. Tom이 어제 지갑을 찾은 곳은 바로 택시에서였다. → **It was** *yesterday* **that** Tom found a wallet in a taxi. Tom이 택시에서 지갑을 찾은 것은 바로 어제였다.

cf. that은 강조하는 말이 사람, 장소나 시간의 부사(구)일 때 각각 who(m), where, when으로 바꿔 쓸 수 있다.

❷ 도치

(1) 부정어 도치: 강조를 위해 부정어(never, hardly, rarely, seldom, not only 등)가 문장 맨 앞에 나오면 주어와 동사는 의문문 어순을 따른다.

I will *never* let you down again.

→ **Never will I let** you down again. 나는 절대로 다시는 너를 실망시키지 않을 거야.

She *hardly* complains about her job.

→ **Hardly does she complain** about her job. 그녀는 거의 자신의 일에 대해 불평하지 않는다.

(2) 부사(구) 도치: 위치나 방향을 강조하기 위해 장소의 부사(구)가 문장 맨 앞에 나오면 주어와 동사의 순서가 바뀐다.

A cozy fireplace is *in the room*.

→ **In the room is a cozy fireplace.** 방 안에 아늑한 벽난로가 있다.

An old apple tree stood *in the garden*.

→ **In the garden stood an old apple tree.** 정원에 오래된 사과 나무 한 그루가 서 있었다.

cf. 주어가 대명사인 경우에는 부사(구) 뒤에 「주어 + 동사」의 어순을 그대로 쓴다.

Here comes the teacher. 선생님이 오신다.
There goes Sarah. Sarah가 저기 간다.
Here is your book. 네 책이 여기 있어.

Here he comes. 그가 온다.
There she goes. 그녀가 저기 간다.
Here it is. 여기 있어.

괄호 안에서 알맞은 것을 고르시오.

1 Sam did (promise, promised) to be here by 7:00 p.m.

2 (It, He) was Sean that recommended this restaurant to us.

3 Never (I have seen, have I seen) a shooting star before.

4 Rarely (he apologizes, does he apologize) for his behavior.

5 On the top of the hill (a castle stood, stood a castle).

6 Down the street (he walked, walked he).

다음 문장을 밑줄 친 부분을 강조하는 문장으로 바꿔 쓰시오.

1 She has a talent for painting.

→ ______________________________

2 I found an old photo album in the attic.

→ ______________________________

3 She never realized that her backpack was open.

→ ______________________________

4 A beautiful lake lies at the top of the mountain.

→ ______________________________

우리말과 일치하도록 괄호 안의 말을 이용하여 문장을 완성하시오.

1 그 피자는 보기만큼이나 정말 맛있었다. (do, taste)

→ The pizza ______________ as good as it looked.

2 내가 그 제과점에서 산 것은 바로 생일 케이크였다. (a birthday cake)

→ It ______________ I bought at the bakery.

3 그는 숙제 하는 것을 잊는 경우가 드물다. (forget)

→ Seldom ______________ to do his homework.

4 입구에 경비원 한 명이 서 있었다. (a security guard, stand)

→ At the entrance ______________.

WRITING FOCUS

A 배열 영작 **우리말과 일치하도록 괄호 안의 말을 바르게 배열하시오.**

1 그녀는 여가 시간에 책을 읽는 것을 정말 즐긴다. (enjoy, books, reading, does, in her free time)

→ She ______________________________.

2 그는 자신의 실수를 정말로 사과했다. (did, mistake, his, for, apologize)

→ He ______________________________.

3 그 쿠키를 먹은 것은 바로 John이었다. (John, the, was, cookies, ate, that)

→ It ______________________________.

4 내가 Ethan을 만난 것은 바로 지난주였다. (I, that, was, met, Ethan, last week)

→ It ______________________________.

5 그녀는 거의 자녀들에게 화를 내지 않는다. (her, angry, she, get, does, children, with)

→ Hardly ______________________________.

6 강을 따라 두 사람이 손을 잡고 걸었다. (two, walked, people, hand in hand)

→ Along the river ______________________________.

B 빈칸 완성 **우리말과 일치하도록 괄호 안의 말을 이용하여 빈칸에 알맞은 말을 쓰시오.**

1 나는 너에게 조심하라고 정말로 말했어! (do, tell)

→ I ________ ________ you to be careful!

2 그 나무를 쓰러뜨린 것은 바로 그 폭풍이었다. (the storm, knock down)

→ It was ________ ________ ________ ________ ________ the tree.

3 우리가 숲에서 본 것은 바로 사슴 한 마리였다. (a deer, see)

→ It was ________ ________ ________ ________ ________ in the forest.

4 그녀는 자신이 유명한 가수가 되리라고는 상상도 하지 못했다. (imagine)

→ Never ________ ________ ________ that she would be a famous singer.

5 그는 출근하기 전에 거의 아침을 거르지 않는다. (skip)

→ Rarely ________ ________ ________ breakfast before going to work.

6 길 아래로 트럭 한 대가 왔다. (a truck, come)

→ Down the street ________ ________ ________.

Answer Key p.31

C 문장 완성 우리말과 일치하도록 괄호 안의 말을 이용하여 문장을 완성하시오.

1 그는 오늘 정말로 피곤해 보인다. (do, look tired)

→ ______________________________ today.

2 거실을 어지럽힌 것은 바로 나의 강아지였다. (puppy, make a mess)

→ It ______________________________ in the living room.

3 그가 지난주에 산 것은 바로 새 차였다. (a new car, buy)

→ It ______________________________ last week.

4 내가 이상한 소리를 들은 것은 한밤중이었다. (in the middle of the night, hear)

→ It ______________________________ a strange noise.

5 그는 지금까지 마감일을 놓친 적이 한 번도 없다. (have missed, a deadline)

→ Never ______________________________ so far.

6 다리 밑으로 유람선 한 척이 지나갔다. (a cruise ship, pass)

→ Under the bridge ______________________________.

D 오류 수정 어법상 틀린 부분을 바르게 고쳐 문장을 다시 쓰시오.

1 They did finished the work on time.

→ ______________________________

2 It was in Hawaii we spent our summer vacation.

→ ______________________________

3 It was this book which she gave me for my birthday.

→ ______________________________

4 That was during the storm that the power went out.

→ ______________________________

5 Little I knew that my friends were planning a surprise party for me.

→ ______________________________

6 In the middle of the room a grand piano stood.

→ ______________________________

ACTUAL TEST

문항 수	객관식 8 / 서술형 12
맞은 개수	/ 20

[01-02] 빈칸에 들어갈 말이 순서대로 짝지어진 것은?

01

- Each of us ________ a responsibility.
- Some of the apples ________ not fresh.
- I think that the old ________ wiser than the young.

① has - is - is ② has - are - is
③ has - are - are ④ have - are - is
⑤ have - are - are

02

- A number of mistakes ________ found in his report.
- The number of club members ________ 120 in total.

① was - is ② was - am
③ was - are ④ were - is
⑤ were - are

빈출

03 주어진 문장을 간접화법으로 바꾼 것 중 잘못된 것은?

① My mom said, "Dinner is ready."
→ My mom said that dinner was ready.
② Ann said, "I want to be a singer."
→ Ann said that she wanted to be a singer.
③ He said, "The weather is hot today."
→ He said that the weather was hot that day.
④ She said to me, "I am going shopping now."
→ She told me that she was going shopping then.
⑤ Lily said to me, "I will visit you tomorrow."
→ Lily told me that she would visit me the day before.

04 다음 중 강조 용법으로 쓰이지 않은 문장은?

① It is a glass of water that she wants.
② It was certain that Ian broke the mirror.
③ It was in the car that I found my umbrella.
④ It was yesterday that the package arrived.
⑤ It was by bus that we went to the museum.

05 밑줄 친 부분을 강조하는 문장으로 틀린 것은?

① Tina knows how to swim
→ Tina does know how to swim.
② He paid the bill at the restaurant.
→ He did pay the bill at the restaurant.
③ I met Ben at the park yesterday.
→ It was Ben that I met at the park yesterday.
④ Emma lost her earrings at the beach.
→ It was at the beach that Emma lost her earrings.
⑤ Mike scored the winning goal in the final.
→ It was Mike scored the winning goal in the final.

빈출

06 다음 중 어법상 올바른 것은?

① Everyone have to follow the rules.
② Amy and Sean is studying together.
③ Twenty dollars are enough for lunch.
④ All of the money was stolen yesterday.
⑤ Physics are very difficult but interesting.

고난도

07 어법상 올바른 문장을 모두 고르면?

ⓐ They asked me if I needed help.
ⓑ He asked me what was my favorite food.
ⓒ She asked me how she could get to the subway station.
ⓓ Mr. Kim told us not cheat on the exam.
ⓔ Judy told me that she has never seen a parrot.

① ⓐ, ⓑ ② ⓐ, ⓒ
③ ⓑ, ⓓ ④ ⓒ, ⓓ
⑤ ⓒ, ⓔ

08 밑줄 친 부분이 어법상 올바른 것의 개수는?

ⓐ Here she comes.
ⓑ Under the tree a bench is.
ⓒ Along the trail walked the hikers.
ⓓ Hardly does he eat any fast food these days.
ⓔ Never I have seen such a beautiful beach.

① 1개 ② 2개 ③ 3개
④ 4개 ⑤ 5개

서술형

09 우리말과 일치하도록 주어진 말을 바르게 배열하시오.

(1) 내 친구들 대부분이 축구하는 것을 좋아한다.
(my, to, most, friends, play, of, like, soccer)

→ ______________________________

(2) 그 그릇에 있는 설탕의 절반이 쏟아졌다.
(sugar, half, was, of, in the bowl, the, spilled)

→ ______________________________

10 밑줄 친 부분을 과거시제로 바꿔 문장을 다시 쓰시오.

(1) He thinks that she will like the gift.

→ ______________________________

(2) I know that the sun is also a star.

→ ______________________________

[11-13] 주어진 문장을 간접화법으로 바꿔 쓰시오.

11

She said to me, "I'm excited about the concert."

→ She told me that ______________________________
______________________________.

12

Mom asked me, "What do you want for your birthday?"

→ Mom asked me ______________________________
______________________________.

13

My brother asked me, "Have you seen my phone?"

→ My brother asked me ______________________________
______________________________.

14 그림을 보고, 각 사람의 말을 간접화법으로 바꿔 쓰시오.

(1) Fill out the form.

(2) Do you want some dessert?

(1) The receptionist told him ______________________

______________________.

(2) The waiter asked me ______________________

______________________.

15 다음 문장을 간접화법으로 바꿀 때 어법상 틀린 부분을 찾아 바르게 고치시오.

> Ms. Jones said to me, "Don't be late again."
> → Ms. Jones told me don't be late again.

______________ → ______________

[16-17] 다음 문장을 밑줄 친 부분을 강조하는 문장으로 바꿔 쓰시오.

16

> Ruth has a good sense of humor.

→ ______________________________

17

> My neighbor borrowed a screwdriver from me yesterday.

→ ______________________________

____

18 다음 문장을 주어진 말로 시작하는 문장으로 바꿔 쓰시오.

(1) He seldom misses a day of exercise.

→ Seldom ______________________________.

(2) A convenience store is across the street.

→ Across the street ______________________.

19 밑줄 친 우리말과 일치하도록 〈조건〉에 맞게 문장을 완성하시오.

> A: The door is open. Did you lock the door before leaving?
> B: Yes, 나는 정말로 문을 잠갔어. (lock, door) Maybe someone is inside the house.

> 조건 1. 동사를 강조하는 문장으로 쓸 것
> 2. 총 5단어로 쓸 것

→ ______________________________

20 빈칸에 알맞은 대답을 〈조건〉에 맞게 완성하시오.

> A: We have a science test on Thursday, right?
> B: No, ______________________________.

> 조건 1. on Friday를 포함할 것
> 2. It is/was ~ that ... 강조 구문을 사용하여 총 10단어로 쓸 것

→ No, ______________________________.

+ Memo

+ Memo

+ Memo

최신개정판

문법을 알면 영작이 쉽다!

Grammar Plus Writing

전지원 | 박혜영

WORKBOOK

중등 내신 · 서술형 시험 완벽 대비

- 중등 필수 영문법을 쉽고 간결하게 설명
- 영작 집중 훈련으로 기초를 탄탄히
- 최신 서술형 연습문제로 실전 대비

DARAKWON

Grammar Plus Writing

WORKBOOK

3

UNIT 01 단순시제, 진행형

Answer Key p.33

A GRAMMAR

괄호 안의 말을 알맞은 형태로 바꿔 문장을 완성하시오.

1 Yesterday, we ______________ packing for our trip. (start)

2 The bus usually ______________ at 8:00 a.m. (arrive)

3 They ______________ for an exam now. (study)

4 The moon ______________ around the Earth. (orbit)

5 I ______________ to the concert next Friday. I bought the ticket. (go)

6 Look! Someone ______________ to open your car door. (try)

7 I ______________ my arm while I was playing badminton. (break)

8 This time tomorrow, we ______________ our holiday. (enjoy)

9 World War II ______________ in 1945. (end)

10 We ______________ a movie when the power went out. (watch)

B WRITING

밑줄 친 부분을 바르게 고쳐 문장을 다시 쓰시오.

1 Dogs wags their tails when they are happy.

→ ____

2 Leonardo da Vinci paints the *Mona Lisa* in the 16th century.

→ ____

3 No one was helping me at the moment.

→ ____

4 The children are playing soccer when it started raining.

→ ____

5 At 5 o'clock tomorrow, I will camping with my friend's family.

→ ____

UNIT 02 완료시제

Answer Key p.33

A GRAMMAR

괄호 안에서 알맞은 것을 고르시오.

1 (Have, Had) you ever been to Europe?

2 We (have finished, will have finished) dinner before you come.

3 Lisa (has, had) just come back after two years in Mexico.

4 They (have, had) visited that museum before it closed down.

5 By next year, I (have studied, will have studied) Italian for two years.

6 I (have, had) already read the book before it became popular.

7 The room is so messy. It (hasn't been, won't have been) cleaned for days.

8 By next month, we (have traveled, will have traveled) to five countries.

9 Bob didn't realize that he (has, had) made a terrible mistake.

10 I can't find my keys. I (have, had) lost them somewhere.

B WRITING

우리말과 일치하도록 괄호 안의 말을 이용하여 문장을 완성하시오.

1 너는 튀르키예 음식을 먹어 본 적이 있니? (ever, try, Turkish food)

→ ______________________________

2 나는 지난주 이후로 그에게서 소식을 듣지 못했다. (hear from)

→ ______________________________

3 내가 그의 집에 도착했을 때 그는 이미 떠난 상태였다. (already, leave)

→ When I got to his house, ____________________.

4 내년이면 그는 10년 동안 이 학교에서 일한 셈이 될 것이다. (work, at this school)

→ By next year, ____________________.

5 그의 부모님이 도착하실 때쯤에는 운동회가 끝나 있을 것이다. (sports day, end)

→ By the time his parents arrive, ____________________.

UNIT
03 완료진행형

Answer Key p.33

A GRAMMAR

괄호 안에서 알맞은 것을 고르시오.

1 Dad (is working, has been working) in the garden since morning.

2 The children (are playing, have been playing) soccer for two hours.

3 It (has been raining, had been raining) all week. I really want to go out.

4 I (have been waiting, had been waiting) for the bus for an hour before it arrived.

5 By next month, he (has been living, will have been living) in L.A. for a year.

6 She (has been practicing, will have been practicing) the piano since 2 o'clock.

7 I (have been studying, had been studying) for hours, so I took a short break.

8 Wendy (has been traveling, had been traveling) in Europe since July.

9 You are sweating a lot. How long (are you running, have you been running)?

10 At noon, Nick (has been sleeping, will have been sleeping) for nine hours.

B WRITING

우리말과 일치하도록 괄호 안의 말을 이용하여 문장을 완성하시오.

1 그 아이들은 한 시간째 진흙놀이를 하고 있다. (play with mud)

→ The children ______________________ for an hour.

2 나는 몇 주째 마라톤을 위해 연습 중이다. (practice for a marathon)

→ I ______________________ for weeks.

3 그는 내가 집에 도착했을 때 하루 종일 TV를 보고 있었다. (watch TV)

→ He ______________________ all day when I got home.

4 내년이면 그는 10년 동안 의사로 일하고 있는 셈이 될 것이다. (work as a doctor)

→ By next year, he ______________________ for ten years.

5 2시가 되면 그들은 한 시간 동안 통화하고 있는 셈이 될 것이다. (talk on the phone)

→ At 2 o'clock, they ______________________ for an hour.

UNIT

01 조동사

Answer Key p.33

A GRAMMAR

괄호 안에서 알맞은 것을 고르시오.

1 (Could, Should) you help me with this assignment? I really need your help.

2 You (must not, don't have to) bring pets into the museum. It is not allowed.

3 You (had better, would) tell him the truth. Otherwise, he might be very upset.

4 Carol (might, used to) bite her fingernails when she was nervous.

5 I (can't, would rather) get a used computer than spend a lot of money on a new one.

6 You (must not, don't have to) apologize. It wasn't your fault.

7 Last night, Claire (must, had to) rush to the hospital because of her son.

8 It (may, cannot) rain tonight. I'll bring my umbrella just in case.

9 What do you think I (would, should) do? Do you have any suggestions?

10 The man (must, can't) be Mike. He has gone to Germany to study.

B WRITING

우리말과 일치하도록 괄호 안의 말을 이용하여 문장을 완성하시오.

1 Susan은 프랑스어를 유창하게 할 수 있다. (able, speak French)

→ Susan ______________________________ fluently.

2 나는 어렸을 때 초콜릿을 매우 좋아했었다. (used, love chocolate)

→ I ______________________________ when I was young.

3 너는 아침을 거르지 않는 것이 좋겠다. (better, skip breakfast)

→ You ______________________________.

4 그가 말한 것은 사실일 리가 없다. (true)

→ What he said ______________________________.

5 Andy는 학교 갈 때 교복을 입을 필요가 없다. (wear a uniform)

→ Andy ______________________________ to school.

UNIT
02 조동사 + have p.p.

Answer Key p.33

A GRAMMAR

괄호 안에서 알맞은 것을 고르시오.

1 Be careful. You (may make, may have made) a mistake.

2 Sally didn't answer my phone. She (may go, may have gone) to sleep.

3 I can't find my book. I (must leave, must have left) it on the bus.

4 Why don't you ask him for help? He (may help, may have helped) you.

5 What you said to Ann made her upset. You (should, shouldn't) have said that.

6 Ben didn't come to the party. He (may not know, may not have known) about it.

7 I (shouldn't snooze, shouldn't have snoozed) the alarm. Now I'm running late.

8 Sally hates exercising. She (can't go, can't have gone) to the gym every day.

9 My boss missed the meeting. He (must forget, must have forgotten) about it.

10 Why did you act so carelessly? You (may hurt, may have hurt) yourself.

B WRITING

우리말과 일치하도록 괄호 안의 말을 이용하여 문장을 완성하시오.

1 그는 시험공부를 열심히 했음에 틀림없다. (study for the exam)

→ He ______________________________ so hard.

2 상황은 이보다 더 나빠졌을지도 모른다. (get worse)

→ Things ______________________________ than this.

3 그들은 주말에 집에 없었을지도 모른다. (at home)

→ They ______________________________ over the weekend.

4 나는 영어에 더 많은 시간을 썼어야 했다. (spend more time)

→ I ______________________________ on English.

5 그녀가 나에 대해 그런 말을 했을 리가 없다. (say such a thing)

→ She ______________________________ about me.

UNIT
01 수동태의 의미와 형태

Answer Key p.34

A GRAMMAR

다음 문장을 수동태로 바꿔 쓰시오.

1 They clean the house every day.

→ The house ______________________ every day by them.

2 Someone wrote this old book thousands of years ago.

→ This old book ______________________ thousands of years ago.

3 We are planting trees in the garden.

→ Trees ______________________ in the garden by us.

4 People have used umbrellas since ancient times.

→ Umbrellas ______________________ since ancient times.

5 A famous chef will cook tonight's dinner.

→ Tonight's dinner ______________________ by a famous chef.

B WRITING

주어진 말을 순서대로 활용하여 수동태 문장을 완성하시오.

1 the window / break / a boy / last week

→ ____

2 the restaurant / renovate / at the moment

→ ____

3 the Olympic Games / hold / since 1896

→ ____

4 my new dress / deliver / tomorrow

→ ____

5 this problem / cannot / solve / me

→ ____

UNIT

02 4형식, 5형식 문장의 수동태

Answer Key p.34

A GRAMMAR

다음 문장을 〈보기〉와 같이 주어진 말로 시작하는 수동태로 바꿔 쓰시오.

| 보기 | The teacher gave us a lot of homework.
→ We were given a lot of homework by the teacher.

1 My father bought me a new game.

→ A new game ________________________________.

2 They call the boy Sammi.

→ The boy ________________________________.

3 The police made us stay away from the crime scene.

→ We ________________________________.

4 We saw a famous actor filming a movie.

→ A famous actor ________________________________.

B WRITING

주어진 말을 바르게 배열하여 문장을 완성하시오.

1 were / to / sent / the flowers / Jane

→ ________________________________ on her birthday.

2 made / me / for / this bag / was

→ ________________________________ by my sister.

3 will / the fence / yellow / painted / be

→ ________________________________ by the workers.

4 named / the baby girl / Olivia / was

→ ________________________________ by her parents.

5 put away / to / the kids / made / their toys / were

→ ________________________________ by their teacher.

UNIT
03 주의해야 할 수동태

Answer Key p.34

A GRAMMAR

다음 문장을 〈보기〉와 같이 주어진 말로 시작하는 수동태로 바꿔 쓰시오.

| 보기 | Mindy takes care of the dogs.
→ The dogs are taken care of by Mindy.

1 We will deal with the problem properly.

→ The problem ______________________________.

2 People believe that silence is golden.

→ It ______________________________.

3 People say that Mark is a nice person.

→ Mark ______________________________.

4 The scent of flowers filled the shop.

→ The shop ______________________________.

B WRITING

우리말과 일치하도록 괄호 안의 말을 이용하여 문장을 완성하시오.

1 그 컴퓨터는 나에 의해 켜졌다. (the computer, turn on)

→ ______________________________

2 그 보고서는 금요일까지 제출되어야 한다. (the report, must, hand in, by)

→ ______________________________

3 그 영화는 아주 흥미진진하다고 말해진다. (it, the movie, really exciting)

→ ______________________________

4 날씨가 화창할 것으로 예상된다. (the weather, expect, to, sunny)

→ ______________________________

5 나는 그의 지루한 농담을 듣는 것에 싫증이 난다. (tired, hearing his dull jokes)

→ ______________________________

to부정사의 용법

Answer Key p.34

A GRAMMAR

〈보기〉에서 알맞은 말을 골라 to부정사를 사용하여 문장을 완성하시오.

보기	do	go	hear	help
	play	read	run	win

1 My plan is __________ this entire book in a day.

2 It is extremely difficult __________ an Olympic gold medal.

3 I haven't decided where __________ for my next vacation.

4 He wants __________ a half-marathon next month.

5 We need time __________ our homework.

6 They volunteered at the shelter __________ homeless animals.

7 He is relieved __________ the good news.

8 This board game is fun __________.

B WRITING

주어진 말을 바르게 배열하여 문장을 완성하시오.

1 goal is / language / to / my / a / learn / new

→ ______________________________

2 haven't / they / decided / car / buy / to / which

→ ______________________________

3 I / read / interesting / to / need something

→ ______________________________

4 we / hotel room / stay / a / during / at / booked / to / our vacation

→ ______________________________

5 he / be / great / a / grew up / to / musician

→ ______________________________

UNIT 02 to부정사의 의미상 주어와 부정, 주요 구문

Answer Key p.34

A GRAMMAR

괄호 안에서 알맞은 것을 고르시오.

1 It is difficult (for, of) children to eat spicy food.

2 It is necessary (for, of) drivers to obey traffic rules.

3 It was thoughtful (for, of) her to remember my birthday.

4 She promised (to not tell, not to tell) anyone the secret.

5 The box is (so, too) small to fit all the items.

6 The suitcase is so heavy (to, that) I can't carry it.

7 The park is (big enough, enough big) for us to spend a day.

8 The book is so short that I (can, can't) read it in one sitting.

9 It seems (to, that) the movie is interesting.

10 Mary seems (being, to be) upset about something.

B WRITING

밑줄 친 부분을 바르게 고쳐 문장을 다시 쓰시오.

1 It is kind for her to help me with my homework.

→ ______________________________

2 It is difficult of beginners to play a musical instrument.

→ ______________________________

3 I use a calendar to not forget important dates.

→ ______________________________

4 This book is enough easy for me to understand.

→ ______________________________

5 She seems that dislike the new restaurant.

→ ______________________________

UNIT

03 다양한 형태의 목적격보어

Answer Key p.35

A GRAMMAR

괄호 안에서 알맞은 것을 고르시오.

1 The clerk asked us (take, to take) a number.

2 Let me (introduce, to introduce) myself.

3 They got me (joining, to join) their team.

4 I will have my hair (cut, cutting) this week.

5 He helped me (finding, to find) my way home.

6 Did you get your car (repair, repaired) yesterday?

7 I can smell something (burning, to burn) in the kitchen.

8 She heard her name (calling, called) by someone.

9 Nobody expected him (winning, to win) the race.

10 They made us (show, showing) our passports at the airport.

B WRITING

밑줄 친 부분을 바르게 고쳐 문장을 다시 쓰시오.

1 My friend told me stay calm.

→ ______________________________

2 She had her son washed the dishes.

→ ______________________________

3 We would like you bringing your own drinks.

→ ______________________________

4 She felt the wind to blow through her hair.

→ ______________________________

5 My brother didn't let me riding his bike.

→ ______________________________

UNIT 04 동명사

Answer Key p.35

A GRAMMAR

괄호 안의 말을 알맞은 형태로 바꿔 문장을 완성하시오.

1 She enjoys ____________ delicious meals for her friends. (cook)

2 We hope ____________ you again in the near future. (see)

3 Please turn down the music. I am trying ____________ here. (study)

4 The girls are busy ____________ pictures of themselves. (take)

5 We are looking forward to ____________ you soon. (meet)

6 We regret ____________ you that the flight has been delayed. (inform)

7 Do you mind ____________ me where you are from? (tell)

8 The children are excited about ____________ on a field trip. (go)

9 I usually spend a lot of money ____________ books for myself. (buy)

10 The actor refused ____________ about his private life. (talk)

B WRITING

우리말과 일치하도록 괄호 안의 말을 이용하여 문장을 완성하시오.

1 우리는 그 지루한 영화 보는 것을 멈추었다. (stop, watch, the boring movie)

→ ____

2 Teddy는 7시까지 돌아오겠다고 약속했다. (promise, come back, by 7 o'clock)

→ ____

3 나는 좋은 식당을 찾는 데 어려움을 겪었다. (difficulty, find, a good restaurant)

→ ____

4 그는 외국에 사는 것에 익숙하다. (used, live, in a foreign country)

→ ____

5 나는 히터 끄는 것을 잊어버렸다. (forget, turn off, the heater)

→ ____

UNIT
01 현재분사와 과거분사

Answer Key p.35

A GRAMMAR

괄호 안에서 알맞은 것을 고르시오.

1 The (smiling, smiled) children played with their toys.

2 The (baking, baked) cake smelled delicious.

3 My dad is fixing the (breaking, broken) door.

4 Who is the man (carrying, carried) your bags over there?

5 The bridge (building, built) over the river connects two towns.

6 I found him (watching, watched) TV on the sofa.

7 When he came in, he looked (exhausting, exhausted).

8 I think his jokes are always (amusing, amused).

9 You stayed up all night. It is not (surprising, surprised) that you feel tired.

10 It was a terrible experience. Everyone was (shocking, shocked).

B WRITING

밑줄 친 부분을 바르게 고쳐 문장을 다시 쓰시오.

1 The boy sat next to Amy is my brother.

→ ______________________________

2 It is excited that we can go swimming all together.

→ ______________________________

3 Can you think of a word begin with A?

→ ______________________________

4 They repaired the house damaging by the typhoon.

→ ______________________________

5 Was the food at the new restaurant satisfied?

→ ______________________________

UNIT 02 분사구문

Answer Key p.35

A GRAMMAR

다음 문장을 〈보기〉와 같이 분사구문으로 바꿔 쓰시오.

| 보기 | Because I felt tired, I went to bed early.
→ Feeling tired, I went to bed early.

1 When he drives to work, he listens to his favorite songs.

→ ______________________, he listens to his favorite songs.

2 If you exercise regularly, you will become healthier.

→ ______________________, you will become healthier.

3 Although he was busy, he made time to help his friend.

→ ______________________, he made time to help his friend.

4 Because I didn't want to be late, I woke up early.

→ ______________________, I woke up early.

B WRITING

우리말과 일치하도록 괄호 안의 말을 이용하여 문장을 완성하시오. (단, 분사구문으로 쓸 것)

1 그는 그 피아노를 옮기려고 하다가 허리를 다쳤다. (try to, move the piano)

→ He hurt his back ______________________.

2 휴대폰이 없어서, 나는 내 친구에게 전화할 수 없었다. (have a cellphone)

→ ______________________, I couldn't call my friend.

3 숙제를 마치고, 나는 공원으로 산책을 나갔다. (after, finish my homework)

→ ______________________, I went for a walk in the park.

4 노래를 잘해서, 그녀는 종종 무대에서 공연한다. (be good at, singing)

→ ______________________, she often performs on stage.

5 직진하면 당신은 버스 정류장이 보일 것입니다. (go straight)

→ ______________________, you will see the bus stop.

UNIT 03 주의해야 할 분사구문

Answer Key p.35

A GRAMMAR

밑줄 친 부분을 분사구문으로 바꿔 쓰시오.

1 As she grew up in Japan, she speaks Japanese fluently.

→ ______________________, she speaks Japanese fluently.

2 Since I haven't visited that museum, I plan to go there next week.

→ ______________________, I plan to go there next week.

3 Because he was badly hurt in the accident, he couldn't go to work.

→ ______________________, he couldn't go to work.

4 Although I was invited to the wedding, I can't attend it.

→ ______________________, I couldn't attend it.

5 Because it was too cold, we had to stay indoors.

→ ______________________, we had to stay indoors.

B WRITING

밑줄 친 부분을 바르게 고쳐 문장을 다시 쓰시오.

1 Having not checked the map, he got lost.

→ ______________________________________

2 Decorating with flowers, the cake looks beautiful.

→ ______________________________________

3 The dog greeted us with its tail wagged.

→ ______________________________________

4 He started talking with his eyes closing.

→ ______________________________________

5 Consider her age, she has a good memory.

→ ______________________________________

UNIT

01 원급, 비교급, 최상급

Answer Key p.36

A GRAMMAR

괄호 안에서 알맞은 것을 고르시오.

1 Dylan is as (tall, taller) as his mother.

2 Kate likes animals as (much, better) as I do.

3 Canada is not as (big, biggest) as Russia.

4 Steel is (stronger, strongest) than wood.

5 This quiz is (more, much) easier than the last one.

6 The roller coaster was (more, most) thrilling than the Viking.

7 Mount Everest is the (higher, highest) mountain in the world.

8 Jessica is (a, the) most intelligent student of the three.

9 This is the (more, most) delicious pizza I have ever tasted.

10 The Great Wall of China is one of the longest (wall, walls) in the world.

B WRITING

우리말과 일치하도록 괄호 안의 말을 이용하여 문장을 완성하시오.

1 이 자동차는 스포츠카만큼 빠르다. (fast, a sports car)

→ This car is ______________________________.

2 그녀의 영어 실력은 그녀의 언니만큼 좋지 않다. (good, her sister's)

→ Her English is ______________________________.

3 그는 그 팀에서 최고의 선수이다. (good, player, on the team)

→ He is ______________________________.

4 그의 스마트폰은 내 것보다 훨씬 더 발전된 것이다. (advanced)

→ His smartphone is ______________________________.

5 이것은 내가 지금까지 치른 것 중 가장 어려운 시험이었다. (difficult, test, take)

→ This was ______________________________.

UNIT
02 여러 가지 비교 표현

Answer Key p.36

A GRAMMAR

괄호 안에서 알맞은 것을 고르시오.

1 The green building is (two, twice) as tall as the red one.

2 This house is (four times bigger, bigger four times) than that one.

3 Mr. Lee left the office as quickly as he (can, could).

4 Lily types (more accurately, as accurately as) possible to avoid mistakes.

5 The music is getting (louder and louder, the loudest).

6 The party became (better and better, more and more) exciting.

7 The more you practice, the (better, best) you will become.

8 The higher you climb, the (far, farther) you can see.

9 John is funnier than any other (student, students) in the class.

10 No other dessert in the bakery is (as sweet as, the sweetest) this one.

B WRITING

우리말과 일치하도록 괄호 안의 말을 이용하여 문장을 완성하시오.

1 새 차는 중고차보다 다섯 배 더 비싸다. (expensive)

→ The new car is ______________________________ than the used car.

2 그는 자신의 직장 동료의 절반만큼 번다. (half, much)

→ He earns ______________________________ his coworker.

3 그 강좌는 점점 더 어려워지고 있다. (difficult)

→ The course is becoming ______________________________.

4 너는 더 많이 운동할수록 더 건강해질 것이다. (healthy)

→ _______________ you exercise, _______________ you will become.

5 Grace는 다른 어떤 주자보다 더 빨리 결승점을 통과했다. (fast, runner)

→ Grace crossed the finish line ______________________________.

UNIT
01 부사절 접속사

Answer Key p.36

CHAPTER 07 접속사

A GRAMMAR

괄호 안에서 알맞은 것을 고르시오.

1 I listened to music (while, though) I was cooking dinner.

2 Christina has studied in New York (when, since) 2020.

3 You can't go out (until, because) you finish your homework.

4 (If, Even though) it rains tomorrow, we will stay indoors.

5 You won't pass the test (if, unless) you review the material.

6 You can borrow my car (unless, as long as) you bring it back by tonight.

7 (Because, Though) it was too hot, we couldn't go for a walk.

8 (As, Although) she was tired, she continued working.

9 I bought a new laptop (unless, so that) I can work more efficiently.

10 Mark likes coffee (because, while) Tim prefers tea.

B WRITING

우리말과 일치하도록 괄호 안의 말을 이용하여 문장을 완성하시오.

1 그는 기타를 연주하면서 노래를 불렀다. (as, play the guitar)

→ He sang a song ____________________.

2 해가 질 때, 하늘은 오렌지색으로 변한다. (when, the sun, set)

→ ____________________, the sky turns orange.

3 Jane은 활동적인 반면에 그녀의 여동생은 수줍음이 많다. (while, her sister, shy)

→ Jane is outgoing ____________________.

4 비가 내리고 있었지만, 우리는 캠핑을 가기로 결정했다. (although, it, rain)

→ ____________________, we decided to go camping.

5 영화가 시작하자마자, 그들은 휴대폰을 껐다. (as soon as, the movie, start)

→ ____________________, they turned off their cellphones.

UNIT
02 상관접속사, 명사절 접속사

Answer Key p.36

A
GRAMMAR

다음 문장을 〈보기〉와 같이 간접의문문으로 바꿔 쓰시오.

| 보기 | I don't know. Why is she late for the meeting?
→ I don't know why she is late for the meeting.

1 Please tell me. Who is responsible for the project?

→ Please tell me ______________________.

2 I wonder. Is she going to attend the concert?

→ I wonder ______________________.

3 I don't know. What time will he arrive?

→ I don't know ______________________.

4 I want to know. How did they solve the problem?

→ I want to know ______________________.

B
WRITING

우리말과 일치하도록 괄호 안의 말을 이용하여 문장을 완성하시오.

1 축구와 농구 모두 전 세계에서 인기가 있다. (both, soccer, basketball)

→ ______________________ popular around the world.

2 너는 그 파티에 가거나 집에 있을 수 있다. (either, go to the party, stay home)

→ You can ______________________.

3 고양이도 개도 목욕하기를 좋아하지 않는다. (neither, cats, dogs, like)

→ ______________________ to take baths.

4 Helen뿐만 아니라 Elaine도 춤을 잘 춘다. (only, also)

→ ______________________ good at dancing.

5 Emily는 노래를 부르는 것뿐만 아니라 곡을 쓰는 것도 즐긴다. (well, sing, write songs)

→ Emily enjoys ______________________.

관계대명사

Answer Key p.36

A GRAMMAR

괄호 안에서 알맞은 것을 고르시오.

1 The boy (who, which) is standing over there is my cousin.
2 The dog (that, what) Silvia adopted is very playful.
3 I have a friend (what, whose) father is a politician.
4 She showed me the photos (who, which) were taken in Hawaii.
5 I saw a house (which, whose) roof is pink.
6 I work with people (who, which) are friendly and generous.
7 The car (that, who) I bought last month broke down.
8 Frank found the bag (that, what) he had lost.
9 Just tell me (that, what) you need.
10 Nick did (what, whose) he planned to do.

B WRITING

어법상 틀린 부분을 바르게 고쳐 문장을 다시 쓰시오.

1 I met a woman whose won a gold medal at the Olympics.
→ ______________________________

2 The young man who live next door seems nice.
→ ______________________________

3 The child that parents are doctors wants to be a doctor, too.
→ ______________________________

4 The movie that we watched it last night was boring.
→ ______________________________

5 The teacher explained that we needed to do for the test.
→ ______________________________

UNIT
02 관계부사, 복합관계사

Answer Key p.37

A
GRAMMAR

괄호 안에서 알맞은 것을 고르시오.

1 This is the park (where, when) we used to play as children.

2 I remember the day (when, why) we first dated.

3 Do you know the reason (when, why) he canceled the trip?

4 Tom taught me (how, the way how) he baked the chocolate cake.

5 This town is (where, which) I was born and raised.

6 The house in (which, where) I lived is now a restaurant.

7 I won't believe (whatever, whichever) he says.

8 I don't care (whoever, wherever) you go.

9 (Whoever, Whenever) needs help can ask me.

10 (Whenever, However) you need help, you can call me.

B
WRITING

밑줄 친 부분을 바르게 고쳐 문장을 다시 쓰시오.

1 Do you remember the night where we saw the fireworks?

→ ______________________________

2 Nobody knows the reason how he was absent.

→ ______________________________

3 I don't know the way how he fixed the air conditioner.

→ ______________________________

4 However you try hard, you can't change my mind.

→ ______________________________

5 This is the room which my father often works.

→ ______________________________

UNIT 03 주의해야 할 관계사 용법

Answer Key p.37

A GRAMMAR

다음 문장에서 생략할 수 있는 부분을 괄호로 묶으시오.

1 The bag which I bought last week is bright red.

2 Tiffany has a brother who is studying abroad.

3 Have you seen the pen which was on the table?

4 Steve bought a car which he can't afford.

5 Erin is wearing a dress that she bought online.

6 The music which I am listening to is great.

7 The bus that I was waiting for was late.

8 The person whom I voted for did not win the election.

9 The island that we spent our vacation on was fantastic.

10 Jisoo is the student who is responsible for the event.

B WRITING

우리말과 일치하도록 괄호 안의 말을 이용하여 문장을 완성하시오.

1 그는 축구를 함께 하는 친구가 있다. (play soccer)

→ He has a friend with ______________________.

2 Rosa는 그녀가 찾고 있던 반지를 마침내 찾았다. (look for)

→ Rosa finally found her ring for ______________________.

3 내 남동생 Dave는 의사인데, 그 병원에서 일한다. (a doctor)

→ My brother Dave, ______________________, works at the hospital.

4 보스턴은 내가 가장 좋아하는 도시인데, 뉴욕과 가깝다. (my favorite city)

→ Boston, ______________________, is close to New York.

5 기말고사가 취소되었는데, 그것은 좋은 소식이다. (good news)

→ The final exams are canceled, ______________________.

UNIT
01 가정법 과거, 가정법 과거완료

Answer Key p.37

A
GRAMMAR

괄호 안에서 알맞은 것을 고르시오.

1 If it doesn't rain, we (will, would) go on a picnic.

2 If Susan (is, were) here, she would give us a hand.

3 If we (live, lived) closer, we could see more often.

4 If I had time, I (will, would) learn to play the drums.

5 If he had invited me, I (would accept, would have accepted) the invitation.

6 If Eric (didn't miss, hadn't missed) the bus, he wouldn't have been late.

7 If I (listened, had listened) to his advice, I might have avoided the mistake.

8 If I were taller, I (may, might) be a basketball player.

9 If Bob lived abroad, he (would learn, would have learned) a new language.

10 If we (bought, had bought) the tickets, we could have gone to the concert.

B
WRITING

우리말과 일치하도록 괄호 안의 말을 이용하여 문장을 완성하시오.

1 내가 복권에 당첨된다면, 나는 세계를 여행할 텐데. (win, the lottery)

→ ______________________________, I would travel the world.

2 내가 미국인이라면, 영어를 공부할 필요가 없을 텐데. (American)

→ ______________________________, I wouldn't need to study English.

3 그가 더 열심히 공부했다면, 하버드에 들어갔을지도 모를 텐데. (study harder)

→ ______________________________, he might have gotten into Harvard.

4 내가 그녀의 전화번호를 안다면, 그녀에게 지금 당장 전화할 텐데. (call, right now)

→ If I knew her phone number, ______________________________.

5 Sue가 그녀의 일을 더 일찍 끝냈다면, 그 파티에 갔을 텐데. (go to the party)

→ If Sue had finished her work earlier, ______________________________.

UNIT

02 I wish 가정법, as if 가정법

Answer Key p.37

A GRAMMAR

다음 문장을 〈보기〉와 같이 가정법 문장으로 바꿔 쓰시오.

| 보기 | I am sorry that I don't have my own garden.
→ I wish I had my own garden.

1 I am sorry that I can't speak English better.

→ I wish ______________________.

2 I am sorry that I didn't study harder for the test.

→ I wish ______________________.

3 In fact, she is not a ballerina.

→ She dances as if ______________________.

4 In fact, they didn't attend the event.

→ They talk as if ______________________.

B WRITING

우리말과 일치하도록 괄호 안의 말을 이용하여 문장을 완성하시오.

1 내가 좀 더 자신감이 있다면 좋을 텐데. (more confident)

→ I wish ______________________.

2 내가 내 꿈을 포기하지 않았더라면 좋을 텐데. (give up, my dream)

→ I wish ______________________.

3 그녀는 마치 자신이 그 회사의 사장인 것처럼 행동한다. (the boss of the company)

→ She acts as if ______________________.

4 그는 마치 우리가 외계인인 것처럼 우리를 바라보았다. (aliens)

→ He looked at us as if ______________________.

5 Tim은 마치 그가 그 가수를 만났던 것처럼 말한다. (meet, the singer)

→ Tim talks as if ______________________.

UNIT
03 주의해야 할 가정법

Answer Key p.37

A GRAMMAR

괄호 안에서 알맞은 것을 고르시오.

1 If we had left earlier, we (would be, would have been) at school now.

2 If Kate (took, had taken) a nap, she would feel more energized.

3 If it (didn't snow, hadn't snowed) a lot last night, schools wouldn't be closed.

4 (Without, But) your support, I wouldn't have achieved my goals.

5 (Without, But) for the rain, we would have gone to the beach.

6 If it (were not, had not been) for water, plants would not grow.

7 If it (were not, had not been) for the treatment, I would have been worse.

8 (Were, Had) I taller, I could sit in the back of the classroom.

9 (Were, Had) I known about the event, I would have attended it.

10 Had I been you, I (wouldn't miss, wouldn't have missed) the opportunity.

B WRITING

우리말과 일치하도록 괄호 안의 말을 이용하여 문장을 완성하시오.

1 내가 내 우산을 가져왔다면, 지금 젖지 않을 텐데. (bring, get wet)

→ If I ______________ my umbrella, I ______________ now.

2 공기가 없다면, 우리는 소리를 들을 수 없을 텐데. (hear)

→ If it ______________ air, we ______________ sound.

3 당신의 지원이 없었다면, 나는 실패했을 텐데. (fail)

→ If it ______________ your support, I ______________.

4 내가 좀 더 계획적이라면, 내 시간을 더 잘 관리할 수 있을 텐데. (manage)

→ __________ I more organized, I ______________ my time better.

5 그에게 조금 더 참을성이 있었다면, 화를 내지 않았을 텐데. (lose)

→ __________ he been more patient, he ______________ his temper.

일치

Answer Key p.38

괄호 안에서 알맞은 것을 고르시오.

1 Everybody in the room (has, have) a chair.

2 Each of the students (has, have) a textbook.

3 The Netherlands (is, are) the member of the European Union.

4 Physics (is, are) one of the most difficult subjects to learn.

5 Five dollars (is, are) the price of admission to the museum.

6 Both the parents and the children (enjoy, enjoys) the family outings.

7 The poor (face, faces) a lot of challenges in life.

8 A number of hotel guests (is, are) waiting in the lobby.

9 The number of people in the room (is, are) approximately 50.

10 Some of the cars (is, are) parked in the wrong spots.

B
WRITING

밑줄 친 부분을 바르게 고쳐 문장을 다시 쓰시오.

1 Ten years are a long time.

→ ______________________________

2 Each of the flowers need to be watered daily.

→ ______________________________

3 Half of the movie were boring.

→ ______________________________

4 I thought she is very upset then.

→ ______________________________

5 We expected he will come to the party yesterday.

→ ______________________________

UNIT

02 화법

Answer Key p.38

A GRAMMAR

다음 문장을 〈보기〉와 같이 간접화법으로 바꿔 쓰시오.

| 보기 | She said to me, "I want to learn how to dance."
→ She told me (that) she wanted to learn how to dance.

1 Bob said to me, "When will you go home?"

→ Bob asked me ______________________.

2 My friend said to me, "Can you cook rice?"

→ My friend asked me ______________________.

3 She said to Tim, "Pass me the salt."

→ She asked Tim ______________________.

4 Emily said to me, "Don't close the window."

→ Emily told me ______________________.

B WRITING

주어진 말을 바르게 배열하여 문장을 완성하시오.

1 we / a / have / that / would / test

→ The teacher told us ______________________.

2 I / my / put / where / had / keys

→ Mom asked me ______________________.

3 I / the way / if / knew / the museum / to

→ She asked me ______________________.

4 the / drive / to / driver / slowly / told

→ Amy ______________________.

5 forget / not / buy / to / milk / to

→ He told me ______________________.

UNIT

03 강조, 도치

Answer Key p.38

A GRAMMAR

괄호 안에서 알맞은 것을 고르시오.

1 She does (drink, drinks) coffee in the morning.

2 They (do, did) go hiking last Saturday.

3 Mark and Alex (do, does) miss going to their granddad's.

4 (It, They) was Tom and Jane that I saw last weekend.

5 Rarely (they are, are they) late for work.

6 Hardly (she complains, does she complain) about anything.

7 Never (I have seen, have I seen) such a talented musician.

8 Not only (he finished, did he finish) the project, but he also received an A.

9 Behind the fence (a peaceful garden is, is a peaceful garden).

10 At the door (the package arrived, arrived the package).

B WRITING

우리말과 일치하도록 괄호 안의 말을 이용하여 문장을 완성하시오.

1 우리는 하늘에서 유성을 정말로 보았다. (do, see)

→ We ______________________________ a shooting star in the sky.

2 내가 책을 발견한 곳은 바로 선반 위였다. (on the shelf)

→ It ______________________________ I found the book.

3 그 노트북을 고장 낸 사람은 바로 Liam이었다.

→ It ______________________________ broke the laptop.

4 그들은 저녁을 먹으러 거의 나가지 않는다. (go out)

→ Hardly ______________________________ for dinner.

5 그 오래된 동굴에는 해적의 보물 상자가 있다. (a pirate's treasure chest)

→ In the old cave ______________________________.

+ Memo

+ Memo

최신개정판

문법을 알면 영작이 쉽다!

Grammar Plus Writing

ANSWER KEY

3

DARAKWON

Grammar Plus Writing

ANSWER KEY

3

Chapter 01
시제

UNIT 01 단순시제, 진행형

GRAMMAR FOCUS p.11

EXERCISE A

1 am watching
2 boils
3 was
4 broke
5 am going
6 will be camping
7 I'll have

해석

1 나는 지금 TV를 보고 있다.
2 물은 섭씨 100도에서 끓는다.
3 Emma는 내가 방에 들어갔을 때 공부하고 있었다.
4 그의 차는 그가 운전해서 출근하는 동안 고장이 났다.
5 나는 너와 함께 갈 수 없어. 나는 오늘 할아버지와 할머니를 방문할 예정이야.
6 다음 주 이맘때쯤, 우리는 산에서 캠핑하고 있을 것이다.
7 A: 주문할 준비가 되셨나요?
B: 네, 저는 스테이크로 할게요.

EXERCISE B

1 drinks
2 is shining
3 have
4 was reading
5 will be studying
6 will[is going to] be

해석

1 그녀는 주로 아침에 커피를 마신다.
2 (날씨가) 좋은 날이다. 태양이 빛나고 있다.
3 나에게는 오빠 한 명과 언니 한 명이 있다.
4 어젯밤에 나는 침대에서 책을 읽다가 잠이 들었다.
5 Ann은 오후 3시까지 공부할 계획이다. 오후 2시 50분에 그녀는 공부하고 있을 것이다.
6 일기 예보에 따르면, 이번 주말은 추울 것이다.

EXERCISE C

1 went
2 were, doing
3 closes
4 am looking
5 saw
6 will[is going to] be
7 will be watching

해석

1 어제, 우리는 박물관으로 현장 학습을 갔다.
2 내가 너에게 전화했을 때 너는 무엇을 하고 있었니?
3 도서관은 토요일에 오후 5시에 문을 닫는다.
4 나는 내 가방을 찾고 있어. 너는 그게 어디 있는지 아니?
5 Jack은 해변을 걷고 있는 동안 거북이를 보았다.
6 나의 할머니는 다음 달에 80세가 되실 것이다.
7 영화가 지금 시작한다. 우리는 몇 분 후에 그것을 보고 있을 것이다.

WRITING FOCUS pp.12-13

A

1 He takes vitamins with a glass of water
2 Rachel traveled to Europe for vacation
3 It will get colder
4 He is making pizza and spaghetti
5 He was driving on the highway
6 I will be relaxing at home

B

1 is singing
2 were you doing
3 did he study
4 is going to rain
5 arrives
6 is going

C

1 eats sandwiches for lunch
2 runs every 30 minutes
3 bought an interesting book
4 is learning a new language
5 was practicing the piano
6 are going to leave for Busan / are leaving for Busan

D

1 Mary likes her new job.
2 She always makes her bed in the morning.
3 The temperature dropped below freezing last night.
4 Pedro was taking a shower when the water stopped.
5 What will you be doing at 10 o'clock tomorrow?
6 I promise I will be there on time.

UNIT 02 완료시제

GRAMMAR FOCUS p.15

EXERCISE A

1 have eaten
2 started

3 has
4 had
5 will have lived
6 haven't gone

해석

1 나는 그 새로운 식당에서 두 번 먹어 봤다.
2 그녀는 일곱 살 때 피아노를 치기 시작했다.
3 Emily는 그녀의 지갑을 잃어버려서 돈이 조금도 없다.
4 우리가 극장에 도착했을 때, 그 영화는 이미 시작했다.
5 내년이면 우리는 5년 동안 이 도시에서 산 셈이 될 것이다.
6 그들은 지난 여름 이후로 가족 여행을 가지 않았다.

EXERCISE B

1 since
2 Have you ever tried
3 hasn't come
4 had forgotten
5 will have finished
6 had seen

해석

1 우리는 지난달 이후로 서로를 보지 못했다.
2 너는 전에 초밥을 먹어 본 적이 있니? 그것은 맛있어.
3 Luke는 아직도 버스를 기다리고 있다. 그것은 아직 오지 않았다.
4 엄마는 내가 전화하는 걸 깜빡해서 화가 나셨다.
5 그들은 손님들이 도착할 때까지 요리를 끝마칠 것이다.
6 나는 전에 어딘가에서 그녀를 본 적이 있다고 생각했다.

EXERCISE C

1 have just arrived
2 have taught
3 had been
4 will have studied

WRITING FOCUS

pp.16-17

A

1 Joe has gained a lot of weight
2 Have you ever eaten
3 How long has she been
4 Chris has already spent
5 he had left his cellphone at home
6 Amy will have graduated from university

B

1 have been, were
2 haven't washed
3 have you read
4 had already ordered
5 had never seen
6 will have stopped

C

1 have never played the violin
2 have just arrived at the train station
3 has had the same job for thirteen years
4 he had worked in London before
5 his old one had broken down
6 she will have completed her project

D

1 Have you ever learned to dance?
2 Mr. Brown has been to Egypt twice.
3 The old couple has lived in the country for many years.
4 He didn't know that someone had stolen his wallet.
5 My brother had already eaten the cake when I got home.
6 By the time I wake up, my mom will have gone to work.

UNIT 03 완료진행형

GRAMMAR FOCUS

p.19

EXERCISE A

1 is raining
2 has been studying
3 has had
4 has been listening
5 have you been painting
6 has been singing

해석

1 밖을 봐. 지금 비가 내리고 있어.
2 Chris는 2시부터 공부를 하고 있다.
3 나의 아버지는 10년 동안 그의 차를 갖고 계신다.
4 Lisa는 하루 종일 크리스마스 음악을 듣고 있다.
5 너는 얼마나 오랫동안 이 그림을 그리고 있니?
6 Judy는 한 시간째 같은 노래를 부르고 있다.

EXERCISE B

1 have been looking
2 had been running
3 will have been driving
4 have been playing
5 had been working
6 will have been waiting

해석

1 나는 오늘 아침부터 내 열쇠를 찾고 있다.
2 Jim은 내가 그에게 전화했을 때 한 시간째 뛰고 있었다.
3 그는 집에 도착할 때까지 세 시간 동안 운전하고 있는 셈이 될 것이다.
4 Sue와 Eric은 테니스를 치고 있다. 그들은 두 시간째 그것을 치고 있다.
5 David는 오랫동안 일을 하고 있었기 때문에 피곤했다.

6 Andy는 아직 오지 않았다. 2시가 되면, 나는 그를 한 시간 동안 기다리고 있는 셈이 될 것이다.

EXERCISE C

1 have been walking
2 has been taking
3 had been studying
4 will have been reading

WRITING FOCUS

pp.20-21

A

1 Fred has been playing a computer game
2 How long have you been waiting
3 It has been raining
4 He had been sleeping for ten hours
5 I had been playing on the beach
6 we will have been shopping

B

1 have been talking
2 have been working
3 have you known
4 am not studying, am watching
5 had been using
6 will have been raining

C

1 has been swimming for an hour
2 Is it snowing
3 has been using the computer since 3 o'clock
4 they had been hiking for two hours
5 he will have been sleeping for ten hours
6 will have been living in our new house for a year

D

1 Eric has been taking a nap for 30 minutes.
2 Liam has known Amy for fifteen years.
3 The children have been playing since they woke up.
4 She had been studying for two hours when her friend called.
5 By next June, I will have been attending this school for three years.
6 By tomorrow, Jessica will have been working here for a year.

ACTUAL TEST

pp.22-24

01 ④ 02 ④ 03 ⑤ 04 ⑤
05 ②, ⑤ 06 ③ 07 ② 08 ③
09 (1) finished (2) am going to work
10 (1) I have never worn contact lenses.
(2) The computer has not been working well for days.
11 told me, had lost
12 has been traveling around Europe since
13 (1) didn't have → haven't[have not]
(2) has been having → has had
14 have gone → went
15 (1) was doing the dishes when he arrived
(2) I will be studying at the library
16 (1) is doing her homework
(2) has been doing her homework
17 ⓓ → has been waiting
18 (1) The concert had already started when we arrived.
(2) By tomorrow, he will have fixed the car.
19 Have you ever thought about becoming a vet?
20 What are you doing

01 ④ is sleeping → was sleeping으로 고쳐야 알맞다.

02 〈보기〉와 ④는 미래를 나타내는 현재시제이고, 나머지는 현재의 사실이나 습관을 나타낸다.

03 가까운 미래에 예정된 계획은 현재진행형으로 나타낼 수 있다. (I am going camping with my friends tomorrow.)

04 과거(changed)보다 앞선 과거는 과거완료를 써서 「had+p.p.」 형태로 쓴다.

05 ② didn't go → haven't been to, ⑤ have eaten → ate로 고쳐야 알맞다.

06 과거부터 지금까지 진행 중인 일은 현재완료진행형을 써서 「have/has been+동사원형-ing」 형태로 쓴다.

07 ⓐ have been dancing → are dancing, ⓑ has not studied → did not study, ⓔ have finished → will have finished로 고쳐야 알맞다.

08 ⓐ have been knowing → have known, ⓑ have you reading → have you been reading, ⓔ will be studying → will have been studying으로 고쳐야 알맞다.

09 (1) 30 minutes ago는 과거를 나타내므로 과거시제(finished)를 쓴다.
(2) next month는 미래를 나타내므로 「will+동사원형」 또는 「be going to+동사원형」 형태로 쓴다.

10 (1) '~해 본 적이 한 번도 없다'는 「have/has never+p.p.」로 나타낸다.
(2) 지금도 진행 중인 일이 기간(for days)을 나타내는 말과 함께 쓰이면 현재완료진행형을 써서 「have/has been+동사원형-ing」 형태로 쓴다.

11 친구가 나에게 말한 것은 과거(told)이고, 내 책을 잃어버린 것은 그 이전에 일어난 일이므로 과거완료(had lost)를 쓴다.

12 현재완료진행형은 「have/has been+동사원형-ing」 형태이다. 7월부터 여행을 하고 있으므로 July 앞에는 since가 와야 한다.

13 (1) 현재완료 부정문은 「have/has not+p.p.」 형태이다.
(2) 상태와 소유를 나타내는 동사는 진행형을 쓰지 않으므로 현재완료로 대신한다.

14 과거 특정 시점(last month)을 나타내는 말이 올 경우에는 과거시제를 쓴다.
해석 A: 안녕, 어떻게 지냈니?
B: 잘 지냈어. 너는 어때?
A: 좋아. 나는 지난달에 발리에 갔었어.
B: 와! 어땠어?
A: 거기에 일주일 동안 머물렀는데 그곳의 모든 것이 아주 좋았어.

15 (1) '~하고 있었다'는 과거진행형을 써서 「was/were+동사원형-ing」 형태로 쓴다.
(2) '~하고 있을 것이다'는 미래진행형을 써서 「will be+동사원형-ing」 형태로 쓴다.

16 (1) 지금(now)은 현재진행형과 어울리는 시간 표현이다. 현재진행형은 「am/is/are+동사원형-ing」 형태로 쓴다.
(2) 지금도 진행 중인 일이 기간(for two hours)을 나타내는 말과 함께 쓰이면 현재완료진행형을 써서 「have/has been+동사원형-ing」 형태로 쓴다.

17 과거부터 지금까지 계속 기다리는 상황이므로 ⓓ는 현재완료진행형으로 고쳐야 알맞다.
해석 Chris는 Lucy를 기다리고 있다. 그는 2시에 그녀를 기다리기 시작했다. 지금은 3시다. 그는 한 시간째 그녀를 기다리고 있다. 4시가 되면 그는 Lucy를 두 시간 동안 기다리고 있는 셈이 될 것이다.

18 (1) 도착한 것은 과거이므로 arrived, 콘서트는 그 이전에 시작했으므로 과거완료를 써서 had already started로 나타낸다.
(2) 미래 특정 시점까지 완료될 일은 미래완료를 써서 「will have+p.p.」형태로 쓴다.

[19-20]
해석 A: 너는 수의사가 되는 것을 생각해 본 적이 있니?
B: 응, 해봤어. 나는 동물들, 특히 개와 고양이를 좋아해.
A: 그거 잘됐다. 너는 네 꿈을 이루기 위해 무엇을 하고 있니?
B: 나는 지역 동물 보호소에서 자원봉사 활동을 하고 동물에 관한 책들을 읽고 있어.
A: 훌륭하구나! 나는 네가 훌륭한 수의사가 될 거라고 믿어.

19 '~해 본 적이 있니?'라고 경험을 물을 때는 「Have you ever+p.p. ~?」로 묻는다.

20 현재진행형 의문문은 「의문사+am/is/are+주어+동사원형-ing ~?」 형태이다.

Chapter 02
조동사

UNIT 01 조동사

GRAMMAR FOCUS p.27

EXERCISE A

1 ⓒ 2 ⓓ 3 ⓔ
4 ⓕ 5 ⓑ 6 ⓐ

해석
1 Jessica는 교실에 있을지도 모른다.
2 승객들은 그들의 안전벨트를 착용해야 한다.
3 10대들은 술을 마시면 안 된다.
4 Eric은 정장을 입고 출근할 필요가 없다.
5 너는 내가 휴가 중일 때 내 차를 사용해도 돼.
6 Scott은 그가 열 살 때 기타를 연주할 수 있었다.

EXERCISE B

1 Can 2 can't
3 should 4 don't have to
5 had better not 6 would rather
7 used to

해석
1 집에 오는 길에 우유 좀 사다 줄 수 있니?
2 그 이야기는 말이 안 돼. 그것은 사실일 리가 없어.
3 그는 담배를 끊고 건강에 좋은 음식을 먹어야 한다.
4 우리는 줄을 서서 기다릴 필요가 없다. 우리에게는 VIP 패스가 있다.
5 너는 취업 면접에 늦지 않는 것이 좋겠어.
6 나는 스포츠를 보느니 차라리 체육관에 가겠다.
7 Sally는 초콜릿 먹는 것을 매우 좋아했지만 지금은 그것을 싫어한다.

EXERCISE C

1 am able to 2 has to
3 ought not to 4 would

해석

1 나는 왼손으로 글을 쓸 수 있다.
2 Ryan은 금요일까지 그의 보고서를 끝내야 한다.
3 너는 그 포도를 사면 안 된다. 그것은 안 좋아 보인다.
4 Kim과 Greg은 함께 스노보드를 타러 가곤 했다.

WRITING FOCUS

pp.28-29

A

1 He can run 100m
2 Can I borrow your car
3 It may be sunny
4 I had to finish my science project
5 Visitors must not take pictures
6 You don't have to bring anything

B

1 don't have to do
2 should[must] go
3 has to write
4 had better wear
5 would rather not watch
6 used to make

C

1 must be at the office
2 I may[might] go backpacking in Europe
3 He had to work overtime
4 You don't have to carry cash
5 He will be able to achieve his goal
6 We had better take a taxi

D

1 You don't have to pay for parking.
2 She can't be at home now.
3 In the future, robots will be able to do more jobs.
4 You must[should] not forget your passport.
5 You had better not leave your bag here.
6 I used to have long hair when I was in middle school.

UNIT 02 조동사+have p.p.

GRAMMAR FOCUS

p.31

EXERCISE A

1 be 2 have left 3 should
4 shouldn't 5 can't 6 must

해석

1 서두르자. 우리는 수업에 늦을지도 몰라.
2 나는 내 우산을 찾을 수 없다. 나는 그것을 버스에 두고 내렸을지도 모른다.
3 Joe는 그의 자전거에서 떨어졌다. 그는 좀 더 조심했어야 했다.
4 우리는 그 영화를 보지 말았어야 했다. 그것은 끔찍했다.
5 Tom이 이 편지를 썼을 리가 없다. 이것은 그의 필체가 아니다.
6 그녀는 물 세 잔을 마셨다. 그녀는 매우 목이 말랐음에 틀림없다.

EXERCISE B

1 should have bought
2 must have used
3 can't have gone out
4 may not have read

해석

1 A: 티켓이 금방 매진됐어.
B: 우리는 그것을 미리 샀어야 했어.
2 A: 오븐이 따뜻해.
B: 누군가 그것을 사용한 것임에 틀림없어.
3 A: 개는 어디 있어?
B: 그것은 나갔을 리가 없어. 문이 닫혀 있거든.
4 A: Dave가 내 이메일에 답장을 보내지 않았어.
B: 그는 아직 그것을 읽지 않았을지도 몰라.

EXERCISE C

1 should have done
2 can't have eaten
3 may[might] have lost

WRITING FOCUS

pp.32-33

A

1 Something may have happened to her.
2 Liam may not have gotten my message.
3 He must have forgotten about the meeting.
4 Mr. Jones can't have known the truth.
5 We should have practiced more for the game.
6 He shouldn't have told a lie.

B

1 may[might] have taken
2 may not have started
3 must have used
4 can't have been
5 should have set
6 shouldn't have chosen

C

1 He may[might] have felt sick
2 She must have spent a lot of money
3 The bus can't have left
4 He may[might] have been at the gym
5 You should have talked to me
6 I shouldn't[should not] have stayed up

D

1 Bob may have gone shopping.
2 She may not have seen me there.
3 I must have left my wallet in the car.
4 She can't have forgotten her own birthday.
5 He should have quit smoking a long time ago.
6 Somebody must have stolen my bike last night.

ACTUAL TEST

pp.34-36

01 ③	02 ⑤	03 ②	04 ⑤
05 ⑤	06 ④	07 ⑤	08 ②

09 (1) must (2) shouldn't (3) may not
10 (1) may have missed
(2) must have dropped
(3) should have bought
11 (1) You don't have to wait for me.
(2) You had better think twice
12 (1) You should not have eaten that fish.
(2) Dan can't have won the tennis match.
13 (1) must not (2) must have practiced
14 I used to be afraid of flying.
15 had better not park
16 (1) should have done
(2) must have rained
17 (1) must (2) don't have to
18 (1) should have been
(2) shouldn't have eaten
19 When I was a kid, my sister and I used to go to the beach to collect seashells.
20 I may have become a marine biologist.

01 첫 번째 빈칸에는 의미상 can, can't, may, 두 번째 빈칸에는 may가 적절하므로 ③ may가 알맞다.

02 일주일치 식료품을 구입했으므로, '~할 필요가 없다'는 의미의 ⑤ don't have to를 쓰는 것이 자연스럽다.

03 '~일리가 없다'는 강한 부정적 추측은 cannot[can't]을 사용한다.

04 '~했어야 했다'는 should have p.p. 형태로 쓴다.

05 과거의 상태는 would로 바꿔 쓸 수 없다.

06 had better의 부정형은 had better not이다.

07 시험공부를 하지 않았다는 내용이므로, 앞에는 '공부를 했어야 했다'의 의미인 should have studied를 써야 자연스럽다.

08 ⓑ has to → had to, ⓓ to hurry → hurry, ⓔ am used to → used to로 고쳐야 알맞다.

09 (1) '~임에 틀림없다'는 must를 사용한다. 어떤 근거를 바탕으로 확신을 갖고 추측할 때 쓴다.
(2) '~해서는 안 된다, ~하지 않는 것이 좋다'는 shouldn't를 사용한다.
(3) '~이 아닐지도 모른다'는 may not을 사용한다.

10 (1) '~했을지도 모른다'는 may have p.p.를 사용한다.
(2) '~했음에 틀림없다'는 must have p.p.를 사용한다.
(3) '~했어야 했다'는 should have p.p.를 사용한다.

11 (1) '~할 필요가 없다'는 don't have to를 사용한다.
(2) '~하는 것이 좋겠다'는 had better를 사용한다.

12 (1) '~하지 말았어야 했다'는 should not have p.p.를 사용한다.
(2) '~했을 리가 없다'는 can't have p.p.를 사용한다.

13 (1) '~해서는 안 된다'라는 금지의 뜻은 must not을 사용한다.
(2) '~했음에 틀림없다'라는 과거의 일에 대한 강한 추측은 must have p.p.를 사용한다.

14 '~하곤 했다'라는 과거의 상태는 「used to+동사원형」 형태로 쓴다. 동사 was가 쓰였으므로, used to 뒤에는 원형인 be가 온다.

15 주차 금지 구역임을 말하고 있으므로, '~하지 않는 것이 좋겠다'의 의미의 had better not을 쓸 수 있다.

16 (1) 과거에 하지 않은 일에 대해 후회하는 내용이므로 '~했어야 했다'의 의미인 should have p.p.를 사용한다.
(2) 과거의 일에 대한 강한 추측이나 확신은 '~했음에 틀림없다'의 의미인 must have p.p.를 사용한다.

17 (1) 과학 시험이 내일이라고 했으므로, '~해야 한다'의 의미인 must가 알맞다.
(2) 시험 일정이 변경되었다고 했으므로, '~할 필요가 없다'의 의미인 don't have to가 알맞다.

해석 A: 오, 안 돼! 과학 시험이 내일이야. 우리는 지금 바로 공부를 시작해야 해.
B: 진정해. 시험은 다음 주 금요일로 변경되었어. 우리는 지금 공부할 필요가 없어.
A: 정말 다행이다! 그렇다면 우리는 쉴 수 있겠네.

18 (1) 충분히 주의하지 않았다고 했으므로, '~했어야 했다'는 의미인 should have p.p.가 알맞다.
(2) 단것을 너무 많이 먹어서 이가 아프다고 했으므로, '~하지 말았어야 했다'의 의미인 shouldn't have p.p.가 알맞다.

[19-20]
해석 나는 플로리다의 해변 근처에서 자랐다. 어렸을 때 내

여동생과 나는 조개 껍데기를 모으기 위해 해변에 가곤 했다. 우리는 게와 새우 같은 바다 생물을 관찰하는 것을 좋아했다. 나는 해양 생물학자가 되었을지도 모른다. 하지만 나는 수학 교사가 되기로 했다. 나는 학생들을 가르치는 것을 즐기지만 시간이 나면 다이빙을 하러 가기 위해 작은 섬들을 방문한다. 아무도 가 보지 않은 곳에서 다이빙을 하는 것은 신나는 일이다.

19 '~하곤 했다'는 「used to+동사원형」 형태로 쓴다. (going → go)

20 '~했을지도 모른다'는 may have p.p.를 사용한다.

Chapter 03
수동태

UNIT 01 수동태의 의미와 형태

GRAMMAR FOCUS
p.39

EXERCISE A

1 coaches **2** baking
3 be cooked **4** been watched
5 been stolen **6** clean
7 disappeared

해석

1 John은 그 농구팀을 지도한다.
2 나의 엄마는 한 시간 전에 케이크를 굽고 계셨다.
3 그 음식은 전자레인지로 조리될 수 있다.
4 그 뮤직비디오는 수백만 명에 의해 시청되었다.
5 그 차는 경찰이 도착하기 전에 도난당했다.
6 나는 내 부모님이 집에 오시기 전에 집을 청소할 것이다.
7 그 배는 버뮤다 삼각 지대에서 사라졌다.

EXERCISE B

1 was broken **2** be changed
3 being watered **4** been translated
5 happened **6** don't resemble

해석

1 그 창문은 어젯밤에 폭풍우가 치는 동안 깨졌다.
2 비밀번호는 6개월마다 변경되어야 한다.
3 그 꽃들은 지금 정원사가 물을 주고 있다.
4 그 책은 여러 다른 언어들로 번역되어 왔다.
5 그 사고는 오늘 아침에 고속도로에서 일어났다.
6 내 여동생과 나는 쌍둥이지만, 우리는 서로 닮지 않았다.

EXERCISE C

1 were eaten **2** are being asked
3 have been written **4** will be launched

해석

1 내 남동생은 그 모든 쿠키를 먹었다.
→ 그 모든 쿠키는 내 동생이 먹었다.
2 그 남자는 몇 가지 질문을 하고 있다.
→ 몇 가지 질문이 그 남자에 의해 되고 있다.
3 J.K. Rowling은 많은 책을 썼다.
→ 많은 책이 J.K. Rowling에 의해 쓰였다.
4 그 회사는 신제품을 출시할 것이다.
→ 신제품이 그 회사에 의해 출시될 것이다.

WRITING FOCUS
pp.40-41

A
1 is run by a famous chef
2 was built 30 years ago
3 My computer is being fixed
4 The book can be borrowed
5 The shop has been closed
6 The party had already been canceled

B
1 was enjoyed
2 is being cooked
3 was being played
4 can be charged
5 has been parked
6 had, been completed

C
1 The Earth is being destroyed
2 The test was taken
3 A new bridge will be built
4 Reservations can be made
5 The animation has been loved
6 The room had already been cleaned

D
1 The door was fixed by my father yesterday.
2 The house is being painted by the workers now.
3 Payments can be made through the app.
4 The book belongs to the school library.
5 The flight has been canceled due to the bad weather.
6 New computers will be bought for students.

UNIT 02 4형식, 5형식 문장의 수동태

GRAMMAR FOCUS p.43

EXERCISE A

1 to 2 for 3 to
4 Kitty 5 to stop 6 to study
7 smiling

해석

1 피아노 열 대가 그 학교에 주어질 것이다.
2 그 티켓은 그녀의 친구가 그녀에게 사 준 것이다.
3 그 초대장은 이메일로 당신에게 보내졌다.
4 그 고양이는 내 가족에 의해 Kitty라고 불린다.
5 그 운전자는 경찰관에게 멈추라는 말을 들었다.
6 나는 나의 부모님에 의해 더 열심히 공부하도록 시켜졌다.
7 그 아기가 웃고 있는 모습이 그녀의 어머니에게 보였다.

EXERCISE B

1 was written to me by my friend
2 are taught English by Mr. Jones
3 was seen running away by the police
4 were made to wait in line by the staff

해석

1 내 친구가 나에게 편지를 썼다.
→ 편지는 내 친구가 나에게 써준 것이다.
2 Jones 선생님은 우리에게 영어를 가르치신다.
→ 우리는 Jones 선생님에게 영어를 배운다.
3 경찰은 그 도둑이 도망가고 있는 것을 보았다.
→ 그 도둑이 도망가고 있는 것이 경찰에 의해 목격되었다.
4 직원은 우리에게 줄을 서서 기다리게 시켰다.
→ 우리는 직원에 의해 줄을 서서 기다리도록 시켜졌다.

EXERCISE C

1 Korean 2 to us
3 for me 4 to go
5 crying / to cry 6 to sing

해석

1 그들은 학교에서 한국어를 배운다.
2 놀라운 소식이 Jane에 의해 우리에게 전해졌다.
3 그 수프는 나의 어머니가 나에게 요리해 주신 것이다.
4 그 아이들은 오후 9시 전에 잠자리에 들도록 시켜진다.
5 그녀가 자신의 방에서 혼자 우는 것이 보였다.
6 그는 관객들로부터 노래를 불러 달라는 요청을 받았다.

WRITING FOCUS pp.44-45

A

1 They are taught Spanish
2 The package was sent to me
3 The seaweed soup was made for me
4 I was made happy
5 The kids were made to wash their hands
6 The baby was heard to cry

B

1 was given the necklace
2 was awarded to
3 was called Jerry
4 were told to wait
5 were made to be quiet
6 was seen breaking into

C

1 was given to us by the teacher
2 is cooked for us every Sunday
3 was made angry by his rude comment
4 was heard playing the piano by me
5 was made to sit and stay by him
6 were asked to fasten their seatbelts by the driver

D

1 I was given useful information by Jackie.
2 The book was bought for me by my friend.
3 The story was told to me by my grandmother.
4 They were asked to follow the rules by the coach.
5 He was seen sleeping[to sleep] in class by the teacher.
6 I was made to take piano lessons by my mom.

UNIT 03 주의해야 할 수동태

GRAMMAR FOCUS p.47

EXERCISE A

1 by the vet 2 put off
3 laughed at 4 is reported
5 to be 6 with
7 of

해석

1 그 개는 수의사에 의해 돌봐지고 있다.
2 소풍은 비가 와서 연기되었다.
3 그 코미디언의 농담은 관객들로부터 비웃음을 받았다.
4 그 배우는 새 영화에서 주연을 맡을 것이라고 전해진다.
5 그는 그 나라에서 최고의 축구 선수라고 말해진다.

6 모든 나무들이 폭설 후에 눈으로 덮여 있다.
7 그녀는 위층에서 나는 소음에 지쳤다.

EXERCISE B

1 is said that Emily is kind / is said to be kind
2 is believed that John is a good leader / is believed to be a good leader

해석

1 사람들은 Emily가 친절하다고 말한다.
→ Emily는 친절하다고 말해진다.
2 그들은 John이 좋은 리더라고 믿는다.
→ John은 좋은 리더라고 믿어진다.

EXERCISE C

1 am interested in
2 were satisfied with
3 is known for
4 is made of

WRITING FOCUS pp.48-49

A

1 The goldfish was taken care of by Eric.
2 I won't be laughed at anymore.
3 It is expected that Martin will win the race.
4 The restaurant is said to be the best in the city.
5 The bookshelf is covered with dust.
6 Amy was tired of her job.

B

1 must be handed in
2 is said to be
3 is expected to graduate
4 is believed that
5 was crowded with
6 is satisfied with

C

1 will be dealt with
2 is looked up to by many people
3 is said that Susan is a great singer
4 is expected to give a presentation
5 is filled with paintings
6 is made from flour

D

1 The event was called off due to the pandemic.
2 The TV was turned off by Chris.
3 It is believed that they left the country.
4 Mark is said to be a hardworking man.
5 Sabrina is interested in Latin music.
6 The bag was filled with Christmas gifts.

ACTUAL TEST pp.50-52

01 ⑤ 02 ② 03 ② 04 ④
05 ③, ⑤ 06 ①, ④ 07 ④ 08 ③
09 (1) The buildings were destroyed by the earthquake.
(2) The traffic rules must be followed by all drivers.
10 (1) The national gallery is visited by many people.
(2) The house is being cleaned by Tom.
11 (1) been invited (2) made
12 My grandfather was looked up to by everybody.
13 (1) of (2) in (3) for
14 fix → be fixed
15 The cookies are being made by them.
16 (1) were shown the menu by the waiter
(2) was shown to us by the waiter
17 He is said to speak five languages.
18 ⓒ to → for ⓔ keep → be kept
19 Have his classes been canceled?
20 they are being taught by Ms. Taylor

01 방은 장식되는 것이므로 수동태가 적절하다. is 뒤에서 수동태로 쓸 수 있는 것은 ⑤ being decorated이다.
02 조동사 should가 있는 수동태이므로 「should+be+p.p.」 형태로 쓴다.
03 구동사(turn off)는 수동태에서 한 단어처럼 붙여 쓴다. (The power was turned off by the storm.)
04 ①②③⑤는 with, ④는 at 또는 by를 쓴다.
05 '~는 …라고 말해지다'는 「It is said that+주어+동사」 또는 「주어+is said to+동사원형」 형태로 쓴다.
06 4형식 문장의 수동태는 「간접목적어+be동사+p.p.+직접목적어」 또는 「직접목적어+be동사+p.p.+전치사+간접목적어」 형태로 쓴다. 직접목적어가 주어일 때 수여동사 give는 간접목적어 앞에 to를 쓴다.
07 사역동사의 목적격보어로 쓰인 동사원형은 수동태 문장에서 to부정사로 바뀐다. 따라서 I was made to do the dishes by my mom이 알맞다.
08 ⓒ were built → built, ⓔ has been canceled → has canceled로 고쳐야 알맞다.
09 (1) 과거시제의 수동태는 「was/were +p.p.」의 형태로 쓴다.

(2) 조동사가 있는 문장의 수동태는 「조동사+be+p.p.」 형태로 쓴다.

10 (1) 현재시제의 수동태는 「am/is/are+p.p.」의 형태로 쓴다.
(2) 진행형의 수동태는 「be동사+being+p.p.」의 형태로 쓴다.

11 (1) 파티에 초대된 것이므로 수동태를 써야 한다.
(2) My mom은 행위의 주체이므로 능동태를 써야 한다.

12 구동사(look up to)는 수동태에서 한 단어처럼 붙여 쓴다.

13 (1) be tired of: ~에 싫증나다
(2) be interested in: ~ 에 관심[흥미]이 있다.
(3) be known for: ~로 알려져 있다[유명하다]

14 에어컨은 수리되는 것이므로 will fix를 will be fixed로 고쳐야 알맞다.
해석 A: 오늘은 너무 더워. 에어컨 좀 틀어주실 수 있니?
B: 미안해. 고장 났어. 그것은 내일 고쳐질 거야.

15 진행형의 수동태는 「be동사+being+p.p.」의 형태로 쓴다.

16 4형식 문장의 수동태는 「간접목적어+be동사+p.p.+직접목적어」 또는 「직접목적어+be동사+p.p.+전치사+간접목적어」 형태로 쓴다. 직접목적어가 주어일 때 수여동사 show는 간접목적어 앞에 to를 쓴다.

17 '~는 …라고 말해지다'는 「It is said that+주어+동사」 또는 「주어+is said to+동사원형」 형태로 쓴다.

18 ⓒ 수여동사 buy는 직접목적어가 문장의 주어일 때 간접목적어 앞에 for를 쓴다.
ⓔ 치즈는 냉장고에 보관되는 것이므로 should be kept로 써야 알맞다.

[19-20]
해석 A: 과학 선생님이 독감에 걸리셨다는 소식 들었니?
B: 오, 안 돼! 지금 침대에 누워 계시겠구나.
A: 응, 며칠 동안은 돌아오시지 않을 거야.
B: 그분의 수업들은 취소되었니?
A: 아니, 그것들은 Taylor 선생님이 가르치고 계셔.
B: 그거 잘됐다. 선생님이 빨리 나으셨으면 좋겠어.

19 완료형의 수동태는 의문문일 때 「Have/Has/Had+주어+been+p.p. ~?」 형태로 쓴다.

20 진행형의 수동태는 「be동사+being+p.p.」의 형태로 쓴다.

Chapter 04
부정사와 동명사

UNIT 01 to부정사의 용법

GRAMMAR FOCUS
p.55

EXERCISE A
1 It
2 to play
3 go
4 to pronounce
5 live in
6 fun to do
7 to find

해석
1 더운 날씨에는 물을 마시는 것이 필수적이다.
2 그의 꿈은 NBA에서 농구를 하는 것이다.
3 우리는 오늘 식료품을 사러 가야 한다.
4 그는 그 단어를 어떻게 발음해야 할지 몰랐다.
5 그들은 공원 근처에 살기 좋은 집을 찾았다.
6 이번 주말에 할 재미있는 무언가를 찾아보자.
7 그녀는 자신의 지갑에서 잃어버린 열쇠를 발견하고 놀랐다.

EXERCISE B
1 where to park
2 how to use
3 what to buy

해석
1 그녀는 나에게 자신의 차를 어디에 주차해야 할지 물었다.
2 그는 나에게 복사기 사용하는 법을 보여 주었다.
3 Cathy는 언니의 생일을 위해 무엇을 사야 할지 생각하고 있다.

EXERCISE C
1 to win
2 to say
3 to lift
4 to be
5 to use

해석
1 그 팀은 그 경기에서 이기기 위해 열심히 연습했다.
2 그녀는 자신의 친구들에게 작별 인사를 해서 슬펐다.
3 저 무거운 상자를 들다니 그는 힘이 센 것임에 틀림없다.
4 그 소년은 자라서 유명한 배우가 되었다.
5 그 새로운 태블릿 PC는 정말 사용하기 쉽다.

WRITING FOCUS
pp.56-57

A
1 It is not easy to finish the book

2 My childhood dream was to travel
3 decided to start a business together
4 sweet to eat after dinner
5 He turned off the air conditioner to save
6 Lisa was surprised to find a present

B

1 expensive to eat
2 promised to help
3 what to wear
4 report to write
5 brave to go
6 grew up to be

C

1 difficult to learn a foreign language
2 His goal is to win a gold medal
3 where to go on vacation this year
4 two chairs to sit on
5 meditate to calm your mind
6 The table was easy to assemble

D

1 It is wonderful to have close friends.
2 The most important thing is to have a positive attitude.
3 My dad promised to buy me a new cellphone.
4 I don't know how to solve this problem.
5 I went to the library to borrow some books.
6 You need something warm to wear for camping.

UNIT 02 to부정사의 의미상 주어와 부정, 주요 구문

GRAMMAR FOCUS p.59

EXERCISE A

1 for me
2 of you
3 for dogs
4 of her
5 for Jack
6 of them

해석

1 나는 대중 앞에서 말하는 것이 어렵다.
2 네가 나에게 생일 카드를 준 것은 친절하다.
3 개들이 낯선 사람들을 보고 짖는 것은 자연스럽다.
4 그녀가 그 접시들을 깨뜨린 것은 부주의했다.
5 Jack은 비 오는 날 집에 있는 것이 지루하다.
6 그들이 미래를 위해 약간의 돈을 저축하는 것은 현명하다.

EXERCISE B

1 for you
2 of them
3 not to be
4 too long
5 loud enough
6 couldn't eat

해석

1 네가 주의 깊게 듣는 것은 중요하다.
2 그들이 선물을 가져온 것은 사려 깊었다.
3 John은 다시는 늦지 않겠다고 약속했다.
4 그 하이킹은 너무 오래 걸려서 어두워지기 전에 완료할 수 없었다.
5 그 전화 통화는 대화를 들을 수 있을 만큼 충분히 컸다.
6 그 아이스크림은 너무 녹아서 나는 그것을 먹을 수 없었다.

EXERCISE C

1 too hot for me to drink
2 warm enough for us to swim
3 seems to know
4 have lost

해석

1 그 커피는 너무 뜨거워서 내가 마실 수 없었다.
2 날씨는 우리가 바다에서 수영할 수 있을 만큼 충분히 따뜻했다.
3 그 노인은 모든 것을 아는 것처럼 보인다.
4 그녀는 어딘가에서 자신의 휴대폰을 잃어버린 것 같다.

WRITING FOCUS pp.60-61

A

1 It was kind of him to give up his seat
2 It is impossible for me to finish the work
3 too small for three of us to sit on
4 smart enough to solve the problem
5 It seems that the restaurant is
6 She seems to be talented

B

1 necessary for us to understand
2 careless of him to lose
3 not to be lonely
4 too scary to watch
5 fast enough to win
6 seems to be

C

1 unusual for him to get angry
2 nice of you to see me off
3 not to participate in the race
4 too small for five people to live in
5 You are old enough to vote
6 She seems to be in a bad mood

D

1 It was foolish of him to say that.
2 It is important not to bother a guided dog.

3 Linda is too busy to cook dinner.
4 He is tall enough to go on the ride.
5 The package is so heavy that I can't lift it.
6 Mary seems to have finished her homework.

UNIT 03 다양한 형태의 목적격보어

GRAMMAR FOCUS
p.63

EXERCISE A

1 to read	2 to get	3 fall
4 singing	5 do	6 to postpone
7 washed		

해석

1 나는 네가 이 책을 읽기를 원해.
2 그 의사는 그에게 충분한 휴식을 취하라고 조언했다.
3 Carol은 비가 그녀의 머리 위로 떨어지는 것을 느꼈다.
4 나는 그 소녀들이 아름다운 노래를 부르는 소리를 들었다.
5 나의 부모님은 나에게 저녁 식사 전에 숙제를 하도록 시키셨다.
6 그 학생들은 선생님에게 시험을 연기해 달라고 했다.
7 나의 삼촌은 한 달에 한 번 그의 차를 세차한다.

EXERCISE B

1 had the repairman fix the computer
2 made everyone leave the building
3 lets his kids watch TV after 8 p.m.
4 got her husband to give up smoking

해석

1 John은 수리 기사에게 그 컴퓨터를 고치게 했다.
2 경찰은 모두에게 그 건물을 떠나라고 했다.
3 Smith 씨는 절대로 그의 아이들이 오후 8시 이후에 TV 보는 것을 허락하지 않는다.
4 Sue는 그녀의 남편이 담배를 끊게 했다.

EXERCISE C

1 to finish	2 not to download
3 happen[happening]	4 cut
5 come	6 checked

해석

1 그녀는 그 학생들이 수업 프로젝트를 끝내도록 격려했다.
2 나의 형은 나에게 그 파일을 다운로드하지 말라고 경고했다.
3 너는 어젯밤에 그 사고가 일어난 것을 보았니?
4 Kevin은 이발사에게 그의 머리를 자르게 했다.
5 엄마는 내가 오후 7시 전에 집에 돌아오게 하셨다.
6 James는 그의 차를 정기적으로 점검받는다.

WRITING FOCUS
pp.64-65

A

1 want me to be a doctor
2 The doctor asked the nurse to take
3 helps my grandfather hear better
4 saw the thief steal a purse
5 I heard someone call my name
6 made us study harder

B

1 told us not to park
2 help me move
3 felt someone touch[touching]
4 let me go
5 had me buy
6 get it done

C

1 told his roommate to turn down
2 allow me to stay out late
3 helped me (to) do my homework
4 saw the school band perform[performing]
5 makes me feel good
6 gets her nails done

D

1 Ann asked me to go shopping with her.
2 We expect him to be a great leader.
3 This herbal tea helped me (to) sleep well at night.
4 She heard her baby cry[crying] in the room.
5 Mr. Kim had the students write an essay.
6 I had my wisdom tooth pulled out at the dentist's.

UNIT 04 동명사

GRAMMAR FOCUS
p.67

EXERCISE A

1 Eating	2 cleaning	3 living
4 my	5 not going	6 wearing

해석

1 단것을 너무 많이 먹는 것은 치아에 좋지 않다.
2 집에서 그녀의 임무 중 하나는 자신의 방을 청소하는 것이다.
3 Jin과 그녀의 남편은 대도시에 사는 것에 싫증이 났다.

4 Jerry는 내가 회의에 늦는 것을 신경 쓰지 않았다.
5 나는 파티에 가지 않을 것을 고려하고 있다.
6 Angela는 아직도 안경을 쓰는 것이 익숙하지 않다.

EXERCISE B

1 feel like doing
2 had difficulty walking
3 looking forward to seeing
4 couldn't help laughing

EXERCISE C

1 forgetting
2 to find
3 to buy
4 going
5 to water
6 to fix
7 working

해석

1 Jessica는 그녀의 비밀번호들을 자꾸 잊어버린다.
2 Karen은 졸업하기 전에 일자리를 찾고 싶어 한다.
3 그는 새 차를 살 여유가 없다.
4 나는 지난여름에 해변에 갔던 것을 기억한다.
5 일주일에 두 번 그 식물에 물을 주는 것을 잊지 마세요.
6 그 정비사는 두 시간 동안 내 차를 고치려고 노력했지만 실패했다.
7 그들은 휴식을 취하기 위해 일하는 것을 멈췄다.

WRITING FOCUS

pp.68-69

A

1 is reading poetry and short stories
2 enjoys going skiing in winter
3 going to the movies with me
4 was having difficulty breathing
5 Do you mind helping me translate
6 forgets to turn off the gas

B

1 telling me
2 goes hiking
3 are busy preparing
4 agreed to cancel
5 quit working
6 couldn't afford to buy

C

1 I am thinking of signing up
2 She avoided making eye contact
3 They started singing[to sing] together
4 He stopped eating
5 It is no use buying a boat
6 I couldn't help yawning

D

1 The workers don't mind working at night.
2 He left the party without saying goodbye.
3 I am tired of her complaining.
4 His problem is not coming to class on time.
5 They are looking forward to going to Paris next week.
6 I remember traveling abroad for the first time.

ACTUAL TEST

pp.70-72

01 ③ 02 ④ 03 ①, ④ 04 ③
05 ⑤ 06 ④ 07 ③ 08 ②
09 how I should prepare
10 Tim is looking for a friend to play with.
11 She hurried not to miss the train.
12 (1) It is difficult for her to understand
(2) It was kind of him to help
13 well so → so well
14 (1) The laptop is so expensive that I can't buy it.
(2) The laptop is too expensive for me to buy.
15 (1) told us to wait (2) had me water
16 made me stop playing computer games
17 (1) to rest (2) walking (3) repaired
18 (1) playing (2) to bring (3) studying
19 Was it easy to get the concert ticket
20 ⓑ getting → to get ⓓ see → seeing

01 ③은 대명사이고, 나머지는 가주어 it이다.
02 「의문사+to부정사」에서 why는 쓰이지 않는다.
03 ② talk → talk to[with], ③ delicious something to eat → something delicious to eat, ⑤ stay → stay at으로 고쳐야 알맞다.
04 〈보기〉와 ③은 형용사적 용법, ①②⑤는 부사적 용법, ④는 명사적 용법의 to부정사이다.
05 to부정사의 의미상 주어로 「of+목적격」이 쓰였으므로 빈칸에는 사람의 성격이나 성품을 나타내는 형용사가 와야 한다.
06 ①은 He is too busy to take a break, ②는 She is too tired to stay awake, ③은 I was so surprised that I couldn't believe it, ⑤는 He is talented enough to play any instrument로 고쳐야 알맞다.
07 ⓑ of you → you, ⓔ changing → change, ⓕ helped → to help로 고쳐야 알맞다.

08 ② '~하는 것에 익숙하다'는 「be used to+동명사」 형태로 쓴다.

09 「의문사+to부정사」는 「의문사+주어+should+동사원형」으로 바꿔 쓸 수 있다.

10 '함께 놀'은 to play with로 나타내고, a friend를 뒤에서 꾸며 준다.

11 '그 기차를 놓치지 않기 위해'는 목적을 나타내는 부사적 용법의 to부정사 앞에 not을 써서 not to miss the train으로 나타낸다.

12 (1) 「It(가주어)+be동사+형용사+for+목적격+to부정사(진주어)」 어순으로 배열한다.
(2) kind가 쓰였으므로 「It(가주어)+be동사+형용사+of+목적격+to부정사(진주어)」 어순으로 배열한다.

13 「형용사/부사+enough+to부정사」는 '~할 만큼 충분히 …하다'의 의미로 「so+형용사/부사+that+주어+can+동사원형」으로 바꿔 쓸 수 있다.

14 '너무 ~해서 …할 수 없다'는 「so+형용사/부사+that+주어+can't+동사원형」 또는 「too+형용사/부사(+for+목적격)+to부정사」 형태로 쓴다.

15 (1) tell은 목적격보어로 to부정사가 온다.
(2) 사역동사(have)는 목적격보어로 동사원형이 온다.

16 사역동사(make)는 목적격보어로 동사원형이 온다.

17 (1) advise는 목적격보어로 to부정사가 온다.
(2) 지각동사(see)는 목적어와 목적격보어가 능동의 관계일 때 목적격보어로 동사원형이나 현재분사가 온다.
(3) 사역동사 get은 목적어와 목적격보어가 수동의 관계일 때 목적격보어로 과거분사가 온다. 전화기는 수리되는 것이므로 repaired가 와야 한다.

18 (1) '~한 것을 기억하다'는 「remember+동명사」 형태로 쓴다.
(2) '~할 것을 잊다'는 「forget+to부정사」 형태로 쓴다.
(3) '~한 것을 후회하다'는 「regret+동명사」 형태로 쓴다.

[19-20]

해석 A: 너 오늘 신나 보이는구나. 무슨 일이야?
B: 오늘 밤에 내가 제일 좋아하는 밴드의 콘서트를 보러 갈 거야.
A: 내가 맞혀볼게. BTA?
B: 맞아.
A: 콘서트 티켓 구하기는 쉬웠니?
B: 그걸 구하는 것은 거의 불가능에 가까웠어, 그래도 계속 시도해 봤지.
A: 잘됐네! 의지가 있으면 길이 있는 법이야.
B: 고마워. 나는 그들의 공연을 보는 것을 정말 고대하고 있어.

19 의문문이므로 「Be동사+it(가주어)+형용사+to부정사(진주어) ~?」 어순으로 배열한다.

20 ⓑ 가주어 it 뒤에는 일반적으로 to부정사가 진주어로 사용된다.
ⓓ '~하는 것을 고대하다'는 「look forward to+동명사」로 나타낸다.

Chapter 05
분사와 분사구문

UNIT 01 현재분사와 과거분사

GRAMMAR FOCUS

p.75

EXERCISE A

1 boiled 2 fallen 3 waving
4 stolen 5 typing 6 parked

해석
1 나는 아침으로 삶은 달걀과 샐러드를 먹었다.
2 그는 정원에서 떨어진 나뭇잎들을 긁어 모았다.
3 나에게 손을 흔드는 키 큰 소년은 내 남동생이다.
4 그들은 미술관에서 도난당한 그림을 발견했다.
5 나는 방에서 누군가 키보드를 두드리는 소리를 들었다.
6 우리는 우리 집 앞에 낯선 차가 주차되어 있는 것을 보았다.

EXERCISE B

1 polluted 2 interesting 3 waiting
4 sent 5 amazing 6 confused

해석
1 오염된 물을 마시는 것은 위험하다.
2 나는 새에 관한 흥미로운 TV 프로그램을 시청했다.
3 관광버스를 기다리는 학생들은 매우 행복해 보인다.
4 Mike는 아직 자신에게 보내진 이메일을 확인하지 않았다.
5 그 마술사는 우리에게 카드로 놀라운 마술 몇 가지를 보여주었다.
6 그 혼란스러운 학생은 질문을 하기 위해 손을 들었다.

EXERCISE C

1 exciting 2 satisfied
3 disappointing 4 tired

WRITING FOCUS

pp.76-77

A

1 The shirt made of silk
2 The woman talking on the phone
3 novels written in English
4 The passengers waiting for the train
5 saw her crossing the street
6 had my picture taken

B

1 rolling stone
2 freezing weather
3 students studying
4 instruments made
5 spilled
6 running around

C

1 boiling water
2 a dog named Patrick
3 I felt disappointed
4 The car parked in front of this building
5 when you hear your name called
6 I watched the sun rising

D

1 The movie was so boring that I fell asleep.
2 Who is the boy talking to Mina?
3 Climbing Mt. Everest is exhausting.
4 She was very surprised to see us again.
5 What is the main language spoken in India?
6 He found the front door locked.

UNIT 02 분사구문

GRAMMAR FOCUS p.79

EXERCISE A

1 Feeling
2 Preparing
3 Being
4 Taking
5 Not wanting
6 Building

해석

1 피곤해서 나는 일찍 잠자리에 들었다.
2 저녁 식사를 준비하다가 그녀는 손가락을 베었다.
3 키가 매우 커서 그는 농구 선수가 되었다.
4 이 약을 복용하면 당신은 더 나아질 것이다.
5 그를 깨우고 싶지 않아서 나는 조용히 집을 나왔다.
6 모래성을 쌓으면서 그 아이들은 해변에 앉아 있었다.

EXERCISE B

1 Driving to work
2 Not knowing his phone number
3 (Being) Kind and friendly
4 Cleaning my room

해석

1 차로 출근할 때 그는 라디오를 듣는다.
2 그의 전화번호를 몰라서 나는 그에게 연락할 수 없었다.
3 친절하고 상냥했기 때문에 그녀는 자신의 반 친구들에게 인기가 많았다.
4 내 방을 청소하다가 나는 오래된 사진 몇 장을 발견했다.

EXERCISE C

1 Working out
2 Not needing
3 waiting
4 Going

WRITING FOCUS pp.80-81

A

1 Playing ice hockey last week, he hurt
2 Having nothing to do, the children were
3 Being only five years old, Mozart could
4 Not wanting to be late for class, he started
5 Having more practice, you will
6 Shopping at the department store, I saw

B

1 Walking home
2 Taking a pizza
3 Reading this novel
4 Being very old
5 watching TV
6 Not knowing

C

1 Opening the door
2 Listening to music
3 (Being) Hot and thirsty
4 Joining our club
5 Having no food at home
6 Not having enough money

D

1 Parking my car, I hit the one behind me.
2 Not feeling well, he stayed in bed.
3 Hurrying up, we won't be late for the concert.
4 Not having any homework, I played computer games.
5 She was in New York working at a travel agency.
6 Although living next door, we rarely see each other.

UNIT 03 주의해야 할 분사구문

GRAMMAR FOCUS p.83

EXERCISE A

1 Having baked
2 Made
3 It being
4 locked

5 running
6 Considering

해석

1 케이크를 구운 후 그녀는 파티에서 그것을 제공했다.
2 유리로 만들어졌기 때문에 그 꽃병은 쉽게 깨질 수 있다.
3 비가 오는 날이라서 우리는 실내에 머물기로 결정했다.
4 Janet은 문을 잠근 채 그녀의 방에서 울고 있었다.
5 엄마는 나에게 수돗물을 틀어놓은 채로 이를 닦지 말라고 말씀하셨다.
6 모든 증거를 고려하면 그 소문은 아마도 사실일 것이다.

EXERCISE B

1 Having spent all the money
2 Not having seen him for ages
3 (Being) Tired
4 It being a small suitcase

해석

1 돈을 다 썼기 때문에 Mary는 그 원피스를 살 수 없었다.
2 오랫동안 그를 보지 못했기 때문에 나는 그를 알아보지 못했다.
3 피곤했지만 나는 계속 시험공부를 했다.
4 그것은 작은 여행 가방이었기 때문에 그 소년은 그것을 쉽게 들고 다닐 수 있었다.

EXERCISE C

1 Having arrived
2 Painted
3 shining
4 Frankly speaking

WRITING FOCUS pp.84-85

A

1 Having finished my homework, I went out
2 Having been there many times, I know
3 Decorated with lights, the house looked
4 The lights having gone out, we couldn't see
5 with a little rain falling
6 Judging from the look

B

1 Having studied
2 Having saved
3 Fixed
4 It being a holiday
5 with her eyes closed
6 Frankly speaking

C

1 Having slept well during the night
2 Having lost my passport
3 (Being) Located in the city center
4 (Having been) Warned of the eruption
5 with his arms crossed
6 Considering his age

D

1 Having turned off the lights
2 Not having slept for two days
3 (Being) Made of steel
4 (Having been) Interested in astronomy since childhood
5 It being a stormy day
6 The sun having set

ACTUAL TEST pp.86-88

01 ④ 02 ④ 03 ⑤ 04 ④
05 ② 06 ④ 07 ③ 08 ④
09 (1) sitting (2) stolen
10 disappointing
11 Not knowing the way
12 (Being) Asked the question
13 If you turn left
14 Although[Though] he was interested in the book
15 with his arms crossed
16 (1) Being busy (2) Having seen the movie
17 (1) While he was driving to work
(2) Driving to work
18 The weather being nice
19 Judged → Judging
20 ⓒ → Not having ⓓ → exploring

01 '울고 있는'과 '만드는'은 능동, 진행의 의미이므로 crying과 making이 알맞고, '주차된'은 수동의 의미이므로 parked가 알맞다.

02 ①②③⑤는 현재분사, ④는 enjoy의 목적어로 쓰인 동명사이다.

03 ⑤ '지어진'은 수동의 의미이므로 과거분사(built)를 써야 한다.

04 ①②③⑤는 감정을 느끼게 하는 것이므로 현재분사, ④는 감정을 느끼는 것이므로 과거분사로 써야 한다.

05 분사구문에서 부정어 not은 분사 앞에 쓴다.

06 ①은 Feeling sick, ②는 (Being) Left alone, ③은 Reading a book, ⑤는 It being fine tomorrow로 고쳐야 알맞다.

07 ⓐ waited → waiting, ⓓ turning → turned, ⓔ spoken → speaking으로 고쳐야 알맞다.

08 ⓓ는 문맥상 '많은 시간을 잤지만'으로 해석해야 알맞다.

09 (1) '앉아 있는'은 능동, 진행의 의미이므로 현재분사를 써야 한다.

(2) '도난당한'은 수동, 완료의 의미이므로 과거분사를 써야 한다.

10 '실망스러운' 감정을 느끼게 하는 것이므로 현재분사를 써야 한다.

해석 A: 새로 생긴 식당에서의 저녁 식사는 어땠니?
B: 음식은 맛있었지만 서비스는 매우 실망스러웠어.

11 분사구문의 부정은 분사구문 앞에 not을 붙인다.

12 수동형 분사구문으로 Being은 생략할 수 있다.

13 '좌회전을 하면 당신의 오른편에 도서관이 보일 것이다'의 의미이므로 조건의 접속사 if를 사용해서 부사절로 바꾼다.

14 '그 책에 관심이 있었지만 그는 그것을 사지 않았다'의 의미이므로 양보의 접속사 although[though]를 사용해서 부사절로 바꾼다.

15 '~한[된] 채로'는 「with+목적어+분사」 형태로 쓴다. '팔짱을 낀 채로'는 목적어와 분사가 수동의 관계이므로 과거분사 crossed를 써야 한다.

16 (1) Because I am busy에서 접속사와 주어를 생략하고 am을 현재분사로 전환하면 Being busy가 된다.
(2) 주절보다 앞선 과거는 완료형 분사구문을 써서 「having+p.p.」 형태로 쓴다.

17 (1) '차로 출근하는 동안'은 과거진행형을 사용해서 부사절을 만든다.
(2) 분사구문이 진행형일 때는 being을 생략하고 현재분사로 시작한다.

18 부사절과 주절의 주어가 다를 때는 분사 앞에 부사절의 주어를 써 준다.

19 '~로 판단해 보면'은 Judging from ~으로 나타낸다.

20 ⓒ 분사구문에서 부정어 not은 분사 앞에 쓴다.
ⓓ '도시를 탐험하면서'라는 능동의 의미이므로 exploring을 써야 한다.

Chapter 06

비교

UNIT 01 원급, 비교급, 최상급

GRAMMAR FOCUS p.91

EXERCISE A

1 big 2 better 3 long
4 much 5 largest 6 nicest
7 students

해석

1 브라질은 캐나다만큼 크지 않다.
2 나의 형은 나보다 수영을 더 잘한다.
3 내 휴대폰 배터리는 예전보다 덜 오래간다.
4 오늘 날씨는 지난주보다 훨씬 더 따뜻하다.
5 시드니는 호주에서 가장 큰 도시이다.
6 Anthony는 내가 지금까지 만난 사람 중 가장 좋은 사람이다.
7 Ron은 우리 반에서 가장 똑똑한 학생 중 한 명이다.

EXERCISE B

1 as tall as 2 more difficult than
3 the fastest of

해석

1 Tom은 그의 아버지만큼 키가 크다.
2 나는 중국어를 배우는 것이 영어를 배우는 것보다 더 어렵다.
3 Sam은 셋 중 가장 빠르다.

EXERCISE C

1 not as high as
2 less popular than
3 the worst movie, have ever seen
4 one of the most famous paintings

WRITING FOCUS pp.92-93

A

1 enjoys reading as much as I do
2 wasn't as friendly as he usually is
3 is much farther away than I thought
4 the most historical building in the town
5 one of the saltiest seas in the world
6 the most beautiful sunset I've ever seen

B

1 as expensive as
2 not as spacious as
3 more quickly than
4 the biggest bag
5 one of the best players
6 the most delicious, ever tasted

C

1 as popular as her last song
2 not as serious as I thought
3 more important than money and wealth
4 much[even, still, far, a lot] more difficult than English
5 the busiest day of the month

6 one of the greatest inventions in history

D

1 She drinks tea as much as she drinks water.
2 The blue dress is not as pretty as the pink one.
3 This hotel is cheaper than the one we stayed at the last time.
4 Peter's sister is much[even, still, far, a lot] younger than him.
5 That was the funniest joke I've ever heard.
6 The Eiffel Tower is one of the most famous landmarks in Paris.

UNIT 02 여러 가지 비교 표현

GRAMMAR FOCUS p.95

EXERCISE A

1 possible	2 could
3 three times taller	4 heavier and heavier
5 less	6 city
7 more beautiful	

해석

1 나는 가능한 한 빨리 이 프로젝트를 끝내야 한다.
2 그녀는 마라톤에서 가능한 한 멀리 달렸다.
3 그 새 건물은 예전 것보다 세 배 더 높다.
4 교통 체증이 점점 더 심해지고 있다.
5 더 많이 운동할수록 당신은 더 적게 스트레스를 받는다.
6 서울은 한국의 다른 어떤 도시보다 더 크다.
7 자연 그 자체보다 더 아름다운 것은 없다.

EXERCISE B

1 as hard as possible
2 twice as old as
3 bigger than
4 The more, the smarter

해석

1 시험에 합격하기 위해 그는 최대한 열심히 공부했다.
2 John은 그의 여동생의 두 배만큼 나이가 많다.
3 그 큰 피자는 작은 피자보다 세 배 더 크다.
4 더 많이 읽을수록 당신은 더 똑똑해진다.

EXERCISE C

1 colder than any other continent
2 as cold as
3 colder than

해석

1 남극 대륙은 지구상의 다른 어떤 대륙보다 더 춥다.
2 지구상의 다른 어떤 대륙도 남극 대륙만큼 춥지 않다.
3 지구상의 다른 어떤 대륙도 남극 대륙보다 더 춥지 않다.

WRITING FOCUS pp.96-97

A

1 She ran as fast as she could
2 is three times thicker than the magazine
3 are getting higher and higher
4 The more you listen, the less you speak.
5 Mangos are sweeter than any other fruit.
6 No other boy in the class is taller than Roy.

B

1 as soon as possible
2 twice as heavy as
3 more and more popular
4 The harder, the fewer mistakes
5 is as cold as
6 any other planet

C

1 as realistically as he could
2 ten times more expensive than the gold ring
3 The more, the more tired
4 hotter than any other month
5 No other man, as strong as
6 No other continent, smaller than

D

1 I try to exercise as often as possible. / I try to exercise as often as I can.
2 The building is three times taller than the house.
3 She is becoming more and more fluent in English.
4 The more you eat, the fatter you become.
5 The tree is older than any other tree in the garden.
6 No other metal is as useful as iron.

ACTUAL TEST pp.98-100

01 ①	02 ⑤	03 ②	04 ③, ④
05 ①	06 ⑤	07 ④	08 ③

09 (1) sweet (2) funnier (3) largest
10 (1) taller → tall (2) pianist → pianists

11 as slowly as she could
12 (1) twice as heavy as
(2) three times longer than
13 as well as Lily
14 The later I go to bed, the more tired I feel.
15 (1) less expensive than
(2) twice as expensive as
(3) more expensive than, item
16 (1) colder and colder
(2) more and more nervous
17 (1) better than any other player
(2) No other player, as good as
18 ⓑ little → less ⓒ more wise → wiser
19 more I practice, better I become
20 What is the best dish you have ever made?

01 「as+원급+as」: ~만큼 …한/하게

02 「the+최상급(+that)+주어+have ever p.p.」: 지금까지 ~한 것 중 가장 …한

03 far, a lot, even, much 등은 '훨씬'의 의미로 비교급을 강조한다. ② very는 비교급을 수식할 수 없다.

04 ① John은 16세, Tom은 18세로 John이 Tom보다 더 어리다. ③ Tom은 183cm, Mike는 173cm이므로 Tom이 Mike보다 더 키가 크다. ⑤ 셋 중 가장 어린 사람은 John이다.

05 ① 'Jane의 머리는 Emily만큼 길지 않다'는 Jane's hair is shorter than Emily's hair 또는 Emily's hair is longer than Jane's hair로 바꿔 쓸 수 있다.

06 ①②③④는 Sam이 그 반에서 가장 부지런하다는 내용이고, ⑤는 Sam이 그 반의 다른 학생들만큼 부지런하지 않다는 의미이다.

07 ① he possible → possible 또는 he could, ② loud and loud → louder and louder, ③ the much → the more, ⑤ much more younger → much younger로 고쳐야 알맞다.

08 ⓓ your bill will be higher → the higher your bill will be, ⓔ months → month로 고쳐야 알맞다.

09 (1) as ~ as 사이에는 원급이 온다.
(2) than 앞에는 비교급이 온다.
(3) the 뒤에는 최상급이 온다.

10 (1) 「as+원급+as」: ~만큼 …한/하게
(2) 「one of the 최상급+복수명사」: 가장 ~한 것 중 하나

11 「as+원급+as possible」 = 「as+원급+as+주어+can[could]」: 가능한 한 ~한/하게

12 (1) 「배수사+as+원급+as」: ~의 몇 배만큼 더 …한/하게
(2) 「배수사+비교급+than」: ~보다 몇 배 더 …한/하게

13 'Lily는 Ethan보다 노래를 더 잘 부를 수 있다'이므로, 'Ethan은 Lily만큼 노래를 잘 부를 수 없다'의 의미가 되어야 한다.

14 「the+비교급, the+비교급」: 더 ~할수록 더 …하다

15 (1) 「less+원급+than」: ~보다 덜 …한/하게
(2) 「배수사+as+원급+as」: ~의 몇 배만큼 …한
(3) 「the+최상급」은 뒤에 any other가 있는 경우 「비교급+than+any other+단수명사」로 바꿔 쓸 수 있다.

16 '점점 더 …한/하게'는 「비교급+and+비교급」 구문을 사용하고, 2음절 이상일 때는 「more and more+원급」 형태로 쓴다.

17 「the+최상급」 = 「비교급+than+any other+단수명사」 = 「부정 주어 ~ as+원급+as」 / 「부정 주어 ~ than+비교급」

18 ⓑ 「the+비교급 ~, the+비교급 …」이므로 little의 비교급 less를 써야 한다.
ⓒ wise의 비교급은 wiser이다.

[19-20]
해석 A: 나는 요리를 배우고 있어. 더 많이 연습할수록 나는 더 잘하게 돼.
B: 멋지다! 네가 지금까지 만든 요리 중 최고의 요리는 무엇이니?
A: 당연히 라자냐지. 모두가 그것을 매우 좋아했거든.

19 '더 ~할수록 더 …하다'는 「the+비교급 ~, the+비교급 …」으로 나타낸다.

20 '지금까지 ~한 것 중 가장 …한'은 「the+최상급(+that)+주어+have ever p.p.」 구문을 이용한다.

Chapter 07
접속사

UNIT 01 부사절 접속사

GRAMMAR FOCUS
p.103

EXERCISE A

1 while	**2** When	**3** since
4 travel	**5** during	**6** Because of

해석
1 John은 테니스를 치는 동안 팔을 다쳤다.
2 그녀는 여섯 살 때 읽고 쓰기 시작했다.
3 나의 어머니는 고양이 털 알레르기가 있기 때문에 고양이를 싫어하신다.
4 그들은 아프리카로 여행하기 전에 예방 접종을 받을

것이다.

5 그 소녀는 대화 중에 웃음을 터뜨렸다.

6 그 소문 때문에 사람들은 Nancy에게 무슨 일이 일어났었는지 궁금해했다.

EXERCISE B

1 If you want to stay here

2 because he lies a lot

3 Although my computer is old

4 so that he could improve his skills

해석

1 여기에 머물고 싶다면 너는 그 규칙을 따라야 한다.

2 그들은 그가 거짓말을 많이 하기 때문에 그를 전혀 믿지 않는다.

3 내 컴퓨터는 오래되었지만 아주 잘 작동한다.

4 그는 자신의 실력을 향상시키기 위해 매일 피아노를 연습했다.

EXERCISE C

1 unless 2 so that 3 Despite

WRITING FOCUS

pp.104-105

A

1 While I was having lunch

2 As soon as you find out the answer

3 Because he didn't get enough sleep

4 Even though she felt exhausted

5 so that I could remember it

6 because of the loud music

B

1 since 2 until[till] 3 unless

4 As long as 5 Even though 6 so that

C

1 When you help people in need

2 As Andrew grew older

3 until it recovered

4 Because[As, Since] I felt hungry

5 so that[in order that] he could work from home

6 so expensive that we booked

D

1 Although[Though, Even though] it was 4:00 a.m., he couldn't sleep.

2 Come here as soon as you finish work.

3 When you come back from the trip, I won't be here.

4 John had worked for the same company until he retired.

5 It rained so heavily that the streets were flooded.

6 I spent most of my time at home during the winter break.

UNIT 02 상관접속사, 명사절 접속사

GRAMMAR FOCUS

p.107

EXERCISE A

1 either, or 2 not only, but also

3 Both, and, are 4 Neither, nor, were

EXERCISE B

1 Her problem is (V) she lacks confidence.

2 It is a fact (V) smoking is harmful to health.

3 He quickly realized (V) he was on the wrong bus.

4 (V) They are getting married is not surprising at all.

해석

1 그녀의 문제는 자신감이 부족하다는 것이다.

2 흡연이 건강에 해롭다는 것은 사실이다.

3 그는 자신이 잘못된 버스를 탔다는 것을 재빨리 깨달았다.

4 그들이 결혼한다는 것은 전혀 놀라운 일이 아니다.

EXERCISE C

1 I don't know what his name is.

2 She wants to know why he left for America.

3 Let's see what is on the menu today.

4 I wonder if[whether] anyone lives in that house.

5 Who do you think the best player on the team is?

해석

1 나는 그의 이름이 무엇인지 모른다.

2 그녀는 그가 왜 미국으로 떠났는지 알고 싶어 한다.

3 오늘 메뉴에 무엇이 있는지 보자.

4 나는 저 집에 누군가 살고 있는지 궁금하다.

5 너는 누가 그 팀에서 최고의 선수라고 생각하니?

WRITING FOCUS

pp.108-109

A

1 Both his life and his work inspired

2 either at a shop or online

3 is not only pretty but also functional

4 knew that he was in great danger
5 where I can take a taxi
6 if I am pronouncing the name

B

1 Both coffee and tea are
2 neither denied nor admitted
3 It is possible that
4 what he was doing
5 if[whether] he would attend
6 Who do you think broke

C

1 both a study room and a bedroom
2 neither good nor bad
3 others as well as yourself
4 (that) he will stay here one more year
5 if[whether] there is a stationery store
6 what was happening

D

1 Both he and I are going to join the drama club.
2 Either Joseph or Mary has to take responsibility for it.
3 You as well as Jake deserve to win the prize.
4 I wonder why Mark changed his mind.
5 Whether we can go there depends on the cost.
6 Who do you think the right person for the job is?

ACTUAL TEST

pp.110-112

01 ②	02 ③	03 ③	04 ③
05 ③	06 ②	07 ③	08 ④

09 (1) while (2) since (3) although
10 (1) will arrive → arrives (2) will be → is
11 unless you have
12 so that I could buy
13 was neither informative nor interesting
14 I wonder if she likes flowers.
15 (1) not only, but also (2) Both, and (3) Neither, nor
16 We should realize that time is valuable.
17 (1) Do you know how she goes to work?
(2) Tom wants to know if[whether] the test was easy.
18 (1) While (2) despite (3) because
19 because of the fine dust
20 ⓓ → How long do you think it will take?

01 첫 번째 빈칸에는 since(~ 때문에)와 when(~할 때), 두 번째 빈칸에는 since(~ 이후로)를 쓸 수 있으므로 ② since가 알맞다.

02 ③ Unless는 '만일 ~하지 않으면'의 의미로 부정어와 함께 쓰지 않는다. 따라서 Unless → If로 고쳐야 알맞다.

03 「so as to[in order to]+동사원형」은 '~하기 위해, ~하도록'의 의미로 목적을 나타내며, 「so that[in order that]+주어+동사」 형태의 절로 바꿔 쓸 수 있다. ③의 「so+형용사/부사+that ~」은 '너무 …해서 ~하다'라는 결과의 의미를 나타낸다.

04 ① speak → speaks, ② am → are, ④ are → is, ⑤ need → needs로 고쳐야 알맞다.

05 ①②④⑤는 명사절을 이끄는 접속사 that, ③은 girl을 가리키는 지시형용사이다.

06 ① how she is old → how old she is, ③ where did she go → where she went, ④ Do you think when → When do you think, ⑤ I wonder → I wonder if[whether]로 고쳐야 알맞다.

07 ① or not 바로 앞, ② 전치사의 목적어 자리, ④ 주어 자리, ⑤ to부정사 앞에는 if를 쓸 수 없고 whether만 쓸 수 있다.

08 ⓓ '네가 원하지 않더라도 너는 이것을 해야 한다'의 의미가 되어야 하므로 빈칸에는 양보의 접속사 although, thought, even though 등이 알맞다.

09 (1) while: ~ 동안에
(2) since: ~ 때문에
(3) although: 비록 ~이지만

10 시간과 조건의 부사절에서는 미래시제 대신 현재시제를 쓴다.

11 'if ... not ~'은 '만일~하지 않으면'의 의미인 unless로 바꿔 쓸 수 있다.

12 「in order to+동사원형」은 '~하기 위해, ~하도록'의 의미로 목적을 나타내며, 「so that+주어+동사」 형태의 절로 바꿔 쓸 수 있는데 주로 조동사 can, could 등과 함께 자주 쓰인다.

13 'A도 B도 아닌'의 의미는 상관접속사 「neither *A* nor *B*」를 이용해 쓴다.

14 '~인지 (아닌지)'의 의미는 접속사 if나 whether를 쓰고, 간접의문문이므로 「if[whether]+주어+동사」 어순으로 쓴다.

15 (1) Amy는 수영과 테니스를 둘 다 즐기므로 'A뿐만 아니라 B도'의 의미인 「not only *A* but also *B*」 구문을 이용한다.
(2) Leo와 Jane 모두 사진 찍기를 즐기므로 'A와 B 둘 다'의 의미인 「both *A* and *B*」 구문을 이용한다.
(3) Leo와 Alex 모두 책 읽기를 즐기지 않으므로 'A도 B도 아닌'의 의미인 「neither *A* nor *B*」 구문을 이용한다.

16 목적어로 절이 올 때는 접속사 that을 사용해서 「(that+) 주어+동사」 형태로 쓴다.

17 (1) 의문사가 있는 의문문의 간접의문문은 「의문사+주어+동사」 어순으로 쓴다.

(2) 의문사가 없는 의문문의 간접의문문은 「if[whether]+주어+동사」 어순으로 쓴다.

18 (1) 뒤에 「주어+동사」 형태의 절이 이어지므로 접속사 While이 알맞다.

(2) 뒤에 명사구가 이어지므로 전치사 despite가 알맞다.

(3) 뒤에 「주어+동사」 형태의 절이 이어지므로 접속사 because가 알맞다.

19 기침을 하는 이유에 대해 말하고 있고 전치사 of가 있으므로 「because of+명사(구)」를 이용해 문장을 만든다.

해석 A: 왜 그렇게 기침을 많이 하니?

B: 미세먼지 때문에 기침하는 것 같아.

A: 밖에 나갈 때는 마스크를 쓰도록 해야겠구나.

20 간접의문문에서 주절에 think, believe, guess, imagine, suppose 등의 동사가 쓰인 경우에는 의문사를 맨 앞에 쓴다.

해석 A: 안녕, Brian. 오늘 밤에 영화 볼래?

B: 글쎄, 갈 수 있을지 없을지 잘 모르겠어.

A: 왜?

B: 과학 보고서를 먼저 끝내야 하거든. 끝내면 너에게 바로 알려 줄게.

A: 좋아, 네가 끝날 때까지 기다릴게. 얼마나 오래 걸릴 것 같니?

B: 한 시간 정도 걸릴 것 같아.

Chapter 08 관계사

UNIT 01 관계대명사

GRAMMAR FOCUS p.115

EXERCISE A

1 who **2** whose **3** which
4 that **5** What **6** that

해석

1 그는 강에 빠진 소년을 구했다.
2 그녀는 베스트셀러 책을 낸 작가이다.
3 내가 어제 산 코트는 비쌌다.
4 이분은 제가 지난번에 당신에게 소개했던 사람입니다.
5 그녀가 어제 한 말은 나를 화나게 했다.
6 그가 원했던 유일한 것은 가족의 행복이었다.

EXERCISE B

1 which[that] have lots of violent scenes
2 who(m)[that] I wanted to see canceled her concert
3 whose native language is not English
4 that are playing with a ball together

해석

1 나는 폭력적인 장면이 많은 영화를 좋아하지 않는다.
2 내가 보고 싶었던 가수는 그녀의 콘서트를 취소했다.
3 그녀는 모국어가 영어가 아닌 학생들을 가르친다.
4 함께 공을 가지고 놀고 있는 남자와 개를 봐.

EXERCISE C

1 whose **2** which[that]
3 who[that] **4** what

WRITING FOCUS pp.116-117

A

1 People who were born or live in Paris
2 everything that happens at the campsite
3 The man that she married has
4 a sister whose English pronunciation is perfect
5 what you just said
6 What the child needs is

B

1 who[that] directs
2 which[that] you want
3 whose desire is
4 which[that] contains
5 which[that] was taking
6 What I like

C

1 the hamster which[that] I got from my neighbor
2 a person who[that] writes music
3 The movie which[that] you recommended
4 some good news which[that] will surprise you
5 What I liked most about the movie
6 whose parents died in the accident

D

1 The man who[that] is standing over there is my father.
2 I can't find the book which[that] I borrowed from you.

3 We helped the people whose houses were destroyed by the hurricane.
4 All the students who received the medal were proud.
5 This is the poem which my brother wrote.
6 Mary couldn't believe what she heard.

UNIT 02 관계부사, 복합관계사

GRAMMAR FOCUS

p.119

EXERCISE A

1 where	2 when	3 how
4 why	5 during which	6 in which

해석

1 그가 자란 마을은 매우 작았다.
2 가을은 나무들이 잎을 떨어뜨리기 시작하는 계절이다.
3 그는 나에게 그 기계가 작동하는 방법을 보여주었다.
4 우리는 그 차에서 이상한 소리가 나는 이유를 알지 못했다.
5 7월과 8월은 많은 사람들이 휴가를 가는 달이다.
6 이곳은 모차르트가 태어나서 그의 가족과 함께 살았던 집이다.

EXERCISE B

1 The hotel where we stayed was nice.
2 I like how she sings that song.
3 Do you know the reason why he missed the bus?
4 The time when we arrived home was late.

해석

1 우리가 묵었던 호텔은 좋았다.
2 나는 그녀가 그 노래를 부르는 방식이 마음에 든다.
3 너는 그가 버스를 놓친 이유를 아니?
4 우리가 집에 도착한 시간은 늦었다.

EXERCISE C

1 Whatever	2 Whoever	3 wherever
4 whenever	5 However	6 whichever

해석

1 엄마가 요리한 것은 무엇이든지 맛있다.
2 먼저 오는 사람이 좋은 자리를 차지할 것이다.
3 Tim은 어디에 가든지 빨리 친구를 사귄다.
4 질문이 있으면 언제든지 제게 물어봐도 됩니다.
5 아무리 노력해도 그는 일자리를 찾을 수 없었다.
6 그 경기는 어느 팀이 이기더라도 흥미진진할 것이다.

WRITING FOCUS

pp.120-121

A

1 the year when he graduated from high school
2 a shop where I can buy hiking boots
3 The reason why the restaurant is crowded
4 the way I rearranged the living room
5 give this book to whoever wants it
6 However busy he is

B

1 the time when
2 the city where
3 the reason why
4 the way she
5 wherever we are
6 Whichever way you take

C

1 The day when we went for a swim
2 The school where I studied
3 why she was late
4 how she made homemade candles
5 whatever he wants
6 whenever you need it

D

1 June is the month when[in which] I was born.
2 This is the place where[at which] I last saw him.
3 This is the house where[in which] they lived two years ago.
4 Technology has changed how[the way] we live.
5 Whoever broke the window will have to pay for it.
6 However cold it is, he always goes swimming.

UNIT 03 주의해야 할 관계사 용법

GRAMMAR FOCUS

p.123

EXERCISE A

1 who is	2 that is	3 ×
4 that	5 ×	6 ×

해석

1 노란색 원피스를 입은 소녀는 내 여동생이다.
2 차량은 육지에서 사람이나 물건을 운반하는 데 사용되는 것이다.
3 어제 나는 쇼핑몰에서 너와 비슷한 사람을 보았다.

4 나의 아버지는 사고 싶어 했던 차를 사셨다.
5 그녀는 자신의 방을 파란색으로 칠했는데, 그것은 그녀가 가장 좋아하는 색이다.
6 한국과 일본은 월드컵을 공동 개최한 최초의 국가였다.

EXERCISE B

1 to whom John is talking
2 at which she is looking
3 on which he was sitting
4 for whom we were waiting

해석

1 너는 John이 이야기하고 있는 그 여자아이를 아니?
2 그녀가 보고 있는 그림은 아름답다.
3 그가 앉아 있던 의자는 낡았지만 안락했다.
4 우리가 기다리고 있던 사람들은 늦었다.

EXERCISE C

1 who
2 which
3 where
4 which

WRITING FOCUS pp.124-125

A

1 the man talking to Jenny
2 The alarm clock set for 7:00 a.m.
3 The candidate that I voted for
4 the book you told me about yesterday
5 where she found a job
6 which made him very proud

B

1 playing the guitar
2 five things you like
3 the friend with whom
4 The island on which
5 who lives
6 which keeps

C

1 (who is) responsible for the project
2 (which[that]) we saw yesterday
3 whom she is dancing
4 which my friend played
5 who has great musical talent
6 which was a shock

D

1 in the cupboard
2 I bought last week
3 we had dinner at
4 who had attended
5 where we took
6 which

ACTUAL TEST pp.126-128

01 ③ 02 ④ 03 ③ 04 ④
05 ②, ⑤ 06 ④ 07 ⑤ 08 ③
09 (1) which (2) whose (3) whom
10 (1) These are the pictures that he took in Iceland.
(2) What they want is a better education.
11 (1) live → lives (2) whose → who[that]
12 that → what
13 (1) I remember the day when I adopted my puppy.
(2) I remember the day on which I adopted my puppy.
14 (1) Anyone who (2) No matter what
15 (1) The boy whose backpack is blue is talking to his friend.
(2) The girl whose hair is blond is eating ice cream.
16 (1) This is the house which my parents built.
(2) This is the house where my parents lived.
17 (1) which (2) that (3) where
18 This book is about King Sejong, who invented Hangeul.
19 The boy won the first prize at the contest, which surprised everyone.
20 However difficult the problem is

01 선행사가 사람일 때 주격 관계대명사는 who나 that을 쓰고, 명사 앞의 빈칸에는 소유격 관계대명사 whose가 알맞다.

02 앞 문장 전체를 선행사로 취하는 계속적 용법의 관계대명사는 which를 쓴다.

03 ①②④⑤는 관계대명사 what, ③은 명사절 접속사 that이 알맞다. what을 포함한 모든 관계대명사 뒤에는 불완전한 문장이 오고, 명사절 접속사 that 뒤에는 완전한 문장이 온다.

04 선행사 the way는 관계부사 how와 함께 쓰지 않는다.

05 두 번째 문장은 at the café를 where 또는 at which로 바꿔 관계대명사절로 만들 수 있다. ②는 전치사 뒤에 that이 쓰였으므로 알맞지 않고, ⑤는 관계부사 where가 쓰였으므로 at을 빼야 한다.

06 ①은 전치사 뒤에 that을 쓸 수 없으므로 that → which, ②는 when이 on Sunday를 대신하므로 of which → on which, ③은 why가 for the reason을 대신하므로 at which → for which, ⑤는 which를 삭제하거나 how가 in the way를 대신하므로 which → in which로 고쳐야 알맞다.

07 문맥상 '내가 가는 곳 어디든지'라고 해야 자연스러우므로

wherever가 알맞다.

08 ⓑ which → what, ⓒ don't → doesn't, ⓓ where → which로 고쳐야 알맞다.

09 (1) 선행사가 사물일 때 주격 관계대명사는 which가 알맞다.
(2) 명사 앞의 빈칸에는 소유격 관계대명사 whose가 알맞다.
(3) 선행사가 사람일 때 목적격 관계대명사는 who(m)이 알맞다.

10 (1) 선행사가 the pictures이고, 목적격 관계대명사 that이 이끄는 절이 뒤에서 수식하여 「선행사+that+주어+동사」 어순으로 문장을 완성한다.
(2) 관계대명사 what이 이끄는 명사절인 「What+주어+동사」를 주어로 사용해 문장을 완성한다.

11 (1) 선행사 My aunt가 단수이므로 주격 관계대명사의 동사는 lives가 알맞다.
(2) 관계대명사 뒤에 동사가 이어지므로 whose 대신 주격 관계대명사 who나 that을 써야 한다.

12 선행사가 없고 '~하는 것'의 의미는 what을 사용해서 나타낸다.
해석 A: 실례합니다. 이것은 제가 주문한 것이 아닙니다. 저는 피자가 아니라 스파게티를 원했어요.
B: 오, 죄송합니다. 주문하신 음식을 바로 가져다 드리겠습니다.

13 부사구 on the day는 when 또는 on which로 바꿔 쓸 수 있다.

14 (1) whoever는 '~하는 누구든지'의 의미일 때 anyone who로 바꿔 쓸 수 있다.
(2) whatever는 '무엇을 ~할지라도'의 의미일 때 no matter what으로 바꿔 쓸 수 있다.

15 (1)의 His와 (2)의 Her 대신 소유격 관계대명사 whose를 써서 관계대명사절을 만들고, 선행사인 The boy와 The girl 뒤에 넣어 한 문장으로 바꾼다.

16 (1) 관계사절에서 built의 목적어 역할을 하는 관계대명사가 필요하므로 which를 사용해 문장을 만든다.
(2) 관계사절에서 부사구(in the house) 역할을 하는 관계부사가 필요하므로 where를 사용해 문장을 만든다.

17 (1) 전치사 뒤에는 관계대명사 whom과 which만 쓸 수 있다. 선행사가 The pool이므로 which가 알맞다.
(2) 관계사절에서 painted의 목적어 역할을 하는 관계대명사가 필요하므로 which나 that이 알맞다.
(3) 관계사절에서 부사구(at the library) 역할을 하는 관계부사가 필요하므로 where가 알맞다.

18 계속적 용법에서 선행사가 사람일 때 주격 관계대명사는 who만 쓸 수 있으며, 관계대명사 앞에 콤마(,)를 붙인다.

19 앞 문장 전체를 선행사로 취하는 계속적 용법의 관계대명사는 which를 쓴다.

20 '아무리 ~하더라도'는 「however+형용사/부사+주어+동사」의 어순으로 배열한다.

Chapter 09
가정법

UNIT 01 가정법 과거, 가정법 과거완료

GRAMMAR FOCUS p.131

EXERCISE A

1 is
2 were
3 will miss
4 would go
5 had called
6 would have greeted

해석
1 내일 날씨가 맑다면, 우리는 동물원에 갈 것이다.
2 내가 너라면, 그런 결정을 내리지 않을 텐데.
3 서두르지 않으면, 너는 그 기차를 놓칠 거야.
4 내가 수영하는 법을 안다면, 너와 함께 해변에 갈 텐데.
5 네가 나에게 전화했다면, 나는 너를 도우러 왔을 텐데.
6 내가 너를 학교에서 봤다면, 너에게 인사했을 텐데.

EXERCISE B

1 had
2 were
3 would send
4 had been
5 would have seen
6 had allowed

해석
1 그에게 친구가 더 많다면, 외롭지 않을 텐데.
2 그 소년이 키가 더 크다면, 롤러코스터를 탈 수 있을 텐데.
3 내가 그녀의 주소를 안다면, 그녀에게 카드를 보낼 텐데.
4 그 텐트가 더 컸다면, 우리 모두 거기서 잘 수 있었을 텐데.
5 내가 더 일찍 도착했다면 그 파티에서 너를 봤을 텐데.
6 Nick은 그의 엄마가 허락했다면 강아지를 입양했을 텐데.

EXERCISE C

1 had, would grow
2 were not, could go
3 had set, would not have woken
4 had not been, could have borrowed

해석
1 우리에게 정원이 있다면, 직접 채소를 키울 텐데.
2 비가 오고 있지 않다면, 우리는 산책하러 갈 수 있을 텐데.
3 내가 알람을 맞춰 놓았다면, 늦게 일어나지 않았을 텐데.
4 도서관이 문을 닫지 않았다면, 우리는 책을 빌릴 수 있었을 텐데.

WRITING FOCUS pp.132-133

A

1 I were you, I would refuse
2 I had a car, I would give
3 everyone were kind, the world would be
4 had saved money, could have bought
5 had called ahead, wouldn't have waited
6 hadn't eaten it, wouldn't have had

B

1 were
2 saw
3 would lend
4 had been
5 had read
6 wouldn't have happened

C

1 weren't[were not], could buy
2 visited, would be
3 were, could participate
4 had studied, could have passed
5 had known, would have told
6 had been, would have asked

D

1 What would you do if you had one million dollars?
2 We could have a snowball fight if there were snow.
3 If I were a teacher, I wouldn't[would not] give students tests.
4 If it hadn't[had not] rained, we would have gone to the park.
5 If you had taken care of your health, you might have avoided getting sick.
6 If he had gone to bed earlier, he wouldn't have been so tired.

UNIT 02 I wish 가정법, as if 가정법

GRAMMAR FOCUS p.135

EXERCISE A

1 weren't	2 had driven
3 were	4 hadn't heard
5 had talked	6 hadn't lost

해석

1 지금은 비가 오고 있다. 비가 오지 않으면 좋을 텐데.
2 그가 어제 더 조심히 운전했더라면 좋을 텐데.
3 나의 형은 가끔씩 마치 그가 내 아버지인 것처럼 말한다.
4 Steve는 마치 그 소식을 듣지 않은 것처럼 행동한다.
5 내가 그 문제에 대해 더 나빠지기 전에 이야기했더라면 좋을 텐데.
6 나의 아버지는 작년에 직장을 잃으셨다. 아버지가 직장을 잃지 않았더라면 좋을 텐데.

EXERCISE B

1 had	2 had listened
3 were	4 had seen

해석

1 나에게 운동할 충분한 시간이 있다면 좋을 텐데.
2 내가 나의 부모님의 조언을 들었더라면 좋을 텐데.
3 그녀는 마치 내가 아이인 것처럼 나에게 말한다.
4 그는 마치 하늘에서 UFO가 날아다니는 것을 본 것처럼 말한다.

EXERCISE C

1 weren't	2 knew
3 hadn't spent	4 had traveled

WRITING FOCUS pp.136-137

A

1 I wish I had an umbrella.
2 I wish I were taller than my friend Lisa.
3 I wish I had learned to drive a car.
4 as if he were a little baby
5 as if he had been to Thailand
6 as if she had seen a ghost

B

1 were	2 didn't live
3 had enjoyed	4 were
5 had won	6 had heard

C

1 I were more outgoing and sociable
2 I didn't have to wake up early
3 we had made a reservation
4 he didn't care about the results
5 my father were at my graduation
6 they had won the lottery

D

1 I wish I knew more about computers.
2 I wish I had been kinder to him.

3 I wish I hadn't[had not] lost my cellphone.
4 She acts as if she were a famous celebrity.
5 I feel as if I were walking on clouds.
6 She talks as if she had read the book.

UNIT 03 주의해야 할 가정법

GRAMMAR FOCUS

p.139

EXERCISE A

1 be
2 had finished
3 exist
4 But
5 Were I
6 Had I known

해석

1 내가 규칙적으로 운동했다면, 지금은 더 건강할 텐데.
2 그가 숙제를 끝냈다면, 지금 놀 수 있을 텐데.
3 물이 없다면, 어떤 생명체도 지구상에 존재할 수 없을 텐데.
4 교통 체증이 없었다면, 우리는 정시에 도착했을 텐데.
5 내가 백만장자라면, 직장을 그만두고 사업을 시작할지도 모를 텐데.
6 내가 너의 전화번호를 알았다면, 너에게 전화했을 텐데.

EXERCISE B

1 had taken, would be
2 had missed, would regret
3 hadn't bought, would live

EXERCISE C

1 Without
2 But for
3 Were I
4 Had he been

해석

1 기술이 없다면, 우리의 삶은 덜 편리할 텐데.
2 그녀의 조언이 없었다면, 나는 실수를 했을 텐데.
3 내가 그 동아리의 리더라면, 더 많은 모임을 가질 텐데.
4 그가 조심했더라면, 넘어지지 않았을 텐데.

WRITING FOCUS

pp.140-141

A

1 had studied harder, would be
2 had learned Spanish, could talk
3 If it were not for email
4 If it had not been for your help
5 Were it warmer outside
6 Had I read the book

B

1 had closed
2 had planted
3 Without, would try
4 But for, couldn't have passed
5 Were I
6 Had we arrived

C

1 hadn't[had not] eaten, would be
2 had checked, wouldn't[would not] be
3 were not for the supercomputer
4 had not been for his hard work
5 I were you
6 I had heard

D

1 I would be in a better position now
2 If we had bought some food
3 But for music
4 If it were not for the Internet
5 If it had not been for the storm
6 Had I been you

ACTUAL TEST

pp.142-144

01 ② 02 ⑤ 03 ⑤ 04 ③
05 ② 06 ⑤ 07 ① 08 ②
09 (1) had, would travel
(2) had invited, would have gone
10 isn't → weren't
11 could avoid → could have avoided
12 is not, have to go
13 had remembered, would not have been
14 had, could go
15 (1) lived in Hawaii
(2) had been more careful
16 (1) I could fly (2) I had listened
17 (1) as if he knew
(2) as if she had been
18 hadn't[had not] left, could call
19 Without the scholarship
20 Were I you

01 가정법 과거 문장은 「If+주어+동사의 과거형, 주어+조동사의 과거형+동사원형」 형태로 쓴다.

02 가정법 과거완료 문장은 「If+주어+had p.p., 주어+조동사의 과거형+have p.p.」 형태로 쓴다.

03 과거에 이루지 못한 일에 대한 아쉬움은 「I wish+가정법 과거완료」로 나타낸다.

04 가정법 과거완료에서 '~이 없다면'은 'Without ~', 'But for ~', 'Had it not been for ~', 'If it had not been for ~'로 나타낼 수 있다.

05 ②는 현재에 반대되는 소망이므로, 「I wish+가정법 과거」를 사용해서 have → had로 고쳐야 알맞다.

06 ⑤는 '(과거에) 요리를 배웠다면, 지금 요리를 즐길 텐데'라는 의미의 혼합 가정법이다. 「If+주어+had p.p., 주어+조동사의 과거형+동사원형」을 사용해서 would have enjoyed → would enjoy로 고쳐야 알맞다.

07 ①의 바뀐 문장은 '(과거에) 샌드위치를 먹지 않았다면 (지금) 배가 고플 것이다'라는 의미의 혼합 가정법이다. 주절에 조동사의 과거형인 would를 사용하여 were → would be로 고쳐야 알맞다.

08 ⓑ can play → could have played(가정법 과거완료) 또는 can play(혼합 가정법), ⓓ are → were로 고쳐야 알맞다.

09 (1) 가정법 과거 문장은 「If+주어+동사의 과거형, 주어+조동사의 과거형+동사원형」 형태로 쓴다.
(2) 가정법 과거완료 문장은 「If+주어+had p.p., 주어+조동사의 과거형+have p.p.」 형태로 쓴다.

10 가정법 과거 문장은 「If+주어+동사의 과거형, 주어+조동사의 과거형+동사원형」 형태로 쓴다.

11 가정법 과거완료 문장은 「If+주어+had p.p., 주어+조동사의 과거형+have p.p.」 형태로 쓴다.

12 가정법 과거를 직설법으로 바꿀 때는 긍정은 부정으로 바꾸고, 시제는 현재형으로 바꾼다.

13 가정법 과거완료 문장은 「If+주어+had p.p., 주어+조동사의 과거형+have p.p.」 형태로 쓴다.

14 가정법 과거 문장은 「If+주어+동사의 과거형, 주어+조동사의 과거형+동사원형」 형태로 쓴다.
해석 A: 만약 네가 어떤 초능력이라도 가질 수 있다면, 너는 무엇을 갖고 싶니?
B: 나는 초고속 능력을 갖고 싶어. 너는 어때?
A: 그럴 수 있다면, 나는 날 수 있는 능력을 갖고 싶어. 나에게 그런 능력이 있다면 차 없이도 어디든지 갈 수 있을 텐데.

15 (1) 가정법 과거 문장은 「If+주어+동사의 과거형, 주어+조동사의 과거형+동사원형」 형태로 쓴다.
(2) 가정법 과거완료 문장은 「If+주어+had p.p., 주어+조동사의 과거형+have p.p.」 형태로 쓴다.

16 (1) 현재 사실에 반대되는 소망은 「I wish+가정법 과거」를 사용해서 나타낸다.
(2) 과거에 이루지 못한 일에 대한 아쉬움은 「I wish+가정법 과거완료」를 사용해서 나타낸다.

17 (1) 현재 사실에 반대되는 가정은 「as if+가정법 과거」를 사용해서 나타낸다.
(2) 과거 사실에 반대되는 가정은 「as if+가정법 과거완료」를 사용해서 나타낸다.

18 혼합 가정법이므로 「If+주어+had p.p., 주어+조동사의 과거형+동사원형」 형태로 쓴다.

19 '~이 없었다면'의 의미인 'If it had not been for ~'는 'Without ~' 또는 'But for ~'로 바꿔 쓸 수 있다.

20 가정법 과거 문장에서 if절의 동사가 were일 때, if를 생략하고 주어와 동사의 위치를 바꿔 쓸 수 있다

Chapter 10 일치, 화법, 강조, 도치

UNIT 01 일치

GRAMMAR FOCUS

p.147

EXERCISE A

1 has to **2** is **3** is
4 is **5** is **6** is
7 were **8** are **9** is
10 were **11** is **12** are

해석
1 모든 학생은 그 문제에 답해야 한다.
2 각 시험지 세트는 완전히 봉인되어 있다.
3 여섯 시간은 쉬지 않고 운전하기에 긴 시간이다.
4 50달러는 저 청바지의 적당한 가격이다.
5 수학은 나에게 가장 어려운 과목이다.
6 미국은 세계에서 네 번째로 큰 나라이다.
7 노숙자들은 쉴 곳을 찾고 있었다.
8 많은 자원봉사자들이 공원을 청소하고 있다.
9 도시에 거주하는 사람들의 수가 증가하고 있다.
10 거리의 자동차 몇 대는 견인 구역에 주차되어 있었다.
11 그 케이크의 절반은 네 것이고, 나머지는 내 것이다.
12 경험과 지식 둘 다 그의 일에 필수적이다.

EXERCISE B

1 looked **2** would arrive
3 could go **4** has
5 had worked **6** fell

해석
1 나는 Ethan이 그의 발표에 자신감이 있어 보인다고

생각한다.
→ 나는 Ethan이 그의 발표에 자신감이 있어 보였다고 생각했다.

2 나는 내 소포가 곧 도착할 것으로 예상한다.
→ 나는 내 소포가 곧 도착할 것으로 예상했다.

3 Angela는 우리와 함께 하이킹을 갈 수 있다고 말한다.
→ Angela는 우리와 함께 하이킹을 갈 수 있다고 말했다.

4 그는 인간의 몸에 약 206개의 뼈가 있다는 것을 안다.
→ 그는 인간의 몸에 약 206개의 뼈가 있다는 것을 알았다.

5 그녀는 파리에서 2년 동안 일을 했다고 말한다.
→ 그녀는 파리에서 2년 동안 일을 했었다고 말했다.

6 우리 선생님은 우리에게 베를린 장벽이 1989년에 무너졌다고 가르쳐 주신다.
→ 우리 선생님은 우리에게 베를린 장벽이 1989년에 무너졌다고 가르쳐 주셨다.

WRITING FOCUS

pp.148-149

A

1 Everyone is going to be served
2 Each of the flowers has
3 Physics is the most interesting subject
4 The injured were taken
5 Half of the coffee was spilled
6 She said that she had visited

B

1 desk has
2 consists of
3 was spent
4 are sitting
5 thought, would take
6 believed, moves

C

1 Every member, is wearing
2 Forty minutes is a proper amount of time
3 Most of the food, has gone bad
4 The number of tourists, is increasing
5 A number of houses were damaged
6 water boils at 100 degrees Celsius

D

1 The Netherlands is known for its windmills and tulips.
2 The number of players on a soccer team is eleven.
3 Ten dollars is a reasonable price for the hat.
4 Every child was given a piece of cake.
5 I thought that he would be surprised by the news.
6 Some of the trees on the roadside were cut down.

UNIT 02 화법

GRAMMAR FOCUS

p.151

EXERCISE A

1 was
2 would
3 it was
4 I exercised
5 if
6 to turn off

해석

1 Ann은 나에게 학교에 가는 중이라고 말했다.
2 Kevin은 다음날 나를 보겠다고 말했다.
3 한 여자가 나에게 그때가 몇 시냐고 물었다.
4 그 의사는 나에게 얼마나 자주 운동하는지 물었다.
5 Sue의 오빠는 그녀가 그에게 돈을 좀 빌려줄 수 있는지 물었다.
6 내 룸메이트는 나에게 나가기 전에 불을 끄라고 말했다.

EXERCISE B

1 was reading
2 would arrive
3 what the word meant
4 if[whether]
5 to be
6 not to talk

해석

1 John은 그가 책을 읽고 있었다고 말했다.
2 Mary는 나에게 교통 체증 때문에 늦게 도착할 것이라고 말했다.
3 나는 선생님에게 그 단어가 무슨 뜻인지 물었다.
4 그는 나에게 자신과 이야기할 시간이 좀 있는지 물었다.
5 그 사서는 우리에게 도서관에서는 조용히 하라고 말했다.
6 Green 선생님은 그들에게 시험 중에 말하지 말라고 말씀하셨다.

EXERCISE C

1 what I wanted for lunch
2 who was going to teach us
3 if[whether] I had seen her favorite hat
4 to take out the garbage
5 not to touch the hot stove

해석

1 Matt는 나에게 점심으로 무엇을 원하는지 물었다.
2 Jane은 누가 우리를 가르칠 것인지 물었다.
3 내 여동생은 나에게 자신이 좋아하는 모자를 본 적이 있는지 물었다.
4 엄마는 내 남동생에게 쓰레기를 버려 달라고 부탁했다.
5 Emily는 나에게 그 뜨거운 난로를 만지지 말라고 말했다.

WRITING FOCUS

pp.152-153

A

1 Bob told me that he would be there
2 Tom said that he had already finished
3 He asked us how he could get to
4 She asked me if there was a bus stop
5 Carol asked me to wait
6 The park manager told us not to walk

B

1 was going to
2 what my name was
3 who had cleaned
4 if[whether] she could park
5 to bring
6 not to forget

C

1 he wanted to go to the movies
2 why I was late
3 if[whether] I could speak English
4 to take care of his dog
5 to hand in the final report
6 not to be late for the meeting

D

1 He said that he would arrive in Seoul the following day.
2 Lisa told me that she had been to Paris twice.
3 The salesperson asked me which color I preferred.
4 The waiter asked us if[whether] we were ready to order.
5 Mom asked me to help her with the dishes.
6 He told his son not to talk with strangers.

UNIT 03 강조, 도치

GRAMMAR FOCUS

p.155

EXERCISE A

1 promise	2 It
3 have I seen	4 does he apologize
5 stood a castle	6 he walked

해석

1 Sam은 오후 7시까지 오기로 정말 약속했다.
2 우리에게 이 식당을 추천한 사람은 바로 Sean이었다.
3 나는 전에 별똥별을 본 적이 한 번도 없다.
4 그는 자신의 행동에 대해 사과하는 경우가 거의 없다.
5 그 언덕 꼭대기에는 성 한 채가 세워져 있었다.
6 길을 따라 그가 걸었다.

EXERCISE B

1 She does have a talent for painting.
2 It was an old photo album that I found in the attic.
3 Never did she realize that her backpack was open.
4 At the top of the mountain lies a beautiful lake.

해석

1 그녀는 그림에 정말 재능이 있다.
2 내가 다락방에서 발견한 것은 바로 오래된 사진첩이었다.
3 그녀는 자신의 배낭이 열려 있다는 사실을 결코 깨닫지 못했다.
4 그 산 정상에는 아름다운 호수가 있다.

EXERCISE C

1 did taste
2 was a birthday cake that
3 does he forget
4 stood a security guard

WRITING FOCUS

pp.156-157

A

1 does enjoy reading books in her free time
2 did apologize for his mistake
3 was John that ate the cookies
4 was last week that I met Ethan
5 does she get angry with her children
6 walked two people hand in hand

B

1 did tell
2 the storm that knocked down
3 a deer that we saw
4 did she imagine
5 does he skip
6 came a truck

C

1 He does look tired
2 was my puppy that made a mess
3 was a new car that he bought
4 was in the middle of the night that I heard
5 has he missed a deadline

6 passed a cruise ship

D

1 They did finish the work on time.
2 It was in Hawaii that we spent our summer vacation.
3 It was this book that she gave me for my birthday.
4 It was during the storm that the power went out.
5 Little did I know that my friends were planning a surprise party for me.
6 In the middle of the room stood a grand piano.

ACTUAL TEST

pp.158-160

01 ③	02 ④	03 ⑤	04 ②
05 ⑤	06 ④	07 ②	08 ③

09 (1) Most of my friends like to play soccer.
(2) Half of the sugar in the bowl was spilled.
10 (1) He thought that she would like the gift.
(2) I knew that the sun is also a star.
11 she was excited about the concert
12 what I wanted for my birthday
13 if[whether] I had seen his phone
14 (1) to fill out the form
(2) if[whether] I wanted some dessert
15 don't → not to
16 Ruth does have a good sense of humor.
17 It was a screwdriver that my neighbor borrowed from me yesterday.
18 (1) does he miss a day of exercise
(2) is a convenience store
19 I did lock the door.
20 it is on Friday that we have a science test

01 「each of+복수 명사」는 단수 취급하고, 「some of+명사」는 of 뒤에 오는 명사에 동사의 수를 일치시킨다. 「the+형용사」(~한 사람들)는 복수 취급한다.

02 「a number of+복수 명사」(많은 ~)는 복수 취급, 「the number of+복수 명사」(~의 수)는 단수 취급한다.

03 ⑤ tomorrow → the next day 또는 the following day로 고쳐야 알맞다.

04 ②는 가주어 It과 진주어 that절이 쓰인 문장이다.

05 ⑤ It is/was ~ that ... 강조 구문으로, 'It was Mike that scored the winning goal in the final.'로 고쳐야 알맞다.

06 ① have → has, ② is → are, ③ are → is, ⑤ are → is로 고쳐야 알맞다.

07 ⓑ what was my favorite food → what my favorite food was, ⓓ not cheat → not to cheat, ⓔ has → had로 고쳐야 알맞다.

08 ⓑ a bench is → is a bench, ⓔ I have seen → have I seen으로 고쳐야 알맞다.

09 (1) '~의 대부분'은 'most of ~'로 나타내고, of 뒤에 오는 명사에 동사의 수를 일치시킨다.
(2) '~의 절반'은 'half of ~'로 나타내고, of 뒤에 오는 명사에 동사의 수를 일치시킨다.

10 (1) 주절의 동사가 과거이므로 종속절의 동사 will을 would로 바꾼다.
(2) 과학적 사실은 주절의 시제에 상관없이 항상 현재시제를 쓴다.

11 평서문의 간접화법은 that절의 인칭대명사를 전달자의 입장에 맞게 바꾸고 that절의 동사는 시제 일치의 규칙에 맞게 바꾼다.

12 의문사가 있는 의문문의 간접화법은 「의문사+주어+동사」 어순으로 쓴다.

13 의문사가 없는 의문문의 간접화법은 「if[whether]+주어+동사」 어순으로 쓴다.

14 (1) 명령문의 간접화법은 to부정사를 사용해서 바꾼다.
(2) 의문사가 없는 의문문의 간접화법은 「if[whether]+주어+동사」 어순으로 쓴다.

15 부정 명령문의 간접화법은 「동사+목적어+not+to부정사」 어순으로 쓴다.

16 동사를 강조할 때는 「do/does/did+동사원형」을 쓴다.

17 동사 이외의 부분을 강조할 때는 It is/was ~ that ... 구문을 사용해서 강조하고자 하는 부분을 It is/was와 that 사이에 넣는다.

18 (1) 부정어가 문장 맨 앞에 올 때 주어와 동사는 의문문 어순을 따른다.
(2) 장소의 부사구가 문장 맨 앞에 올 때는 주어와 동사의 순서가 바뀐다.

19 동사를 강조할 때는 「do/does/did+동사원형」을 쓴다.
해석 A: 문이 열려 있어. 나가기 전에 문을 잠갔니?
B: 응, 나는 정말로 문을 잠갔어. 어쩌면 누군가 집 안에 있을지도 몰라.

20 동사 이외의 부분을 강조할 때는 It is/was ~ that ... 구문을 사용해서 강조하고자 하는 부분을 It is/was와 that 사이에 넣는다.
해석 A: 우리 목요일에 과학 시험이 있는 거 맞지?
B: 아니, 우리가 과학 시험이 있는 날은 바로 금요일이야.

WORKBOOK ANSWERS

CHAPTER 01 시제

UNIT 01 단순시제, 진행형 p.2

A

1 started
2 arrives
3 are studying
4 orbits
5 am going to go/am going
6 is trying
7 broke
8 will be enjoying
9 ended
10 were watching

B

1 Dogs wag their tails when they are happy.
2 Leonardo da Vinci painted the *Mona Lisa* in the 16th century.
3 No one is helping me at the moment.
4 The children were playing soccer when it started raining.
5 At 5 o'clock tomorrow, I will be camping with my friend's family.

UNIT 02 완료시제 p.3

A

1 Have
2 will have finished
3 has
4 had
5 will have studied
6 had
7 hasn't been
8 will have traveled
9 had
10 have

B

1 Have you ever tried Turkish food?
2 I haven't[have not] heard from him since last week.
3 he had already left
4 he will have worked at this school for ten years
5 sports day will have ended

UNIT 03 완료진행형 p.4

A

1 has been working
2 have been playing
3 has been raining
4 had been waiting
5 will have been living
6 has been practicing
7 had been studying
8 has been traveling
9 have you been running
10 will have been sleeping

B

1 have been playing with mud
2 have been practicing for a marathon
3 had been watching TV
4 will have been working as a doctor
5 will have been talking on the phone

CHAPTER 02 조동사

UNIT 01 조동사 p.5

A

1 Could
2 must not
3 had better
4 used to
5 would rather
6 don't have to
7 had to
8 may
9 should
10 can't

B

1 is able to speak French
2 used to love chocolate
3 had better not skip breakfast
4 can't[cannot] be true
5 doesn't[does not] have to wear a uniform

UNIT 02 조동사+have p.p. p.6

A

1 may make

2 may have gone
3 must have left
4 may help
5 shouldn't
6 may not have known
7 shouldn't have snoozed
8 can't go
9 must have forgotten
10 may have hurt

B

1 must have studied for the exam
2 may[might] have gotten worse
3 may[might] not have been at home
4 should have spent more time
5 can't[cannot] have said such a thing

CHAPTER 03 수동태

UNIT 01 수동태의 의미와 형태 p.7

A

1 is cleaned
2 was written
3 are being planted
4 have been used
5 will be cooked

B

1 The window was broken by a boy last week.
2 The restaurant is being renovated at the moment.
3 The Olympic Games have been held since 1896.
4 My new dress will be delivered tomorrow.
5 This problem cannot be solved by me.

UNIT 02 4형식, 5형식 문장의 수동태 p.8

A

1 was bought for me by my father
2 was called Sammi by them
3 were made to stay away from the crime scene by the police
4 was seen filming a movie by us

B

1 The flowers were sent to Jane
2 This bag was made for me
3 The fence will be painted yellow
4 The baby girl was named Olivia
5 The kids were made to put away their toys

UNIT 03 주의해야 할 수동태 p.9

A

1 will be dealt with properly by us
2 is believed that silence is golden
3 is said to be a nice person
4 was filled with the scent of flowers

B

1 The computer was turned on by me.
2 The report must be handed in by Friday.
3 It is said that the movie is really exciting.
4 The weather is expected to be sunny.
5 I'm[I am] tired of hearing his dull jokes.

CHAPTER 04 부정사와 동명사

UNIT 01 to부정사의 용법 p.10

A

1 to read
2 to win
3 to go
4 to run
5 to do
6 to help
7 to hear
8 to play

B

1 My goal is to learn a new language.
2 They haven't decided which car to buy.
3 I need something interesting to read.
4 We booked a hotel room to stay at during our vacation.
5 He grew up to be a great musician.

UNIT 02 to부정사의 의미상 주어와 부정, 주요 구문 p.11

A

1 for
2 for
3 of
4 not to tell
5 too
6 that
7 big enough
8 can

9 that
10 to be

B

1 It is kind of her to help me with my homework.
2 It is difficult for beginners to play a musical instrument.
3 I use a calendar not to forget important dates.
4 This book is easy enough for me to understand.
5 She seems to dislike the new restaurant.

UNIT 03 다양한 형태의 목적격보어 p.12

A

1 to take
2 introduce
3 to join
4 cut
5 to find
6 repaired
7 burning
8 called
9 to win
10 show

B

1 My friend told me to stay calm.
2 She had her son wash the dishes.
3 We would like you to bring your own drinks.
4 She felt the wind blow[blowing] through her hair.
5 My brother didn't let me ride his bike.

UNIT 04 동명사 p.13

A

1 cooking
2 to see
3 to study
4 taking
5 meeting
6 to inform
7 telling
8 going
9 buying
10 to talk

B

1 We stopped watching the boring movie.
2 Teddy promised to come back by 7 o'clock.
3 I had difficulty finding a good restaurant.
4 He is used to living in a foreign country.
5 I forgot to turn off the heater.

CHAPTER 05 분사와 분사구문

UNIT 01 현재분사와 과거분사 p.14

A

1 smiling
2 baked
3 broken
4 carrying
5 built
6 watching
7 exhausted
8 amusing
9 surprising
10 shocked

B

1 The boy sitting next to Amy is my brother.
2 It is exciting that we can go swimming all together.
3 Can you think of a word beginning with A?
4 They repaired the house damaged by the typhoon.
5 Was the food at the new restaurant satisfying?

UNIT 02 분사구문 p.15

A

1 Driving to work
2 Exercising regularly
3 (Being) Busy
4 Not wanting to be late

B

1 trying to move the piano
2 Not having a cellphone
3 After finishing my homework
4 (Being) Good at singing
5 Going straight

UNIT 03 주의해야 할 분사구문 p.16

A

1 Having grown up in Japan
2 Not having visited that museum
3 (Being) Badly hurt in the accident
4 (Having been) Invited to the wedding
5 It being too cold

B

1 Not having checked the map, he got lost.
2 (Being) Decorated with flowers, the cake looks beautiful.

3 The dog greeted us with its tail wagging.
4 He started talking with his eyes closed.
5 Considering her age, she has a good memory.

CHAPTER 06 비교

UNIT 01 원급, 비교급, 최상급 p.17

A

1 tall	2 much	3 big
4 stronger	5 much	6 more
7 highest	8 the	9 most
10 walls		

B

1 as fast as a sports car
2 not as good as her sister's
3 the best player on the team
4 much[even, still, far, a lot] more advanced than mine
5 the most difficult test I've[I have] ever taken

UNIT 02 여러 가지 비교 표현 p.18

A

1 twice	2 four times bigger
3 could	4 as accurately as
5 louder and louder	6 more and more
7 better	8 farther
9 student	10 as sweet as

B

1 five times more expensive
2 half as much as
3 more and more difficult
4 The more, the healthier
5 faster than any other runner

CHAPTER 07 접속사

UNIT 01 부사절 접속사 p.19

A

1 while	2 since	3 until
4 If	5 unless	6 as long as
7 Because	8 Although	9 so that
10 while		

B

1 as he played the guitar
2 When the sun sets
3 while her sister is shy
4 Although it was raining
5 As soon as the movie started

UNIT 02 상관접속사, 명사절 접속사 p.20

A

1 who is responsible for the project
2 if[whether] she is going to attend the concert
3 what time he will arrive
4 how they solved the problem

B

1 Both soccer and basketball are
2 either go to the party or stay home
3 Neither cats nor dogs like
4 Not only Helen but also Elaine is
5 writing songs as well as singing

CHAPTER 08 관계사

UNIT 01 관계대명사 p.21

A

1 who	2 that	3 whose
4 which	5 whose	6 who
7 that	8 that	9 what
10 what		

B

1 I met a woman who[that] won a gold medal at the Olympics.

2 The young man who lives next door seems nice.
3 The child whose parents are doctors wants to be a doctor, too.
4 The movie that we watched last night was boring.
5 The teacher explained what we needed to do for the test.

UNIT
02 관계부사, 복합관계사 p.22

A

1 where
2 when
3 why
4 how
5 where
6 which
7 whatever
8 wherever
9 Whoever
10 Whenever

B

1 Do you remember the night when we saw the fireworks?
2 Nobody knows the reason why he was absent.
3 I don't know how[the way] he fixed the air conditioner.
4 However hard you try, you can't change my mind.
5 This is the room where[in which] my father often works.

UNIT
03 주의해야 할 관계사 용법 p.23

A

1 which
2 who is
3 which was
4 which
5 that
6 which
7 that
8 whom
9 that
10 who is

B

1 whom he plays soccer
2 which she was looking
3 who is a doctor
4 which is my favorite city
5 which is good news

CHAPTER 09 가정법

UNIT
01 가정법 과거, 가정법 과거완료 p.24

A

1 will
2 were
3 lived
4 would
5 would have accepted
6 hadn't missed
7 had listened
8 might
9 would learn
10 had bought

B

1 If I won the lottery
2 If I were American
3 If he had studied harder
4 I would call her right now
5 she would have gone to the party

UNIT
02 I wish 가정법, as if 가정법 p.25

A

1 I could speak English better
2 I had studied harder for the test
3 she were a ballerina
4 they had attended the event

B

1 I were more confident
2 I hadn't[had not] given up my dream
3 she were the boss of the company
4 we were aliens
5 he had met the singer

UNIT
03 주의해야 할 가정법 p.26

A

1 would be
2 had taken
3 hadn't snowed
4 Without
5 But
6 were not
7 had not been
8 Were
9 Had
10 wouldn't have missed

B

1 had brought, wouldn't[would not] get wet
2 were not for, couldn't[could not] hear
3 had not been for, would have failed
4 Were, could manage

5 Had, wouldn't[would not] have lost

CHAPTER 10 일치, 화법, 강조, 도치

UNIT 01 일치 p.27

A

1 has	2 has	3 is
4 is	5 is	6 enjoy
7 face	8 are	9 is
10 are		

B

1 Ten years is a long time.
2 Each of the flowers needs to be watered daily.
3 Half of the movie was boring.
4 I thought she was very upset then.
5 We expected he would come to the party yesterday.

UNIT 02 화법 p.28

A

1 when I would go home
2 if[whether] I could cook rice
3 to pass her the salt
4 not to close the window

B

1 that we would have a test
2 where I had put my keys
3 if I knew the way to the museum
4 told the driver to drive slowly
5 not to forget to buy milk

UNIT 03 강조, 도치 p.29

A

1 drink	2 did
3 do	4 It
5 are they	6 does she complain
7 have I seen	8 did he finish
9 is a peaceful garden	10 arrived the package

B

1 did see
2 was on the shelf that
3 was Liam that
4 do they go out
5 is a pirate's treasure chest

Grammar
Plus
Writing